SONGWRITING STRATEGIES

A 360° Approach

MARK SIMOS

Berklee Press

Editor in Chief: Jonathan Feist
Vice President of Online Learning and Continuing Education: Debbie Cavalier
Assistant Vice President of Operations for Berklee Media: Robert F. Green
Assistant Vice President of Marketing and Recruitment for Berklee Media: Mike King
Dean of Continuing Education: Carin Nuernberg
Editorial Assistants: Matthew Dunkle, Reilly Garrett, Zoë Lustri, Sarah Walk
Cover Design: Ranya Karifilly, Small Mammoth Design
Cover Photo of Songwriter Conner Snow: Jonathan Feist

ISBN 978-0-87639-151-8

1140 Boylston Street
Boston, MA 02215-3693 USA
(617) 747-2146

Visit Berklee Press Online at
www.berkleepress.com

Study with

■ **BERKLEE ONLINE**

online.berklee.edu

DISTRIBUTED BY

HAL•LEONARD®
CORPORATION
7777 W. BLUEMOUND RD. P.O. BOX 13819
MILWAUKEE, WISCONSIN 53213

Visit Hal Leonard Online at
www.halleonard.com

Berklee Press, a publishing activity of Berklee College of Music, is a not-for-profit educational publisher.
Available proceeds from the sales of our products are contributed to the scholarship funds of the college.

CONTENTS

ACKNOWLEDGMENTS vii

INTRODUCTION ix

CHAPTER 1. **SONG SEEDS** 1
Catching Seeds 2
Seeds and Personal Voice 3
Seed vs. Filler 3
Varieties of Song Seeds 5
Concept Seeds 5
Lyric Seeds 8
Musical Seeds 12
The Art of Seed Catching 15
EXERCISE 1.1. A WEEK OF SONG SEED CATCHING 18
Conclusion: Song Seeds and the Facets 20

CHAPTER 2. **THE SONGWRITER'S COMPASS** 21
The Four Facets 21
Words and Music 21
Sound and Sense 22
The World 23
Sound and Timbre 24
Structure 25
Traversing the Compass: Songwriting Strategies 26
Setting 26
Casting and Framing 27
Structuring Strategies 29
General Creative Strategies 30
Summary of Compass Elements and Moves 32
Example: Hurricane Revisited 33
Framing "Hurricane" 33
Setting "Hurricane" 35
EXERCISE 2.1. CAST FROM A CONCEPT SEED TO EACH FACET 39
On to the Facets 40

CHAPTER 3. **RHYTHM** 41
The Challenge of Rhythm in Songwriting 41
Working with Rhythm 42
Dimensions of Rhythm in the Song 43
Rhythmic Song Seeds 44
EXERCISE 3.1. COMPOSE A "DRY" RHYTHMIC PHRASE 45
Notating Rhythms: Woodblocks and Bagpipes 46
EXERCISE 3.2. WRITE INTERLOCKING ACCOMPANIMENT
AND VOCAL RHYTHMS 47
The Temporal Framework 49
The Flow of Musical Time 49
Strict vs. Loose Time 49
Pulse 50
Time Signature and Tempo 51

Working with the Temporal Framework. 51

EXERCISE 3.3. SONGWRITE-IRAMA: TRANSFORM A RHYTHMIC
IDEA BY ALTERING TEMPO 52

Accompaniment Rhythm 53

EXERCISE 3.4. CAST FROM A GROOVE TO A LYRIC, MELODY, CHORDS . . . 54

The Rhythmic Phrase 55

Attributes of Lyric Rhythm 55

EXERCISE 3.5. REGULAR TO IRREGULAR LYRIC RHYTHM 58

Rhythmic Events. 58

Rhythmic Pace 60

Rhythmic Patterns. 62

Working with the Rhythmic Phrase 63

EXERCISE 3.6. WRITE A RHYTHMIC SONG SECTION. 63

CHAPTER 4. **LYRICS** **65**

Sound Aspects of Lyrics 65

Thought Phrase. 66

Word Boundaries 67

Syllabic Stress Patterns 67

Mapping Lyrics to Syllabic Rhythm 69

Syllabic Rhythm Example 70

EXERCISE 4.1. DEVELOP ALTERNATE SYLLABIC RHYTHMIC
SETTINGS FOR A LYRIC LINE. 73

EXERCISE 4.2. PIVOT: LYRIC LINE → SYLLABIC SETTING → NEW LINE . . . 74

Syllabic Rhythm to Lyric Rhythm 74

Anatomy of a Syllable 76

Sound Color Aspects 76

Additional Rhythmic Aspects 77

Sense/Sound Lyric Strategies 78

Lyric Sense to Sound: Paraphrasing 79

Lyric Sound to Sense 80

Lorem Ipsum: Dummies for Dummies. 80

Sense vs. Sound Approximations 80

The Gibberish Scale: Seven Levels of Nonsense. 82

EXERCISE 4.3. LYRIC-BY-SOUND STRATEGIES 83

Sonic Contours 84

EXERCISE 4.4. MATCH A LYRIC LINE'S SONIC CONTOUR 85

Setting from Rhythm to Lyric. 86

Rhythm to Lyric by Sound 87

Energy Contour of a Rhythmic Phrase. 88

Vowel and Consonant Contours 89

Syllable Buds to Words to Lyrics. 91

A Few Small Repairs. 92

CHAPTER 5. **MELODY** **95**

EXERCISE 5.1. A CAPPELLA, RUBATO MELODY 95

Challenges in Melody Writing 96

Thinking Melody 96

Melodic Memory. 97

EXERCISE 5.2. STRENGTHENING MELODIC MEMORY 97

Melodic Design. 98

Melodic Contour. 99

Melodic Shape: Scales, Arpeggios, and Figures 99

EXERCISE 5.3. WRITE A MELODIC "RIDGELINE" 101

The Power of Pentatonics. 102

Melodic Transformations. 102

Shifting Figure and Field 103
Melodic Range. 104
Melody/Rhythm Connections 105
The Melody/Rhythm Continuum. 105
Rhythm to Melody 105
Melody to Rhythm 106
Melody/Lyric Connections 108
Lyric Sounds and Melody. 108
Natural Intonation and Speech Melody 109
EXERCISE 5.4. "THE WELL." TRANSFORM A
SPOKEN LINE TO VOCAL MELODY 109
Lyric Rhythm and Melodic Contour 111
Review of Syllabic and Lyric Rhythm 111
Melismas and Chanting Tones 112
Lyric Pace and Melodic Pace 113
Redefining Melodic Rhythm 114
Effects and Uses of Melodic Textures. 117
Process Considerations. 117
Melismas and Chanting Tones in Revision 118
Melodic and Lyric Pace Relationships 119
EXERCISE 5.5. INDEPENDENCE IN LYRIC AND MELODIC PACE. 119
Comfort Zones in Melodic/Lyric Pace. 120
Phrasing Templates 120
EXERCISE 5.6. PHRASING TEMPLATES 121
EXERCISE 5.7. ALTERING THE RHYTHM OF A CHANTING-TONE MELODY. . 121

CHAPTER 6.   **HARMONY** **123**
Sound and Sense in Chords. 123
Sound Aspects of Harmony. 124
Sense Aspects of Harmony. 124
Process Considerations. 125
Chordal Song Seeds. 127
Chords as Sound, Shape, and Feel 127
Chords at Your Instrument 128
EXERCISE 6.1. JACKSON POLLOCK 128
Using Your Chord Seeds 131
Chord Seeds Away from Your Instrument 132
Chord Progressions 136
Simple Chords. 136
Chord Roots as Scale Degrees. 137
EXERCISE 6.2. SIX CHORDS IN SEARCH OF A COMPOSER 138
Intervallic Motion in Chord Progressions 138
Directional Effects of Chord Root Movement. 139
Rising and Falling Moves. 141
EXERCISE 6.3. ANALYZE A PROGRESSION BY ROOT MOTION 144
Working with Root Tone Contours. 145
EXERCISE 6.4. WRITE A PROGRESSION USING
SIX INTERVALS OF ROOT MOTION 146
Harmonic Rhythm. 147
Cyclic vs. Narrative Progressions. 149
Cyclic Progressions 149
Narrative Progressions 150
Motivic Progressions. 151
EXERCISE 6.5. UNWINDING A CHORD CYCLE TO A
NARRATIVE PROGRESSION 153

CHAPTER 7.   **MELODY/HARMONY CONNECTIONS** **155**

   Independence of Melody and Harmony. 156

   Melody/Harmony Counterpoint 157

      Species Counterpoint in Melody/Harmony. 158

      Contrapuntal Motion in Melody/Harmony. 159

   Melody/Harmony Contrapuntal Textures. 159

      Pedal-Point Melodies. 159

      Ostinato Melodies 160

      Parallel Textures. 161

      Lazy Melodic Lines against Chords. 163

      EXERCISE 7.1. LAZY MELODY OVER CRAZY CHORDS 164

      Chord-Driven Melodies. 165

      Independent Tonal Melody 167

   Modal Melody/Harmony 169

      Expanding the Songbook. 170

      Counterpoint in Modal Melody/Harmony. .170

      Modal Palettes and Mosaics 172

CHAPTER 8.   **STRUCTURE.** **175**

   Structure in the Song 175

      Starting from Structure 176

      Structural Challenges 177

   Phrase Structure. 177

      EXERCISE 8.1. SHIFT A LYRIC LINE AGAINST THE PHRASE. 178

      Independence in Phrase Structure. 178

      EXERCISE 8.2. SHIFT A CHORD SEQUENCE

         AGAINST A STRUCTURAL PHRASE 180

   Motivic Structure 181

      Motives vs. Song Seeds 181

      Unfolding: Motives into Structure 181

      EXERCISE 8.3. ANSWER THE QUESTION, QUESTION THE ANSWER! 183

      Fulfilling: Structure into Motives 183

      EXERCISE 8.4. JUGGLE PHRASES IN A SECTION 187

   Counterpoint in Motivic Structure. 188

      Counterpoint within Facets 188

      EXERCISE 8.5. CONTRAPUNTAL STRATEGIES IN A LYRIC SECTION. 190

      Counterpoint Across Facets. 191

CHAPTER 9.   **USING THE COMPASS: FURTHER STEPS** **193**

   Revisiting the Compass 193

      The Compass as a Unity. 193

      From Compass to Tetrahedron. 194

      Facets: From Vertices to Edges 195

      Facets as Faces: Facet Triads 196

   From Counterpoint to Irony: Back to the World 198

   Sound and Sense: Facets, World, and Structure 200

CONCLUSION: FROM A SONG TO THE WORLD **201**

ABOUT THE AUTHOR. **203**

INDEX **204**

ACKNOWLEDGMENTS

Chet Atkins once invited jazz guitarist George Van Eps to play a concert for the Nashville chapter of the Musicians' Union. At the show's end, Chet's buddies urged him to play a number himself. "That would be like following behind a snow plow with a spoon," he said.

I feel a lot like that—trying to explicate a bit of the magic in the masterpieces of many songwriters, famous or obscure, whose work still inspires me. My 360º songwriting approach, described in this book, formalizes practices and discoveries made by these songwriters. Though often working intuitively, collectively they have scouted every pathway described in this book, and many more besides.

I developed 360º songwriting over the course of many decades of observing and documenting my own creative process and experience—as a songwriter and co-writer, tunesmith and composer, musician, and teacher. I've learned especially from other writers—from their books and classes, from interviews and anecdotes, and by talking, co-writing, and teaching with them. I've been privileged to co-write with, and thus learn directly from, some truly great writers: Lisa Aschmann, Jon Weisberger, John Pennell, Becky Buller, Catie Curtis, Jimmy Barnes, Bob Carlin, Viktor Krauss, Andy Hall, Lisa Shaffer, Alana Levandoski, and Sarah Siskind, among many others.

If we're lucky, we songwriters also get to learn from artists who sing our songs. Of the many artists who have performed and recorded my songs and tunes, I offer special thanks to Laurie Lewis, who first heard the night bird sing, and to Alison Krauss, who showed some crazy faith.

Many exercises and practices in this book were developed and presented over the years in songwriting workshops, critique sessions, music camps, retreats, and in more extended classes at Club Passim School of Music and New England Conservatory. A teaching tour to New Zealand/Australia in summer 2010, organized by Clare McLeod, and especially a key discussion with Anne Maree Wilshire, began a long new germination period of shaping 360º songwriting principles into this book. The underlying creative philosophy of this book also reflects many sources and influences beyond songwriting and music, especially my studies with master movement teacher Jaimen McMillan, founder of Spacial Dynamics®.

This work came to fruition in an amazing community of musicians and musical thinkers—Berklee College of Music. Since 2005, teaching songwriting at Berklee has provided me with continuing invaluable opportunities to field-test and refine these techniques. I've been able to build on a legacy of seminal work in songwriting pedagogy contributed by my Berklee colleagues, and those working with their approaches—in particular, the published works of

Pat Pattison, Jack Perricone, Jimmy Kachulis, Andrea Stolpe, and John Stevens, among others. Many other colleagues have generously shared their knowledge and experience, as I've observed their classes or cornered them in delightful afternoons of intense conversation: in Songwriting, the late Henry Gaffney, Scarlet Keys, Susan Cattaneo, Jon Aldrich, Stan Swiniarski, Dan Cantor, Melissa Ferrick, Ben Samama, and Bonnie Hayes; throughout the college and wider community, Allen LeVines, Steve Kirby, Scott McCormick, Sarah Brindell, Mick Goodrick, Matthew Nicholl, Joe Mulholland, Kari Juusela, Keppie Coutts, and Christiane Karam. I owe a particular debt to Matt Glaser, Bruce Molsky, Berklee's American Roots Music Program, and Boston's rich and varied quiltwork of roots music communities; and to Michael Wartofsky and members of NOMTI (New England Opera and Musical Theater Initiative).

To pull it all together, I've been privileged to work with a great music book editor—a true old-school editor, ruthless and (almost) always right—my cheerful nemesis Jonathan Feist and his teams at Berklee Press and Hal Leonard. Many colleagues mentioned above served as beta readers and commenters on early drafts of the book, in addition to the keen-eyed close reading of Rujing (Stacy) Huang.

They say if you want to learn something, teach it. At the root of all this has been the privilege of working with many talented, insightful, dedicated, fearless—and tolerant!—student songwriters and friends, who have accompanied me, as coexperimenters and fellow travelers, in developing and refining these ideas.

Three women have deeply shaped my relation to the creative spirit, honored in these pages. I learned first lessons in creativity from my late mother, Bertha Claire Goldfarb Simos, who brought home rolls of butcher paper on which I happily drew endless maps of imaginary countries. My sister Mimi is always a source of inspiration and encouragement—in the truest sense. A well-known writer (under her *nom de broom*), she told me the hardest thing about writing a book, or any extended work, is managing one's own fluctuating emotions. She was right, as usual. My beloved wife Pam—patient, wise, and more forgiving of me than I am of myself—has served a long vigil as midwife to this awkward babe of a book. On an afternoon walk along a tree-lined street in Vancouver, in summer 2010, she challenged me to take the time to make this book what she knew I wanted it to be. Neither of us knew what we were in for.

INTRODUCTION

This book presents a repertoire of *songwriting strategies*: practical strategies for writing songs, and learning strategies and exercises to help you advance as a songwriter. Using the tools and techniques described in this book, you'll be able to draw on a broader range of sources of inspiration and starting points for songs. And you'll be able to work with this material to write songs in more versatile and innovative ways.

I call this approach *360° songwriting*. It's grounded in a comprehensive model that encompasses and integrates four primary facets of songwriting: rhythm, lyrics, melody, and harmony. Each facet can connect directly to imagery, narrative, and emotion in the world, and each can also express structure and form in unique ways. This opens up a rich repertoire of strategies and skills for songwriters. We can start a song from seed material in any facet, and follow pathways to related material in any other facet, or cast content directly to material in any of the facets.

Developing the skills to follow these different creative pathways will expand the productivity, scope, and versatility of your writing. It will help you get stuck songs "unstuck"—unfreezing "writer's block" by accessing alternate processes or pathways. Above all, it will help you write *better songs*: songs with depth, craft, unity, and integrity—songs that take chances and stretch boundaries, for you as a writer and for the art of songwriting. As you expand your abilities to work from "the full 360," you'll be writing songs *from* all directions, *in* all directions.

This approach is simple in principle, but challenging in practice. We all have comfortable, familiar ways of writing songs. These serve us in good stead, until they don't—when, at key points in our development as writers, they begin to hold us back. You can always improve your craft by reflecting on your habitual creative practices and trying new approaches. The 360° approach offers a framework for exploring alternative strategies in a more systematic, comprehensive way. It can be taken up as a discipline for ongoing "creative disruption," as needed, of creative processes that have become routine, safe, and predictable. One habit you *do* need to cultivate for 360° songwriting, therefore, is the habit of breaking habits: seeking out and embracing challenges to your writing process, uncomfortable though they may be, unusable though initial results may seem—maybe even having fun along the way!

In some respects, this work aims to be *descriptive*—providing a detailed *process language* for the "music of what happens" as songwriters write songs. This book does not set out, though, with the primary aim of describing what most songwriters are aware of doing in informal writing—even what I do in my personal approach to songwriting. Nor is it *prescriptive*, in the sense of advising you to write songs one particular way. It gives directions, not instructions—new options to explore. Toward that end, many new musical constructs, techniques, and tools are described herein, including many you're not likely to find in a typical songwriter's notebook—not yet at least! Use these as explanatory and practical aids to observing your own creative process at finer levels of detail—thereby discovering new ways to write songs, new kinds of songs to write.

All examples in the book were composed by me, written specifically for the book to illustrate concepts and techniques, rather than excerpted from contemporary songs or my own working catalogue. Though not intended to illustrate any particular genre or style, the examples will necessarily reflect my musical background and vocabulary, and may or may not be to your taste. Work through the exercises, writing your own music, and I believe you'll find the tools and techniques applicable in your preferred style and genre. Also put these ideas and techniques to the test by listening for examples (and counter-examples), both in widely known songs and in the music you know and love.

The examples and exercises in this book make extensive use of both standard notation and some notational conventions I introduce. Supporting audio tracks for all examples and exercises, along with other supplemental information and resources, are available at www.360songwriting.com.

This is a comprehensive set of strategies for songwriters' *creative* work. The term "360º songwriting" only coincidentally suggests a connection to the now prevalent "360 deals" between artist/writers, record labels, and publishers. Nevertheless, 360º skills will benefit professional songwriters, in a music industry that rewards productivity and innovation, versatility, responsiveness, and an ability to collaborate with partners with widely varying processes and styles.

While my aims are practical, you'll find the tone of this book philosophical at times. Because great songs can move and touch ordinary listeners who have no special musical training, it's easy to underestimate the complexity hidden beneath the surface of sometimes deceptively simple musical materials, and the profound artistic work songwriting demands of us as songwriters. For me, artistic freedom is *mastering unconstrained movement within a creative domain*. Though style constrains vocabulary, we artists explore the infinity of possibilities within any such vocabulary. For dancers, this means moving the body effortlessly and expressively through space with posture and gesture. The space songwriters dance through—the space we'll explore together in this book—is bounded by the four songwriting facets, and the circle or "horizon" encompassing them. Learning to move in and through this space, working freely and independently with these elements, is the artistic path I call 360º songwriting.

CHAPTER 1

Song Seeds

What's the question most frequently asked of songwriters by nonsongwriters? *"Do the words come first, or does the music come first?"* Different songwriters give different answers to this question. My admittedly smart-aleck answer is: "Yes!" Let me explain.

Many songwriters have one, or just a few, preferred processes for starting a song. Some songwriters always start from lyrics, others from melody or from chords. Other writers experience inspirations arriving as fragments of entire songs: bits of lyric, melody, and chords, all together. Hit songwriter Diane Warren describes how in her writing, some songs might start from an "idea," while others begin with her just sitting at the keyboard, playing arbitrary sequences and listening for chords that sound "cool" together.[1] Writers' processes and preferred sources of inspiration also change over the course of their creative development. Paul Simon has written some of the most powerful and eloquent lyrics in contemporary music; yet, he has also worked on projects (many of them collaborations with musicians from varied world music genres) where the lyrics came relatively late, in a compositional process driven heavily by musical source inspirations.

While different writers have favored starting points, and some can start different songs from multiple directions, most often a *particular song* has a distinct starting point, arising primarily from one modality: a lyrical phrase, a melody, a chord progression, a story or situation. So, yes—for the most part— the music comes first, *or* the lyrics come first....

It's true that by the time we become aware of a song idea, it's often already a mélange of lyric, melody, rhythmic phrasing, chord riffs, etc. But this is *after* we've consciously or unconsciously been "working" the initial inspiration in various ways. Only rarely does a starting idea for a song begin with strong, original material in multiple aspects—lyrical or musical—simultaneously. The next time you get an idea for a song, pay attention to the *very moment*, the literal split second, when you first grabbed the idea (or the idea first grabbed you!)—when the starting point came to your awareness. You'll likely find that

---

1. Diane Warren NPR interview with Neil Conan, *Talk of the Nation*. "Insider Secrets to Great Songwriting." June 21, 2010. Interview archived at npr.org.

the stimulus or inspiration began as a small, singular idea, arising from a particular direction: a lyric phrase, a snatch of melody, or an unexpected chord move. I call this initial burst of inspiration or moment of inception a *song seed*.

Song seeds arrive from an endless variety of sources and directions. A lyric starting point may be a title or hook, a great single line, an interesting phrase, or even an unusual word. A snippet of melody, an intriguing move between chords your hands have never found before, or a starting riff on the guitar might serve as a musical seed. Or your seed could be a chance phrase overheard in a café, a story a friend tells you or that you hear on the news, a sudden memory of a past experience, a curious scene that strikes you on the street, or the way light comes through your window at a certain hour of the afternoon. For a hip-hop producer, it might be a "found sound" from a classic recording or a sampled industrial sound.

CATCHING SEEDS

Many experienced songwriters make a regular practice of collecting song seeds, though they may call them by different names. They're perennially vigilant for good song seeds, even throughout their everyday activities. When interviewed, songwriters love to describe serendipitous ways ideas for songs first occurred to them. But for every idea that led to a great song, a songwriter most likely caught, and scribbled down in some way, dozens of other ideas—ideas that still sit as drafts in a journal or on a scratch recording, seeds that haven't yet turned into songs. This is not a failure of the strategy, but an indication of its power.

Some writers are adept at writing songs different ways, precisely by recognizing and capturing these different kinds of starting points. Studying the genesis of different Beatles songs is a tour through every imaginable kind of starting point for a song: a melody remembered from a dream ("Yesterday"), an old circus poster ("For the Benefit of Mr. Kite"), passing phrases ("A Hard Day's Night"), a child's description of a picture ("Lucy in the Sky with Diamonds"), and borrowings or "judicious theft" of musical ideas from model songs ("Come Together," inspired by a particular chord move from Smokey Robinson's "I Heard It through the Grapevine").

We can move from observations about songwriters' informal seed-catching practices to a more intentional strategy and creative practice, by honing our awareness of seminal seed-catching moments. This practice improves our songwriting overall, for in being alert for and catching song seeds, we're practicing finding and recognizing great material for songs. A more disciplined approach to song seed catching also helps us learn to write songs from all directions, and in all directions.

Seeds and Personal Voice

Magpies are known to like to collect shiny things. Each songwriter is like a unique variety of magpie, responding to distinctive kinds of song ideas—our own private "shiny," as it were. (Apologies to magpies and *Firefly* fans.) Some of us delight in downward-tumbling Dorian moans; others are always on the hunt for good double entendres. The primary aspect of any song seed is that it catches *your* interest, attracts *your* attention as a songwriter. While some titles are instantly recognizable as potential hits by almost everyone, many great lyric seeds might catch the attention of one writer, while breezing right by another. (This is why good co-writing partners often act as "song seed catchers" from each other's casual conversation in the session.)

Song seeds can be deliberately sought out/hunted and gathered, as well as caught serendipitously during everyday activities. But the seeds that teach us most about our own songwriter's point of view, voice, and style are often those that we stumble on spontaneously. This requires being attentive for song seeds that leap out of the context of daily life.

You also need to be prepared to catch seeds as close as possible to the moment you notice them. The "half-life" of a song seed can be surprisingly fleeting. At the moment it comes to mind, it seems distinct and unforgettable. By the time you walk to the end of the block, it may be a vague impression. By the time you get home, you've likely not only forgotten the seed, but forgotten you *found* a seed. The remedy is to faithfully record it, in some way, literally within moments of noticing it. You may drive friends and loved ones bonkers, by pulling out your notepad in the midst of intimate conversations or suddenly pausing while discussing what restaurant to go to, with that glassy look in your eye. But that's the price of being (or hanging with) a songwriter.

Because of this need to catch seeds immediately, in the midst of daily life, it's also important to catch the seed quickly, then put down the pen or turn off the recorder and move on. Don't sit down in the hallway where the idea came to you, pull out your notebook, and try to finish the song then and there. Do this a few times, and your wiser, responsible self will simply stop your seed catching the next time an idea comes along.

Seed vs. Filler

Another challenge in the discipline of song seed catching is learning to catch *just the seed* in its most minimal, fragmentary form. Resist the temptation to quickly attach inessential material to the seed. I use the mildly pejorative term *filler* for such "supporting" material, which often gets in the way as we work later with the seed. Just as we can capture true song seeds in any facet, material in any facet can be filler, if it distracts from the seminal, powerful, and inspiring core of the seed idea.

Let's say you become aware of a potential lyric line, sung to a particular rhythm and melody. Chances are, the idea started as *either* a lyrical *or* a musical inspiration—that is, the initial energy came from one or the other direction. How did it get elaborated with that other material, without your conscious effort? As soon as we have the first "burst" of a song seed—sometimes even before we notice it—our songwriter minds go to work to provide scaffolding for the idea. If it's a lyric line, we're likely to grab a melody easy for us to access and remember. Similarly, we might start with a melodic seed and start chanting words to fill up the musical space. Or, discovering an intriguing chord progression at our instrument, we hum filler melody or words over the progression almost immediately.

We may generate filler just as an aid to remembering the seed—the amber in which we catch the fly of inspiration. Or we may be responding to self-imposed pressure to arrive quickly at something that feels more like a complete song, or at least a piece of one. Whatever the motivation, the problem filler presents is that we quickly lose the ability to distinguish seed from filler. Suppose we support a lyric seed with melodic filler. Since we're using the melody to remember a fresh, unexpected lyrical idea, it's playing a supporting role. We don't expect or even want that melody to be as interesting as the lyric. Yet five minutes later, we've forgotten which came first—lyric or melody. We may never revisit the melody again; we treat the fragment as a whole. Now, we're working not with a seed but a sapling.

Listening back later, we could in theory discard the filler melody, peel back to the original lyrical seed, and write a stronger supporting melody. But instead, we tend to uncritically accept the lyric plus hastily thrown-together music as an inseparable chunk. If enamored of the lyric, we may decide we like, or can live with, the music, and the filler music lives on into the final song. Or, listening with more discerning ears (ours, or our publisher's), we may hear that the filler music is clichéd and predictable, or that the piece as a whole lacks coherence. So, we reject the whole song, throwing the lyrical baby out with the musical bathwater (or vice versa). The seed is lost.

This is how we often wind up with evocative lyrics sung to trite melodies or banal progressions, or hooky melodies set to insipid, first-draft quality lyrics. I've had to rescue many song seeds, sometimes long after the fact, by excavating them from surrounding filler material and starting over—after laboriously recapturing the original, fresh idea. Bad lyrics (melodies, chords) can happen to good writers as the result of a simple process misstep—made in the *first few moments* of working with a song seed.

Happily, we can avoid many of these pitfalls via a simple process remedy as well, part of seed catching as a *strategy*: capture *just* the seed idea, sans filler, in stripped-down form rather than compound fragments of a bit of lyric, melody, and chords, bound together. Isolating seed material from the encumbrances of hastily generated filler frees you later, working the seed, to find supporting material that truly matches the seed, for the greater integrity of the song.

To be clear, I'm talking here about filler generated just after the moment the seed first catches your ear—material that you're likely to record *with* the seed. When working on the song in earnest, making associative connections to related material is part of the natural way we write. That's why it feels natural and right to generate filler as quickly as we can. But if we can practice capturing the seed in its original ragged, fragmentary, unadulterated state, it's actually *much* easier later to recognize and recapture the "juice" or essence of the seed, without first needing to extricate it from filler. Learning to separate the song seed "wheat" from the filler "chaff" leaves us with more workable material for our songs. It's also great training for working independently with material in the different facets.

Don't assume a seed idea is filler, though, just because it sounds simple. As you learn to catch seeds, you get used to hearing lyrics, melodies, and chord progressions in a "seed state"—naked, brave, nothing distracting. You may at first want to dismiss some of these ideas—especially melodic ideas, for some reason—as silly, trite, or derivative. Yet they may be strong ideas that will become mighty, anthemic choruses. Learning to strip away the inessentials becomes an act of trust in the power of the seed idea on its own.

VARIETIES OF SONG SEEDS

Let's turn now to an examination of different types of seeds we can catch as songwriters. We'll first discuss catching seeds in the form of ideas or concepts, prior to embodiment as material in facets. We'll then look at distinctive aspects of seeds from lyric and musical sources. Learning to isolate song seeds in terms of individual facets, with precision, will depend on more detailed exploration we'll do in the chapters on each respective facet that follow.

Concept Seeds

A song can begin from a concept or idea, a theme, a character, a situation, or a visual or other sensory image. In casual English usage, "concept" implies something fairly abstract. A song seed can be something more tangible: an image, an emotion triggered by a situation, a memory of a specific person or an imagined character, or a photograph that suggests a story to you. Seeds can thus range from the abstract or "conceptual" to the highly sensory—senses here including sound inspirations, like samples, particular timbres of instruments, etc.

As a simple placeholder or "umbrella term" I'll call *all* these kinds of materials *concept seeds*. This is because, from the standpoint of how we need to handle such seeds in the 360º approach, the process is similar even though the seed material may be of radically differing types or qualities, and degrees of clarity around what the real working "concept" for the seed is going to be. The key is that concept seeds are any seeds *not yet embodied* as specific material in a facet. Rather, they are reminders or prompts you'll use later to generate material in the facets. This distinction is key to the 360° songwriting approach. If we're writing *from* all directions, *in* all directions, then, when working from a concept seed, our next step needn't be searching for a lyric; we might work directly from concept to a melody or chord progression, for example.

This does present a practical problem in distinguishing concept seeds vs. lyric seeds in particular. We jot down lyric seeds in words. When our starting point is a concept seed, not yet set in compelling lyric form, we use words to jot down the idea as well. Yet, it's important to distinguish a lyric seed from a *textual reminder of* a concept seed. A common pitfall is mistaking the concept reminder for a lyric seed later.

Here's an example. I see an old woman get on the bus. She has too many bags to carry and fumbles with her pocketbook while trying to get out her bus card. Something about this scene strikes my fancy. I pull out my song seed notebook and jot down: *"Old woman on the 71 bus, too many bags to carry."* What kind of seed is this, and how will I work with it?[2] Suppose two days later, I find this phrase and treat it as a lyric seed:

> Old woman on the Seventy-One Bus
> Too many bags to carry

Not a bad lyric: there's internal slant rhyme of "on/One," alliteration of "bus/ bags" etc. But these sonic aspects aren't what captured my interest initially; the seed was the image, the scene. Also: do I need the real-life detail of the "71" bus—part of the original context? Especially since it crowds the line? Or I might have jotted down:

> Old woman on the bus
> Carrying way too many shopping bags

Hear the second line's "prose-y" rhythm? This suggests that this is a concept seed, one I want to be careful not to force-fit too hastily into a lyric. When we uncritically accept a concept seed description, jotted down as a reminder of an image or story, as an actual lyric line, we can wind up with sonically or rhythmically awkward lyrics. Later, in revision, we may need to painfully wrestle that idea into an actual line, having already built musical phrasing, rhyme scheme, and form around it. Poor old woman; hasn't she had it hard enough already?

An extreme example of this error is when we mistake a concept seed for a song *title* or *hook*. Such a leap to lyric material can preemptively force decisions about overall song form, theme, and focus that can hamper us later in developing the song. It can also lead to those too on-the-nose titles that "tell" vs. "show"—flaws that creative writing (and lyric writing) teachers love

---

2. Of course, these days I might just snap a photo of the woman as my reminder. Then there's no written phrase to mistake later for a lyric seed. But I also might not remember why I thought the image was a good starting point for a song.

to pounce on. A songwriter's career might pivot on the difference between: "If you don't love me, I can't make you…" and "I Can't Make You Love Me (If You Don't)…"

By all means, capture interesting concept seeds when they strike you. Simply recognize them as such. Of course, you won't always immediately know which kind of seed you have at the time you catch it. Don't dither deciding which song seed list to add your seed to. But remember to be alert for concept seeds as such, and be willing to write them down as is—even if the line doesn't sound right yet, or doesn't rhyme. Don't pass it by; but also, don't try to wrestle it into suitable lyric form on the spot, *before* you write it down.

Let's go back to our old gal. Wanting to feel like a quick and clever songwriter, I reach for and write down this rhymed couplet:

> Old woman on the train
> Stumbles in out of the rain

Writing this instead of a simple description and reminder for the starting image, I've made two mistakes. The rhymed couplet is not the seed, but an off-the-cuff response. Neither the lone line "old woman on the train," nor the rhymed couplet on its own, without the triggering image, would have caught my attention. Worse, in getting distracted by the rhymed couplet, I've *lost* my original idea (besides moving the poor woman from bus to train): the irony of her having too many bags to carry—with all that implies. *That* was the essence of my original observation—the important thing to capture and to work with later. Having lost this, I'll wind up with a weaker, less focused song. Or I may look at the couplet later and say, "Why did I think *that* was worth writing down?" Use your time to capture the why; don't always try to rhyme on the fly.

By recognizing and recording concept seeds as such, and not conflating them with lyric seeds, we're more likely later to take the time to experiment with varied lyrical expressions for the concept before settling. Distinguishing concept from lyric seeds will also expand your openness to lyric seeds that don't immediately suggest a concept: lines that intrigue because you don't (yet!) know what they mean.

SHOULD WE CAPTURE CONTEXT?

How much of the originating context needs to be saved with a captured seed? If it's a chance phrase spoken by a friend telling us about their latest romance, do we need to record *who* gave us the seed, or the (possibly unsavory) specifics of their personal circumstances? I advise that you capture as *little* information as necessary about the initiating context—only what's essential to remembering the seed's "cool" factor later. Strong seeds invite you to lift them out of their original context. With such seeds, your later work doesn't depend on that original context; it may depend on you letting that context go and reframing the seed. Stripping contextual associations from seeds is thus more than a matter of convenience; it's part of the creative work of seed catching.

There are a few pragmatic reasons to capture the generating context for a seed: when you want a memento of the moment of capture, to aid in reflection on your seed-catching practice, when writing a song as personal history or personal gift, or in anticipation of getting interviewed about your hit song years later by *Rolling Stone*. Also, seeds you catch from fellow songwriters (as opposed to the nonsongwriter folks I call "civilians") warrant special handling. In a formal co-writing session, any novel material spoken aloud in the room by either partner is potentially shared seed material, for that session or a later one. I record such seeds with session notes, so that the co-writing context is clear when I return to the seed later. If you do think you'll want context information for a seed, *write it down with the seed*. Trust me—you won't remember unless you do!

Lyric Seeds

For many writers, the easiest kinds of song seeds to recognize are lyric seeds, especially titles and hooks. In genres such as mainstream country, a good title is a big part of getting to a good song.[3] Not surprisingly, typical names for lists of song ideas that songwriters keep on hand are "title books," "hook books," and "idea books." But not all great lyric seeds are necessarily destined to be titles or hooks, or even central lines of the song. Great first lines, or lines that will show up buried within a later verse, passing images, and even striking individual words are all fair game.

Lyric seeds are easy kinds of seeds to catch for several reasons. We're surrounded by language in every aspect of our daily lives: conversations and overheard dialogue; language in books, the news, and other media; even our own thoughts, which we often experience as words heard internally, a kind of silent monologue. It's also easy to transcribe lyric seeds just by jotting them down; we don't need special notation or transcription skills for lyrics, as we do

---

3. Providing just the title or hook for a song is valued as a creative contribution. Even in contexts outside of formal co-writes, I've heard it can be valued as at least 10 percent of the writers' credit.

with melody, chord, or rhythm ideas. For popular song lyrics, where informal conversational language is valued, strong lyric ideas can appear in the midst of everyday activities and interactions.

Attributes of Good Lyric Seeds

Because language is so ubiquitous and inescapable in our lives, it's worth asking: what makes a given fragment of language a good song seed? Here are a few observations about attributes of strong lyric seeds. To ground the discussion, I'll use an example lyric seed of my own: "Nice Day till the Hurricane."

Individuality/Voice

As mentioned earlier, through seed catching you gain a surer feel for specific kinds of lyric material that appeal to you individually. These form the core of your *voice*—your signature style and vocabulary as a writer. I found "Nice Day till the Hurricane" interesting because of the intriguing implied story behind the line. The paradoxical juxtaposition and contrast of a "nice day" and a "hurricane" strikes a casual-yet-ironic tone that I love, and that is very much in my individual style.

Emotional Resonance

Songs are not creative nonfiction or philosophical essays. Effective song seeds move us emotionally, or move our feet, as well as stimulate our minds. Finding the emotional resonance is important in clarifying concept seeds, but essential in working with lyric seeds as well. I wouldn't try to prejudge this aspect too quickly, though, as you learn seed catching. At first, you might need to revel in clever, playful aspects of seed catching, which can become almost a game (like working a crossword puzzle but in real life). But eventually, we recognize that strong seeds—the ones that *matter*—reveal a story worth telling in song.

This ties back to seed catching as a way to find out what *you* care about as a writer. With "Nice Day till the Hurricane," I get an immediate sense for a character, situation, point of view—a wry, ironic attitude about the misfortunes of life… like a blues singer's attitude, but with more of a country feel. Personally, I'm drawn to writing songs about more nuanced emotional situations, not just stark "I love you/I hate you" declarations.

Novelty/Surprise/Unexpectedness

Songwriters are always on the lookout for freshness and originality in their seeds. The phrase "Nice Day till the Hurricane" begins with a bland, cliché opener, like the proverbial smiley-face "Have a nice day," but then surprises with the violent image of the hurricane. It's almost a song seed *about* surprise.

It might seem obvious that we are in search of novelty in lyric seeds. And yet, novice seed catchers often write down pure clichés as song seeds, even when there's nothing unusual or striking about them—no new twist or angle for exploiting them. In these cases, you're counting mostly on *familiarity* of the fragment as a reason to build it into a song. You can sometimes write great songs based on such clichés, particularly if you're the first to grab a new idiom or expression for a song. But for a more conventional cliché, you need that twist, to set it in an innovative context.

Usually, though, seed catching is listening for "anti-clichés!" Some of the Beatles' greatest songs, like "Eight Days a Week," came from awkward expressions or malapropisms (from Ringo, from taxi drivers, from children) that had a fresh sound when pulled out of their original context.

Compactness

A seed is often the shortest, most concise way to capture the essence of an idea that has caught our attention. The unity, cohesiveness, and compactness of the expression of the idea play a focusing role when developing a complete song. This is especially but not exclusively true of titles and hooks. "Nice Day till the Hurricane" is a short, punchy phrase that has the hookiness built right in.

Recontextability

By noticing a song seed, we *lift it out of the original context* where we experienced it, and see or hear it anew, as something bigger or at least different than in its original setting. An everyday phrase like "going for broke" suddenly strikes us as applicable to a relationship. An image seen in everyday life suddenly takes on metaphorical resonance. Skilled seed catchers keep their songwriter's ear to the wind, continually listening "sideways" for associative leaps and reframing of lyric material. (This can make us songwriters annoying dinner companions!)

"Recontextable" is not the same as "vaguely universal." Concrete, small details engage the listener. "She brushed the hair back from her face" may strike you as a great lyrical seed because it conjures a specific, believable picture. The story you build into the song may have nothing to do with the girl who sparks the seed idea for you. As for "Nice Day till the Hurricane," the best evidence that this seed was amenable to being lifted out of its original context is that I can't remember the original context where I caught this seed. (Supporting evidence for my earlier assertion—if you want to remember context, write it down with the seed!)

Collisions of Sound and Sense

The strongest lyric seeds delight and engage ear as well as mind, combining an intriguing thought or insight with compelling sonic qualities in the specific combinations of words and syllables. You can work with a seed that captures an observation, but is not yet a clear title or lyric line. You can work with a great-sounding line, even with no idea (yet) of what it means. But song seeds worth their weight in gold (or even more!) arrive as a harmonious collision: a single, unified expression, generating both the lightning and the thunderclap as the two clouds of sense and sound rub together. We know instantly what a "Hard Day's Night" means. We also know we're hearing it stated in a fresh way. This is the magical art songwriters refer to as the gift of "turning a phrase."

Let's examine some collisions of sound and sense in our example:

- *Rhythm and pace*: The steadiness of "nice day" contrasts with the relative acceleration of "hurricane." This echoes both the theme and the implied movement and narrative of the line.

- *Assonance* (agreement of vowels): The internal rhyme of "day" and "-cane" is the most prominent.

- *Consonance* (agreement of consonants): "**N**ice" and "-ca**n**e" bookend the line. Note this is consonance, but not the more specific effect of alliteration (consonance at the beginning of words), since the "n" is internal to the word "hurricane."

- *Sonic aspects of vowels*: Long vowels ("I," "AY") begin the line, followed by the short "IH" of "till," the cloudy or murky "UR," the assonant return of "AY."

- *Sonic aspects of consonants*: The "n" and "s" are smooth and gentle; "d" moves towards a more percussive sound (a voiced plosive), followed by its harder partner sound "t" (an unvoiced plosive). The "h" is ironic, a smooth aspirant vowel/consonant blend metaphorically suggesting the approaching wind.

I'm not suggesting I was conscious of all these links between sound, imagery, and sense in the moment the line drew my attention as a seed. I'm not that smart—but my seed-catcher's ear is, and yours can be too. Emergent sonic properties of resonance, structure, and correspondence between sound and sense are characteristic of strong seeds. We learn to catch them first. Then, we learn why.

Rhyme Connections

As with jumping to rhyming with a concept seed, generating on-the-fly rhymes can also be problematic in catching true lyric seeds. Even when an individual line is a great seed, in both sound and sense aspects, we may feel we haven't done our job unless we immediately try to rhyme it. But rhymes we come up with this way are rarely strong; they're most likely obvious, top-of-your-head rhymes. And now, we've locked an initial strong seed line into a couplet, closing off many potential ways of working with it.

A specific rhyme or sonic connection may be a seed in its own right, if it's a surprising juxtaposition of words that also resonates in meaning—collisions again. Here, you'd want to capture the rhyme as part of the seed. But you may *not* want to write down too many prototype or "filler" lines fulfilling the rhyme—maybe just the pair or list of resonating words that caught your attention. Of the many creative tasks in lyric writing, rhyming is one where some extra time and help can make a big difference. A rhyming dictionary and a rhyme word list (or worksheet) are highly effective tools for searching for rhymes in response to starting lyric material such as a title or line.

Musical Seeds

Central to the idea of 360° songwriting is writing from all directions. So, we want to catch song seeds, not just in lyric form, but in musical form as well.

There are distinct challenges in capturing musical vs. lyric seeds:

1. *Isolation.* In catching musical song seeds, as compared with lyric seeds, problems of separating the essential seed from associated "filler" material becomes trickier. Until we train ourselves to separate melodic, harmonic, and rhythmic aspects, they tend to be closely intertwined in musical seeds. And yet song seed catching is a perfect first training ground for developing these isolation skills.

2. *Notation.* We must have ways of capturing seed ideas. It's easy to write down lyrics and concepts (though also easy to confuse them for that very reason, as we've seen!). To write down melodies, chords, or rhythms, we need some kind of notation. Use of technology like portable recorders, cell phones, or sequencers expedites the capture of musical performances. When you're ready to work a melodic seed, you can just listen back to the recording and get to work. But the exercise of writing out the musical ideas can sharpen your focus and make you zero in on the precise expression of the seed idea. There's also a power in working directly with notation—and specifically, with fast, informal notations. Curiously, as you get better about notating or transcribing musical ideas, your musical memory will also improve!

3. *Dependence on an instrument.* Most musicians, whether singers or not, can hear melodies, and sing or hum them, away from an instrument. Similarly, we can hear and tap out rhythmic patterns. This is harder for most of us with harmonic ideas and chord progressions. You can cultivate this ability to hear progressions in "mind's ear," away from an instrument. Spend time catching seeds both at and away from your instrument. Listen for musical ideas that arise spontaneously in your "inner musical ear." Be alert for ideas sparked from external sources. This can include other music—if you borrow judiciously, rather than plagiarizing too obviously!

4. *Sense and sound.* Concept vs. lyric seeds can be thought of as a continuum from sense (meaning, ideas, observations in the world) to *sound* (lyric fragments that interest us because of their sonic aspects). We encounter this same polarity with seed material in musical forms. As we'll see in the "Harmony" chapter, sometimes we're not thinking harmonically at all when we find a "chord seed" at the keyboard or on guitar—we're responding mostly to sonorities of the chord. At other times, it might be "sense"—that is, the "sensible" or meaningful as opposed to the "sensory"—aspects of chords in the context of a harmonic progression that forms the seed, the novel discovery we want to capture. This polarity creates significant challenges for the ways we "transcribe" various musical seeds. We need notation that doesn't get in the way when the essence of the seed is more sound-driven. Informal notations, along with recording technology, can be useful tools in these situations.

We also catch pure "sound seeds"—not associated with lyrics or direct musical material. Since the scope of this book does not extend to sound-based production or experimental composition, from a process standpoint here we might treat these—perhaps surprisingly—as concept seeds. A concept seed might be captured in the form of a photo, to use later as a prompt in writing. Similarly, a sample from existing music, or sampled environmental sound, can certainly be a starting point for songwriting. The songwriting-specific work begins when you "cast" those sounds into rhythm, lyric, melody, or chords.

Guidelines for Catching Musical Seeds

Here are some guidelines for catching musical seeds. We'll discuss specific techniques for grabbing rhythmic, lyric, melodic, and harmonic or chordal seeds in each respective chapter on the facets.

Quality

It's easy to be self-critical about the quality of your song seeds. When honing seed-catching skills, I suggest you grab ideas fairly indiscriminately. Don't stop to judge your seeds for quality, just practice snagging them out of the air. As long as it feels like *your* stuff—banal, boring, or not—grab it and worry about it later. This won't be your ongoing working process, but it will rapidly build your inner ear and musical memory. Having written for many decades, I still go through refresher periods where I write a lot of seeds down, then let both seeds and my seed-catching practice sit for a while.

The quality of lyric seeds can be more obvious at a glance (or a listen) than melodic, harmonic, or rhythmic seeds. We're unaccustomed to hearing musical ideas stripped back to their essentials. At first, even potentially strong melodies heard this way may feel trivial, sing-songy, nursery-rhyme-ish, almost embarrassing. Be patient, and overcome your resistance to catching these ideas.

Eventually, this practice will help you recognize and capture stronger, more original melodic ideas and to strip away nonessentials. The same applies to seeds in the other facets. Once you dutifully capture a seed that seems trite or banal, then see it take form and gain interest through the act of crystallizing and recording it, you'll learn to put more trust in your seed-noticing creative mind and feel less reverence for your inner judge and taste filter.

Originality

Closely allied to the issue of quality is concern for originality of seeds. We're surrounded by language in daily life—source material available for transformation into song lyrics. We can capture lyrical clichés and use them as seeds, especially if we give them that "twist." We can also discover fresh lyric lines or "anti-clichés" just by being attentive. But melodies, chords, and rhythms are built on highly repetitive cliché materials: stock progressions, melodic figures, or rhythmic riffs that cue us to genre and groove. We can't quickly assess the freshness or originality of such materials in seed catching.

In addition, one continuing source of seed material is *other people's music*. We can generally (though not always) tell when we're inadvertently "lifting" lyric material directly from lines of someone else's song. Musical borrowings can be more subtle and unconscious. So, some care is in order when a melody "pops into our heads" or a chord progression falls out beneath our hands, before proceeding with confidence that the material is ours to work with.

With these caveats, I still recommend that, especially while building your seed-catching skills, you catch and notate all seeds that come to mind—even if you suspect they're not original. If you quickly recognize your melody as the first line of "Honky Tonk Women," then don't bother. But if you have only a vague sense you've heard it before, don't waste energy worrying about it; write it down. You can intercept possible rip-offs later (before your album comes out!). Even if you find later that you've rewritten the hook of "Smells Like Teen Spirit," your effort was not wasted. You've sharpened your ear, and practiced the skills of grabbing seeds and composing melodies.

In the musical imagination from whence seed ideas spring, memory and invention are closely intertwined. I learned this lesson in the context of traditional folk music, where the lines between old tunes half-remembered, variant versions, and new creations can be hazy and fluid. But the principle applies across genres and styles. Great performers play material they *didn't* compose as if they did—in fact, as if they're composing it *on the spot*. The corollary: great writers can stumble across original ideas that don't *feel* original when they arrive. Famously, Paul McCartney woke from a dream with the melody for "Yesterday" in his head, then spent weeks trying to find which old song he'd half-remembered.

The Work of Not Working the Seed

Another common way that we inadvertently dilute the unity and clarity of seed material, especially with musical seeds, is by overdeveloping or overelaborating before or during the process of capturing it. Many musical seeds are cyclical or looping in nature. You "tumble them 'round" in your mind. Often, you catch yourself humming something you recognize as a seed only after it's been cycling this way a while. (This is especially true of seeds caught during repetitive physical activities like walking.)

These repetitions are never exact; as you cycle the idea, then externalize it with voice and instrument, you experiment with minor variations in notes, timings, and durations. It takes time for these variations to sort themselves out and stabilize. The ideal moment to capture the seed is just when it has clarified and come into focus, but before your mind starts elaborating and varying too much, or pivots from a unified single idea into a response and starts building a larger structural phrase. Err in the direction of early capture. You can always do the same "tumbling" and refining afterward.

THE ART OF SEED CATCHING

We've described some challenges in seed catching in general: separating seed from filler, not prematurely working the seed, capturing the seed without unnecessary context, and, with musical seeds in particular, avoiding the tendency to *elaborate* seeds before capturing them. Let's illustrate some of these pitfalls in seed catching with an example melodic seed.

FIG. 1.1. Melodic Seed Example

This seed is in a minor pentatonic mode, often used for improvisational vocal riffing, but I've made more definite melodic choices in capturing and especially in notating it as a seed. As you practice catching and notating melodic seeds, the melodies get more distinct and shaped, and you'll be able to retain longer, more complex melodic passages in your mind's ear.

This seed is unified, with little inessential material. The repeated melodic figure in the first half of bars 1 and 3, respectively, creates an audible question-answer phrase structure. Yet in an important sense, the seed is *irreducible*. Take either the start or end away, and you lose the asymmetrical phrasing essential to the seed. The one-bar pause at the end, though silent, is integral, building an even four-bar phrasing into the seed. If we loop the seed, we'll loop it with this extra bar of time.

There's no lyric yet associated with the seed. There may be hints, though, of some features of an eventual lyric setting. For example, the slur in bar 3 hints at a lyric melisma (a single syllable sung over a sequence of changing notes). We don't know what that lyric will be, but the slur even now has a textural effect, contrasting with the similar, but articulated, figure in bar 1.

Rhythmic information is interleaved with melody in a more intrinsic way than chords or lyrics we might add to it. It's still possible for the rhythmic component of a melody to be filler. It's also possible that the rhythm is the interesting seed idea and the melody the filler—or that this seed really depends on both aspects together.

One way to test this is by removing rhythmic effects to see if what's left still has the magic that caught your ear. At first, this is painstaking work, but with practice you can learn to more rapidly "stress-test" a seed idea in this way. In the example, the rhythmic effects embedded in the seed, especially the anticipations in bars 2 and 3, do help shape the melodic seed. In particular, the anticipation into bar 3 connects the two halves of the phrase: we hear the figure D, C, A ending on the A, the last note doing double duty initiating the new phrase of bar 3 (a motivic device known as "elision"). The rhythmic effects add structural interest to the melodic seed. Take the anticipations away, and to my songwriter's ear at least, the phrase feels less unified.

FIG. 1.2. Melodic Seed with Simplified Rhythm

Let's see how filler might get captured with this seed. Suppose I get this seed sitting at my instrument. To capture it, I hum the tune and support myself with some chords:

FIG. 1.3. Melodic Seed with "Filler" Chords

I'd call these chords harmonic "filler." The progression isn't inherently very interesting; the melodic seed is rendered no more interesting with the chords than without them. The relation between melody and harmony is slaved: all melody notes sounded with chord attacks are chord tones; and the chords move in parallel with rhythmic accents of the melody. The chords aren't *wrong* for the seed; they're just not essential to the melodic idea. They're an add-on, an amplification. I could find these chords, *or different ones*, later, working from the melodic seed alone. Notating the melody without the chords would be more effective seed catching.

How about lyric filler? Suppose I'm walking down the street, humming this tune. Instinctively I'm drawn to put lyrics to it. A pretty girl passes by, and I sing:

Ba - by you are just the kind of per - son ___ I _____ want to ___ know

FIG. 1.4. Melodic Seed with "Filler" Lyrics

This lyric shows telltale signs of filler—material grabbed on the fly *after* the melodic seed came to me. It lacks intrinsic interest. A good test is asking the question: Would you write this line down on its own as an exciting lyrical seed? It has a cliché aspect, with no redeeming fresh angle. While the lyric arose partially in response to the melodic seed, it's not a compositionally attentive response. (Perhaps, I was attending more to the girl.) The lyric matches the melody only crudely, and thus is not very singable. The abstract, innocuous word "person" is set on a long spotlighted note. Syllabic junctures like "just / the" are crowded on rapid repeated notes. An unimportant connective ("to") is placed on the melisma. And the most telltale sign of lyric filler? It's a "telling" line.

Even a bit of compositional thought could get me to a lyric better matched to the melodic contour, like "If you're gonna leave me for no reason, tell me no lies." That thoughtful lyric work isn't as likely to come as I'm walking down the street. (After all, I haven't even talked to the girl—so we aren't breaking up yet!) If I save the seed as melody only, I can write this lyric (or a better one) later. If I save melody and lyric together, I may pass them both over later. Or, instead of writing my breakthrough hit, I'll wind up with "Just My Kind of Person." In seed catching, sometimes more is less.

We're not finished with our catalog of sins in the fleeting act of catching a song seed. Here's an illustration of starting to overwork or "pre-work" our example seed on the fly:

Would-Be Instrumental Riff

FIG. 1.5. Melodic Seed with Instrumental Phrases

In figure 1.5, measure 4 is now interspersed instrumental material, intermixing an accompanying funky bass line or guitar riff into the vocal melody. It will be hard later to sift out which part was the essential vocal line, destined to take a lyric, and what was embroidery.

In figure 1.6, we've overworked the seed by ornamenting it, filling in some of the very gaps in the rhythmic pattern that made the original idea fresh. As we work seeds in our minds, it's natural to vary them and fill them in, in this way, using the original seed as silent counterpoint. Do too much of this before capturing the seed, and you weaken or obscure outlines of the original idea.

FIG. 1.6. Melodic Seed with Melodic Ornamentation

EXERCISE 1.1. A WEEK OF SONG SEED CATCHING

Here's an intensive regime for a week's "boot camp" of song seed catching, guaranteed to jumpstart your seed-catching skills. For this week, be as uncritical and indiscriminate as possible in seeds you grab (given that day's focus). Don't go hunting for seeds. Wait until they come to you. When they do, don't judge or filter them.

Also during this week, do your best *not* to "work" any song seeds you gather! This is a chance to teach your creative mind the difference between catching and working seeds. Of course, there's a nefarious reverse psychology here. Try this weekly practice at times when you're feeling stuck in your writing, or suffering from a bout of so-called "writer's block." Be strict about the "no working the seed" rule. By the week's end, you'll be itching to start work on a song from one of your seeds!

Day 1	This is your "calibration" day, where you find out about your natural seed-catching rhythm and the facets most familiar to you. Catch seeds of any and all kinds as they come to your attention.
Day 2	For the first of your days of specific attention, focus on *lyrics*, the facet most comfortable and familiar to most writers. Write down any seeds you notice of any sort, but be particularly attuned to lyric seeds. Given the focus of lyrics, though, be alert to any possible sources of inspiration: dialogue, media, or lines that pop into your head, etc.
Day 3	On this day, switch your focus to *concept* and *sound seeds*. By doing this the day after lyric seeds, it will highlight the differences for you. Again, be open to any thematic ideas, images, fleeting memories, or sonic source material that strike your interest. In this case, don't worry about whether the concept would be best suited for a song as opposed to a poem, a short story, a blog post, or a stand-up comedy routine.

Days 4,

5, and 6   On these three days, focus on a different musical facet (melody, chords, rhythm) each day. You can try these in any order, but following the general principle of moving from easier to harder facets, I'd suggest the sequence: melody, rhythm, then chords.

Caveat: This part of the week's exercise may be difficult in advance of working through the chapters that follow on the individual facets. As we saw with our melodic seed example, rhythmic ideas especially tend to be closely interwoven with other material when we grab seeds. You'll get more out of working through each chapter, though, if you've first tried some seed catching focused on that facet, relying on your own intuitive approach. This will provide you an experiential reference point, to ground those later explorations.

On each day, be open to *any* sources of inspiration for that day's facet of focus. For example, listen for melodic ideas from non-musical stimuli like sounds of the natural environment. Listen for chordal ideas *away* from your instrument. Listen to similar snatches of spoken dialogue overheard in coffee shops that sparked lyrical seeds earlier in the week—but listen now for *rhythmic* aspects of that spoken language, or the melodies suggested by the speech tones.

Day 7   For the last day of your week's practice, go back to open-ended seed catching. See how many seeds you catch and from which sources. Compare these with your experience and results from the first "calibration" day.

Finally, as a reward to yourself, on this last day, pick your favorite seed of the week and—at last!—allow yourself to work on it. You should now be better able to distinguish the very different kinds of energy and attention involved in catching vs. working seed material.

Reflection: At the week's end, consider the seeds you've gathered as a whole. What senses, facets, sources of inspiration came most easily to you? Which did you pass over without enough attention?

This seed-catching week requires an intensity and pace that is difficult to sustain over a long period of time. But in this one week of practice, you'll learn a lot about your level of skill in seed catching—particularly, which facets and sources are easier or harder for you to draw from. You can come back to this exercise periodically throughout your development as a writer, using it as a refresher, or to replenish your seed catalog. You can also use the daily focus format to stretch your seed-catching skills in other ways, working with polarities such as: natural vs. man-made sound sources, inner and outer sources of inspiration, catching seeds at vs. away from your instrument, silly and humorous vs. serious and emotionally intense seeds, etc.

CONCLUSION: SONG SEEDS AND THE FACETS

Song seed catching is the master strategy of 360° songwriting. Separating the moment of catching an inspiration from the work of developing it into a song is a process skill that can transform your entire songwriting practice in many ways. Seed-catching practice also provides an experiential foundation for all the work we'll do with individual songwriting facets throughout this book. Instead of working only with unwieldy "lumps" of unfinished songs— fragments combining both strong and weak bits of lyric, melody, chords, etc.— we learn to recognize strong starting points and leave these as far more potent kinds of fragments, yielding strong seed ideas in multiple facets.

Song seeds are not the *only* way songs begin. As we'll see especially in working with the facets of rhythm and harmony, many writers work over loops, riffs, sampled sounds, or by improvising over familiar chords and cycles—a range of processes we could call "jamming." I've focused on song seed catching as an essential technique to prepare us to work more independently with material in the various facets. In addition, as you strengthen seed-catching skills, you'll also get better at the on-the-fly "seed catching" necessary to recognize strong material when jamming over riffs, chords, and loops.

Now that we can get song ideas *from* all directions, it's time to learn to write *in* all directions.

CHAPTER 2

The Songwriter's Compass

Working with song seeds, we've established an experiential reference point for the 360º songwriting approach. You should now have a better idea of which kinds of sources of inspiration come naturally to you as a writer, and which stretch you beyond your comfort zone. In this chapter, we begin work with the 360º songwriting model in detail, as a comprehensive set of strategies for expanding your scope and flexibility as a songwriter.

Songwriters love metaphors. We'll explore the 360º model with the aid of a metaphor that we'll use throughout the book—the Songwriter's Compass. This model involves three main components: the four songwriting facets, the World of content, and structure or form.

THE FOUR FACETS

Creative material we work with in writing songs can be viewed in terms of four distinct *facets*: rhythm, lyrics, melody, and harmony (chords). These facets are *core* to the essence of the song—rather than ancillary material used in *writing* the song, or part of arrangement and production aspects. Picture these four facets as four quadrants or directions around a circle—the four directions of the songwriter's compass.

Words and Music

Let's compare this circular picture of four facets to a more conventional way of breaking up songwriting: with the cut-with-an-ax distinction of *words* or *lyrics* vs. *music*. Like the "mind/body" split, this false dichotomy not only over-simplifies but misleads, in ways that can hold back our work as songwriters.

There are two big problems with this conventional wisdom. First, the words/music split lumps two vital yet separate aspects under the umbrella of "words" or "lyrics"—lyrics as *sound elements* interacting with melody, chords, and rhythm, vs. lyrics as expressing the *theme, meaning,* or *subject matter* of the song—the content. This reinforces a notion that a song's *meaning* is embodied solely in lyrics, with music mere support or accompaniment. In practice, this attitude leads to songs with cool lyrics but thrown-together music, or great music with disconnected lyrics.

Lyrics are more than just content or sense. Their sonic aspects are equally important for songwriters. Conversely, meaning or content is *not* exclusively the province of lyrics. Melodies, chords, and rhythms all carry meaning and emotion in equally important, though different, ways than lyrics. You can start a song from a musical idea and be led directly to content, without lyrics (yet) in the picture. You can be inspired by the *sound* aspects of lyrics, prior to any firm idea of what the song will be "about."

The words/music dichotomy also treats music in an undifferentiated, monolithic way. Songwriters work with melodic, harmonic, and rhythmic aspects of songs in markedly different ways. Lyrics also connect associatively and sonically to these three musical facets in distinct ways. Songwriters are often asked, "Which comes first, the words or the music?" Rarely are we asked, "Which comes first, the melody or the chords?" Yet, differing answers to that question have dramatic effect on the songs and kinds of songs we write.

Sound and Sense

More fruitful for songwriting is recognizing an interplay of *sound* and *sense*, which plays a role in lyrics and each musical facet. This interplay can be considered, not as a dichotomy or split of two distinct components, but more as a continuum or *polarity*. Just as lyrics involve sound as well as sense, the musical facets of rhythm, melody, and harmony each offer their own sense or "meaning," in ways different than the referential meanings of words. The implication is that we can start a song from a concept or idea and move directly, in response, to material in any facet, matching thematically between content and emotion and that material. We can also start directly from seed material in any facet—without a predetermined idea or content. We can then let material in that facet suggest content: themes, subject matter, imagery. And in each facet, *sound* and *sense* aspects of the material might provide different entry points. We get to different kinds of songs by exploring these different strategies.

The compass picture reflects these creative principles by placing lyrics as a peer facet to the three "musical" facets of rhythm, melody, and chords. (I put "musical" in "quotes" because if you take this picture to heart, lyrics are also a musical facet.)

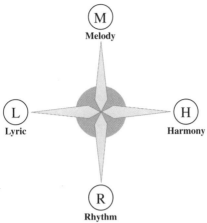

FIG. 2.1. The Songwriter's Compass: Facets

The picture in figure 2.1 lays out the facets (clockwise from the bottom) in the order that we present them in subsequent chapters: rhythm, lyric, melody, and harmony. Despite this specific visual rendering, melody is not primary, at the top; rhythm is not foundational, at the base; lyric is no "farther" from harmony than it is from melody or lyric, etc. Any two-dimensional depiction of the compass inevitably fibs a bit.

THE WORLD

Where does content show up in this picture? Imagine the four facets as circumscribing the realm of song, the domain or magic circle of songwriting. Content—ideas, themes, stories, characters, emotions, meaning, or real-world sense aspects that serve as source material for songs—can be pictured as lying *outside* the perimeter of this circle, in a region we can just call "the World," inherently boundless and infinite.

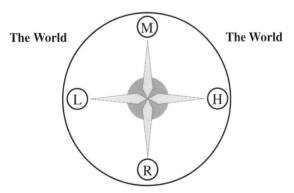

FIG. 2.2. The Songwriter's Compass: Facets and the World

We want to write songs from myriad potential inspirations: a tea kettle's whistle, a fleeting mood, a conversation overheard on the subway, a song half-heard playing on the radio in the other room, a compelling news story. But to carry a particular inspiration or idea into a *song*, we must transform it, at some point engaging directly with materials integral to the song itself—passing our original inspiration through shaping forces of one or more facets. (Our starting inspiration may also, of course, take first form as seed material in a facet.)

It's tempting to try to structure the World itself, defining various categories of "things songs can be about": topics, subject matter, genre, and style. I'll avoid such discussions in this book. I won't try to tell you what to write songs about, first, because I believe songs can and should be written about *everything*. Songs help us connect our heads and hearts—to think and reflect about what we care about, to care about what we think about. Given this mission, anything and everything in the world is worthy of the unique kinds of attention we as songwriters can pay, and songs can draw from us as listeners.

More importantly, changing process can change content. At any stage of our evolution, we're inevitably limiting our concept of "what we can write songs about." By flipping around our habitual creative pathways, we have the potential to dramatically expand that scope. When you write from different directions, and particularly from song seeds without preconceived content, you can find your way to subject matter, source material, stories, and characters you'd *never think* to write about working idea-first, or even lyric-first.

Sound and Timbre

The songwriter's challenges are allied with, but not identical to, those faced by the composer, orchestrator, arranger, performer, studio producer, or sound designer. In each of these creative areas, sonic aspects such as timbre (instrumental as well as vocal) play an integral role. These aspects are, however, only indirectly influential in songwriting.

For many songwriters, specific sonic textures and timbres may spur their creative work toward a song. Vocal melodies may be strongly influenced by your own vocal qualities or those of artists you write for. A chord riff that begins a song may derive its creative force from specific voicings, tone, and resonance of the instrument. A beat maker or track producer may respond to a sampled sound or excerpt by turning it into a groove or instrumental rhythm. Sound and timbre aspects may also end up integrated into a song's final recorded version, and can play a major role in a song's success. Aficionados can recognize many Beatles songs from the first distinctive chord.

Nevertheless, there is a power in recognizing the core facets of songwriting as distinct from these factors. If you can only create sectional contrast in a song by strumming the guitar louder, singing more emotionally, or bringing in a four-on-the-floor kick in the mix, you will not be challenged to learn how to use the elements of melodic range, harmonic rhythm, or lyric phrasing to their fullest effect. You develop further as a songwriter by focusing on core compositional and lyrical design concerns, momentarily at least putting these other concerns in the background. Reflecting this, sound or timbre does not appear as a separate facet or other element in the compass picture. It is best thought of as a central sensory component of the World. Just like concept seeds, sound or timbre seeds can serve as prompts to the songwriter's creative work. But that work turns into a song by embodying sound or timbral material as vocal melody, chords, or rhythm.

STRUCTURE

In the songwriting compass, structure is not a facet, peer to rhythm, lyric, melody, and harmony. Song seeds can be concepts or sound inspirations from the world, or material in any facet. But only rarely is a structural pattern itself the seed or starting point for a song. Yet structure can be expressed directly in the material of any facet—and in several or all facets simultaneously. Thus, structure helps control interactions of material, both within and across facets. These structures can mirror or reinforce each other, or can be in more complex "contrapuntal" relationships. To reflect these aspects of creative process, structure (or form) is best pictured at the center or hub of the compass.

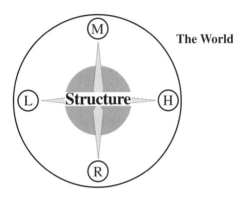

FIG. 2.3. The Songwriter's Compass: Facets, the World, and Structure

Song structure is hierarchical. Larger structures of overall song form arise from varying patterns in lyric and music. Verse/chorus form in *song* arises, for example, out of *contrast* in respective sectional structures of lyric (through-composed verses, repeating chorus, or *ABCB*) and music (repeating music for verse and chorus, or ABAB). Song form divides into *sections* (verse, chorus, etc.), in turn arranged into varying levels of phrases and subphrases. A phrase has duration—a number of measures, each consisting of a number of *beats* in a given time signature. This phrase length forms the bones of a song's structure. It may be indicated by melodic and chordal movement or lyric lines but is not determined by any of them. This freedom of phrasing, especially given the possibility of both balanced and unbalanced phrase structures, allows for complex interleaving between melody, chords, and lyrics, such as overlapping and crisscrossing of lyric lines and musical phrases.

The compass reveals that content—the World—is not the province of lyric alone, or indeed of any one facet. Similarly, structure plays a role in *each* facet: lyric rhyme schemes, melodic and rhythmic phrase structures, chord progressions. Less skilled songwriters may conflate overall song structure with the structure expressed in whatever facet is in the foreground of their attention: lyricists attend to rhyme schemes, guitar players to chord progressions. Developing the ability to work independently with structures in each facet is a major way to advance your songwriting. Try to do this only improvisationally, and you're usually able only to mirror or mimic the foreground structure you're focusing on in other facets. Your rhyme scheme will be echoed by your chord progression, for example. Or else, you'll fall back on simpler, cliché patterns that don't require much compositional attention. By being aware of structural patterns that can be expressed in each facet, and by working with structure in each facet separately, you gain the skill to superimpose or "counterpoint" structures in more complex and expressive ways.

TRAVERSING THE COMPASS: SONGWRITING STRATEGIES

The essence of using 360° songwriting as a discipline lies in developing the skills to work independently with material in each of the facets, and to move freely in any direction between them. We'll address these skills in exploring each facet separately in the chapters that follow.

These skills are *not* part of the intuitive ways most songwriters work on songs. In teaching these techniques, I repeatedly hear some version of this: "As a musician, I pride myself that as soon as I hear a lyric in my head, I hear a melody and rhythm connected with it." This creates an organic, natural, unified *experience* for the songwriter. But it does not necessarily produce the strongest song. If you can't shift the rhythmic phrasing of a lyric line at will, experimenting to find the most expressive and musical setting, you must settle for that first instinctive rhythmic setting and hope for the best.

But we can train ourselves to work independently with material in each facet. We begin by increasing our capacity to catch initial seeds in each facet, and in more independent ways. Even when starting seeds blend elements of several facets, we can pull facet-specific "reductions" or images from such seeds, giving us more options for working creatively with the material.

Different kinds of creative work can be pictured as movements following various pathways between the facets. We'll reference these creative operations—the key *songwriting strategies*—as we discuss each of the facets and their interconnections in the chapters that follow. The descriptive terms are easier to understand by picturing these operations as arrows or "flows" among facets, or crossing between the World and various facets, or between the facets and structure.

Setting

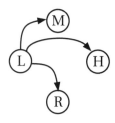

Once we're working with the relatively "isolated" material we get with focused seed catching, we can move between facets by using starting seed material in one facet as a stimulus or prompt for generating responsive material in another facet. This is what we mean when we speak informally of, for example, "setting a lyric to music." In terms of the songwriter's compass, we can speak more precisely about setting a lyric to rhythm, or to melody—or to harmony, for that matter.

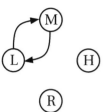

We can also follow any such pathway in reverse: setting a melody to lyric, for example. The informal phrase "setting melody *to* lyric" could be interpreted as movement in either direction or sequence. To make our language unambiguous with respect to the directionality of "lateral" moves across facets, throughout this book, we'll generally say we're "setting *from* X to Y."

While there is a deceptive *logical* symmetry to these various operations, each is a qualitatively distinct kind of creative task—requiring different skills, and yielding different results. For example, in setting "from lyric to melody," we transform a "dry lyric" to a sung lyric. In setting "from melody to lyric," we start with a wordless melody and must derive a lyric to be sung *to that melody*. Many songwriters find the generation of lyrics daunting, in comparison to finding a melody for a lyric. Johnny Mercer was said to have spent a year finishing the lyric to Hoagy Carmichael's music for "Skylark." Similarly, you can say "set from lyric to harmony" fast—without stopping to consider what that creative work would entail, in a strict process scenario: *speaking words*, not yet set to melody or even a definite rhythm, while *searching for the chords for that lyric.* This is a simple and powerful strategy, but one we simply might not try, unless guided by—ah yes, a songwriter's compass!

Casting and Framing

Picturing the World as unstructured territory beyond the compass pulls meaning—theme, story, idea—*out* of the province of lyrics alone. We can work from concept seeds as starting points directly to material in any facet, or begin from musical seeds—or lyrical seeds (when drawn by the *sounds* of the words)—only gradually figuring out what the song is "about." These insights support two complementary strategies: *casting* (from World to facet) and *framing* (from facet to World).

Casting

Casting is the creative work of using content—a starting-point idea for a song—as a prompt for generating material in any facet. We're most familiar with casting from idea to *lyric*, then to music, but we can cast from content directly to material in *any facet.*

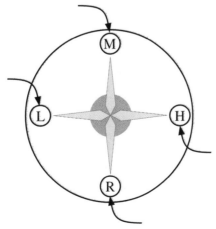

FIG. 2.4. Casting

Suppose you want to write a song about your grandfather. Your first instinct might be to remember pivotal conversations or scenes and to begin generating words, either description or perhaps remembered dialogue. This might be a creative writer's approach, and one can approach writing a song in similar fashion. But as a songwriter, you have other options. Once you know what you want your song to be about, lyrics may not be your next creative step. You can cast from concept straight to a wordless melody or chord progression. For example, you could sit at the piano and search for "grandfather chords" that evoke your emotional connection to him. A bit more challenging would be to search for a rhythmic phrase or accompaniment groove suggested by the subject or theme.[4]

Framing

What about when your starting point is not an idea but a bit of actual song stuff: a fragment of melody, a title or line, a chord move or progression? Adapting a term used in artistic contexts such as film or theater, *framing* is the complementary move to casting: starting from lyrical or musical material, and working *towards* an idea or concept. For a lyric line, framing often takes the form of the questions, "Who would say this? To whom? In what situation?" For a musical starting point, framing can be more like imagining the music as a soundtrack to a movie, and asking what scene is playing on the screen.

Our frames for lyric material in particular are often tacit. Writers tend to bind lyric seeds such as titles to the original context in which the seed arises, or to the first notion of "what the song's about" that pops into mind when catching the seed. But framing can be applied as a more intentional brainstorming technique or strategy, by challenging yourself to come up with several (ideally, at least three) *alternative* frames for a given title or lyric line. (This is an application of the general creative strategy of iterating or "sketching," discussed below.) This "framestorming" strategy is especially useful for those intriguing, ambiguous titles—that sound like they mean something though you can't nail down what something they mean. (These are often lyric seeds captured primarily for their *sound* aspects.) But the strategy can also push us to think beyond the first obvious angle on a cliché or interpretation of a title or lyric phrase. Because the activity of generating alternative frames gets you more conscious and explicit about the frame you eventually choose, framestorming is also particularly useful in co-writing.

In the broader context of the songwriting compass, framing can apply to any song seed—in any facet—not already embedded with a story or theme. That is, just as we can cast not only to lyric, but to melody, harmony, or rhythm, we can also take any musical seed and, prior to fully setting it—in particular, prior to searching for specific *lyrics* for it—inquire about the "story it wants to sing."

---

4. In this book, I'll generally use "theme" with this sense of content or subject, rather than a musical theme, as used in a theme-and-variation form. I'll use the term "motive" for the latter concept.

With musical as opposed to lyrical seeds, therefore, the value of framing is a bit different. It's less about shaking loose preemptively locked-in ideas or themes, resolving ambiguity, or shifting seed material from its original context. It's more about tapping into implicit imagery and narrative in the musical material. I have a strong melodic idea; before grabbing for lyrics to the melody, I ask: "What might a song with this melody be about?" You'll be surprised how readily your creative mind provides possible answers to this backward-thinking, Columbo-style question!

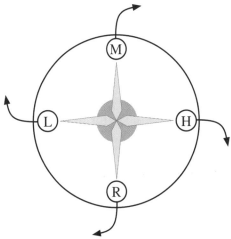

FIG. 2.5. Framing

Structuring Strategies

The work of structuring the song is distinct from setting (associating material across facets), or casting and framing (connecting facets to content and theme). In structuring, we build lyric upon lyric, melody upon melody, etc.

We can structure songs following bottom-up or top-down strategies. Some writers like to work bottom-up, taking a fragment of material (a lyric line, a scrap of melody, a cool chord progression) and building or *unfolding* it into a matching question/answer phrase, a complete phrase, a section, eventually a whole song. For example, from a single lyric line, we might add a rhyming line, then build that couplet into a four-line verse or chorus, etc. Other writers are restless until they

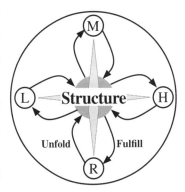

FIG. 2.6. Structuring Strategies

place a starting phrase in the context of an overall form, thus working top down. Is this a title? A line for a chorus? A first line for a verse? Working from a structural pattern or plan, they gradually *fulfill* the structure with material in the facet they're working with. One advantage of this way of working is that you can fulfill a structure out of sequence, sometimes literally working in reverse (e.g., from refrain line to the rest of the verse) of the sequence of elements as they will be heard in the final song.

Those of you who had secret crushes on your third-grade English teachers (*outline* your ideas, dear!) might imagine I'm going to tell you working top-down is preferable. It's true that there are risks in structuring only in bottom-up fashion. With only a "worm's-eye" view of the immediate song section, you can write yourself into a corner. There are risks in trying to complete a section before you know whether it's functioning as chorus or verse, or whether it's verse 1 or verse 2. But working top-down has its own risks. Often, we make early decisions about song form before we see the shape of the song or know the content. Top-level structural commitments are difficult to shift in revision. They affect multiple small compositional decisions throughout the song. Whether building intuitively and organically from a seed, architecturally from an overall song plan, or alternating back and forth, we're wrestling with song *structure* and *form*. There are several advantages to working more intentionally with structure, separate from its expression in individual facets: expanding our repertoire of structures and forms, better supporting the emotion and meaning of the song with our structural choices, and exploring possibilities for using different structures in different facets (structural counterpoint).

General Creative Strategies

For any creative operation or move—setting, casting, framing, unfolding, or fulfilling structure—we can apply a repertoire of techniques or process strategies, made practical by our increased ability to work *independently* with material in various facets, and with structure as a separate element. These strategies can be applied at every stage of songwriting: when first working from seeds, in development work, in revision, in co-writing, and as learning or skill-building exercises.

- *Sequencing.* One significant intervention of a 360° perspective is simply to trace creative work moving *sequentially* through material in various facets, rather than "all at once"—e.g., starting with a melodic seed, setting it to a lyric, then setting from the resulting melody + lyric to chords, etc. But the specific sequence you follow *makes a difference.* You can start in multiple places, and move at each step in multiple directions. Working from melody to chords, then to lyric, will yield different chords, different lyrics—a different song.

- *Iterating.* You could call this strategy: "Even if You Think You've Succeeded, Try, Try Again." By taking multiple, independent passes at any creative step, you challenge your first intuitive, associative creative work through multiple trials. You also stress-test the relative *independence* of material you're working from and toward. If you get stuck on your first trial, you've likely "fused" the material.

  Iterating is the essence of what all artists do when they *sketch*: make multiple, informal, noncommittal, fragmentary attempts at a single problematic feature. In master artisans' studios, apprentices would traditionally learn by being given a small, discrete artistic task—like painting nothing but eyes for a year. Sketching or iterating is, in a sense, a kind of self-apprenticeship.

- *Radiating.* Since facets are peers, almost any creative work you can do involving one facet you can also try with another. If you get stuck following one pathway, you can switch gears and try another. You can also work in parallel, "radiating out" from the same starting material via *different* pathways.

- *Pivoting.* Moving sequentially through creative work in different facets is inherently a messy affair. Once you set from a rhythm to a lyric, sketching till you find what you like, you may find that your lyric requires reworking the original rhythm. This kind of turnabout, a *pivoting* move, can happen at any stage and with any facet. It's what makes songwriting, even with a 360° songwriting approach, still very much art and not a mechanistic procedure.

  Pivoting can also be a powerful *learning* strategy for developing more "ambidextrous" versatility with different facets. As an example exercise, try setting from a melodic phrase to a few different lyric lines (sketches). Pick your favorite of these, and now pivot back, letting the original melody go and finding (sketching) several new ones. Pick your favorite; then compare the melody you started with and the one you wound up with. You can try this pivoting exercise with any combination of facets, and also with framing and casting.

- *Triangulating/converging.* You can also generate material (that is, make stuff up) in response to several converging sources. Most typical is setting across facets in the presence of some reinforcing content frame from the World: e.g., frame a melody, then set from the melody to a lyric, with the additional presence of the *framing context.* This strategy tightens the reins on the creative task. You might think this would make your creative work harder. But the strategy reflects a general principle of creative work: *multiple impinging constraints, especially of different kinds, do not diminish but increase creative energy.*

  Triangulating can also involve sources generated *independently,* such as setting from a rhythm *and* a (separately generated) chord progression to a lyric. When you triangulate from independently generated sources, there's no guarantee the material will lock together; but you might stumble on interesting chance collisions that transform your way of hearing and working with the separate elements.

SUMMARY OF COMPASS ELEMENTS AND MOVES

The basic promise of 360° songwriting is that we can start songs "from any direction." This principle now has more precise meaning in terms of the compass. We've described three components of the compass: the four facets (rhythm, lyric, melody, and harmony), the World of content, and structure at the center. We've also described a starting repertoire of essential creative activities or "moves" among these elements:

- catching *song seeds*, as concepts in the World or as material in any facet
- *casting* from concepts to lyrical or musical material
- *framing* lyrical or musical seeds to concepts
- *setting* from material in one facet to material in another facet
- *structuring* seed material into larger forms, using bottom-up (*unfolding*) or top-down (*fulfilling*) strategies.

Each of these compass-specific moves can be augmented by strategies such as *sequencing, iteration, radiating, pivoting,* and *triangulating* or *converging.*

Since we can start from seeds in any facet, we can set *from* material in any facet *to* material in any facet. Each connection can be traversed in *either direction*: e.g., setting melody to lyric or lyric to melody. This yields a repertoire of *twelve* distinct setting strategies or pathways: setting material in any of four facets *directly* in any of three directions:

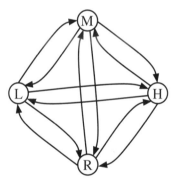

Rhythm → Lyric	Rhythm → Melody	Rhythm → Harmony
Lyric → Rhythm	Lyric → Melody	Lyric → Harmony
Melody → Rhythm	Melody → Lyric	Melody → Harmony
Harmony → Rhythm	Harmony → Lyric	Harmony → Melody

FIG. 2.7. Setting Pathways Across the Facets

While there's a logical symmetry to these pathways, they're experientially unique. Each requires specific skills to traverse, yet also produces *distinctive* creative results. In this book, we'll follow only a few of these pathways in detail, leaving others for your own deeper exploration.

EXAMPLE: HURRICANE REVISITED

To show various elements and moves of the compass at work, let's return to our lyric seed from the previous chapter, "Nice Day till the Hurricane," and show some first steps we can take in developing this seed by first framing, then setting to various facets in succession. We'll also illustrate general creative or process strategies such as iterating or alternatives, as well as radial vs. sequential setting.

Framing "Hurricane"

As discussed earlier, this lyric seed draws largely on the "by sound" side of the spectrum, and is relatively ambiguous in terms of situation and context. A useful first step working with this lyric seed, then, is to frame it: imagining a situation, character, and emotional stance, where the phrase makes sense.

Nice day till the hurricane

Who'd say this to whom, and why? Rather than settling too quickly on the first story or frame that comes to mind, I iterate or "framestorm" several alternative frames. For each alternative, I note reactions and issues that come to mind:

1. A husband just got in an unexpected fight with his wife over something small. (Gender: Does it need to be a husband? Could a wife say this? Are they married? How about a boyfriend/girlfriend?)

2. A victim of abuse dealing with a violent partner. (Makes this a much darker-themed song. Would the lyric seed's casual tone work for this scenario? It would be very ironic—maybe too bitterly ironic….)

3. A more political or societal frame. People go about their lives imagining everything is secure; then the economic (or global warming) meltdown hits. Could be protesting our culture's tendency to stay complacent until the—hurricane—hits the fan….

4. Could combine frames (1) and (3) above: build the song as an arc moving from personal to the political. This frame would immediately suggest constraints on the overall song form to make it work.

5. Last but not least: it could be a song about an actual hurricane! Or again, we could combine this frame with the political one, moving from literal to metaphorical.

I want something closer to frame (1) than frame (2) in tone. I'm less interested in this being a song about a real hurricane, though I do want consistent use of metaphor throughout. I need the Singer to be male to preserve the humorous, lighter emotional quality of the seed; because of the specific metaphor a female point of view might evoke the notion of physical violence, a more serious topic warranting a different kind of song.

Okay, here's my framing statement:

> "A husband/lover in early stages of a new relationship, finds out his partner is "stormier" than he realized. They haven't been together long, and this is the first incident where he discovers this aspect of his partner. So, unlike a more settled relationship, there's some doubt the relationship will survive the storm."

Now that I have my chosen frame, many next steps are possible. I could further develop the frame into a more detailed "back story," including details that might never appear in the song but help me hone in on character, situation, tone of voice, etc. I could generate raw lyric material to develop later into specific lyrics, using tools such as object writing, associative word-lists and rhyming worksheets, etc. I might also begin to make structural decisions about the song, even planning narrative content for various sections to be written. I might also need to tweak the original lyric seed to suit the frame or song structure, or the song's overall direction.

Setting "Hurricane"

With my lyric seed line and accompanying frame, I can also begin setting the lyric to associated material in other facets. Here, I'll show a simplified sequential path: setting first from lyric to rhythm, then from "rhythmic lyric" to melody, then from the combined lyric + rhythm + melody to chords. I'll consider alternative settings at each step, and the frame provides a guideline helping to ensure the emotional consistency of the resulting fully composed line of the song. In the chapters that follow on specific facets, we'll explore some of the technical skills required to work effectively in this independent "isolation" fashion with various elements of the song.

In generating alternative rhythmic settings for the lyric, I'll work with both the emotional tenor of the frame and specific sound aspects and resonances within the seed line. Each rhythmic setting will suggest a particular time signature, tempo and groove, and a certain duration within a phrase structure. These can vary across the different setting trials, as shown in figure 2.8.

FIG. 2.8. Setting from a Lyric Seed to Rhythm

By isolating, focusing initially only on rhythmic settings, not yet considering or not fixing melody or chord choices, I gain flexibility in the range of rhythmic settings I can explore. I take more chances, and can more readily discern the varying effects of each alternative rhythmic setting. As we'll see, I also leave more flexibility in the melody I'll eventually put to the rhythm on which I settle. Extended durations may become single notes or melismatic turns. Melodic contour may follow the rhythm or move more slowly, with repeated notes. Isolation, alternatives, and reflection on the emotional and narrative effects of each choice are closely intertwined in making the strategy work.

In the end, here's the rhythmic setting I settle on. It's a composite of several of my sketches or trials. This is typical: with the various alternatives, you traverse a space of possibilities, feeling out the boundaries of what feels right and the interaction of various compositional and sonic forces at work.

FIG. 2.9. Preferred Rhythmic Setting

I now move from my rhythmically set lyric to a melody. Once again, I'll experiment with several alternatives:

FIG. 2.10. Alternative Melodic Settings. Working from a rhythmic lyric.

My frame provides a sense for the emotion and meaning of the line, particularly the ironic shift from the "nice day" to the oncoming hurricane. The first setting in figure 2.10 conveys this mostly through the descending melodic contour; but the line begins and ends on the stable tonic of the implied tonal center. In the second setting I draw out the more threatening aspect of the word "hurricane" by descending to the sixth, implying the relative minor and widening the overall range. In the third setting, I push the opening figure up to the D. (Here I'm writing melody prior to harmony; later this melodic decision might create a non-chord tone pull against a tonic chord, or suggest a different harmony.) As with my rhythmic alternatives, these sketches can be mixed, matched, and recombined, as in the last setting.

Prior rhythmic decisions about durations of specific syllables now get elaborated by decisions about melodic contour. I can move the melodic contour on downbeats previously de-emphasized by anticipations in lyric rhythm (as in setting 1), or on weak beats (as in the concluding figure of setting 2). In my final melodic setting, shown in figure 2.11, I further tweak setting 4 by swapping melismatic effects: using the softer, delayed melisma on "day," a harder-edged melisma, emphasizing the underlying strong metric beat, on "hurricane."

FIG. 2.11. Final Melodic Setting of the Rhythmic Lyric

Of course, this degree of "word painting" is an over-intensified example. It would be rare to do such polished sketching of a single line without starting to consider structural aspects. In practical songwriting, I'd likely want to know by this point whether I was working on a first line of a verse, a chorus hook, or a refrain line for a verse/refrain.

Now, at last, we can set to our fourth facet, harmonizing the line. Again, I explore several chordal possibilities:

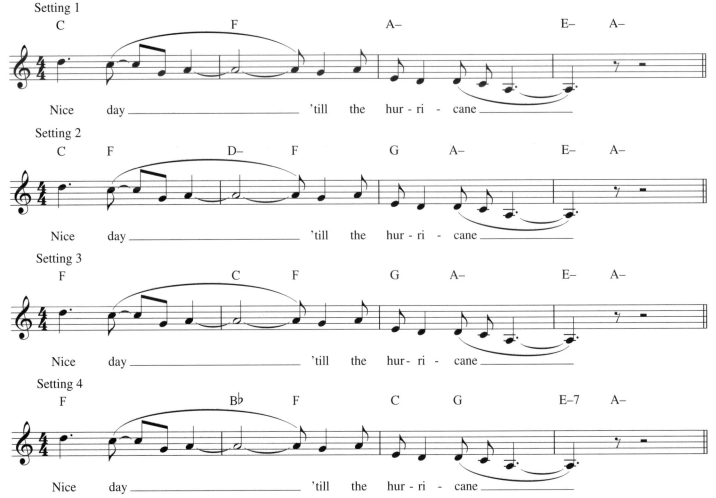

FIG. 2.12. Alternate Harmonic Settings. Working from a rhythmically and melodically set lyric.

I originally conceived the melody with the tonal center of C, and so my first "off the top of my head" harmonization starts on C and ends on the relative minor, A–. Since I developed the melody prior to harmonization, I get a nice non-chord tone relation of the starting D against the C chord. And since my rhythmic setting was a four-bar phrase, I have the option of moving chords in the space after the lyric. Here the "darker" A– chord at the end of the phrase is given an extra punch through the harmonic rhythm of the E– to A– sequence.

But on reflection, I feel that the move to A– at the start of the word "hurricane" telegraphs the change of mood earlier than I'd like. In setting (2), I delay that move until the third syllable "-cane," while creating a strong repeated harmonic-rhythm figure in each bar. In setting (3), I experiment with starting the line on the F (IV) chord instead of C (I). This keeps the D melody note a non-chord tone, but a different non-chord tone relationship, a 6 instead of a 2 (or 9). In the final setting (4), the B♭ (♭VII) "rocking chord" invokes a more tense, Mixolydian feel. The A– is saved for the very end of the phrase, passing quickly through the implied tonic chord C along the way.

These alternatives show how independent melodic and harmonic work opens fresh options. I'm still working here with just a fragment, an individual line. It's always possible to overwrite and overcrowd when you focus on sketching possibilities for a given facet in isolation. But the alternative sketches need not apply only to this one line. As I develop the song section (e.g., verse or chorus), alternatives generated in first stages can later be incorporated as matched question-answer phrases within the sectional structure. This might include variant rhythmic settings, melodic phrases, or chord choices. Thus there's always an advantage in leaving a "trail of bread crumbs" and not discarding unused alternatives. Here, technology, like multiple "takes" in a sequencer, can be useful.

EXERCISE 2.1. CAST FROM A CONCEPT SEED TO EACH FACET

The following exercise reinforces the insight that material in each facet can carry meaning and emotion in different ways.

Phase 1. Cast to Lyric/Iterations

Start with a concept seed from your seed catching. A natural instinct is to look first for a *lyrical* expression of the concept. Don't settle for your first attempt. Use iteration: cast the concept into three *different* lyrics. With each attempt, find a *different* lyrical way of expressing the idea or story. (This iteration helps to confirm that your original seed was more a concept seed than a lyric seed. If, leaving your first lyrical cast behind, you lose the power of the seed idea, you likely started with at least partially a lyric seed!)

Phase 2. Casting

Go back to the original concept seed and *forget* your lyric attempts. Now use a radiating strategy: cast the idea, successively, into: (1) chords, (2) melody, and (3) rhythm. When casting into chords, think of the theme as you play chords at your instrument. The chords will reflect mostly *emotional* associations and responses to the theme. A melodic setting may be more narrative, suggestive of lyrics to come (but remember, no lyrics on this try, and no setting of lyrics you previously wrote!). It may be hardest to cast to rhythm, especially to a *lyric rhythm* for lyrics still to be written. The rhythm should be a response to the theme or idea prompt, not a new rhythmic seed on its own. You'll more likely come up with a beat or rhythmic pattern suggesting an accompaniment and groove.

Phase 3. Setting to a Lyric

You now have your original theme or idea as a guide, as well as musical material generated by several independent "castings"—to chords, melody, and rhythm respectively. Now set *to* a lyric by triangulating or converging from the original concept and one (or more) of these musical castings. This is a kind of "pincer action." You're constraining the lyric generation task in multiple ways, by theme (sense) and by sound. Compare the lyric you obtained by casting straight from the concept in phase 1 with the lyric obtained through this combined radiating/converging strategy.

Other exercises: Start with a seed in any facet and sequentially build the seed into a "complete fragment" by setting successively to the other facets. You can follow the chain as in the extended example above, or try other pathways and sequences. You can try this by first framing the seed and using the frame as a guide for the setting activities. Or "fly blind," and rely on sound relationships to see where you get, framing only at the end. Unlike flying a real airplane, if you crash and burn, only a few syllables will meet their fiery doom.

ON TO THE FACETS

In this chapter, we've introduced the three main components of the 360° songwriting model, as depicted by the songwriter's compass: the four songwriting facets, the World of content, and structure or form.

Each of these components is essential to achieving the full power of the 360° approach. By treating the four facets as peer aspects, we gain *independence* and *flexibility* in ways we can work with different material for songs. By working with the World separately from the facets, we gain expressiveness—an ability to connect every element of the song directly to content, emotion, and narrative. Working with structure as a separate component, we gain the ability to express structure in the material of each facet, to shift those structures in revision, and to combine structures in innovative and even "contrapuntal" ways.

We'll now begin our tour of the four facets. Your self-profiling at the end of the "Song Seeds" chapter may have left you with a clear sense for one facet as your "go to" or "comfort zone" facet—and perhaps one as the scariest for you to tackle. I suggest, though, that you work through the facet chapters in the sequence given. Each chapter progressively introduces concepts and techniques which are then built on in subsequent chapters. So, on to the facets! By the time you're done, you'll know better where your "True North" lies—but you'll have visited some new territory along the way.

CHAPTER 3

Rhythm

Many great songs are defined and made memorable by their rhythmic aspects: a jagged-edged riff in a rock anthem; a compelling, hypnotic beat driving a contemporary pop track; or the complex, master-drummer cadences of skilled rappers in hip-hop. Each of us has favorite songs where the rhythm was an essential part of what grabbed us. My personal list would include the 1982 hip-hop classic "The Message" by Grandmaster Flash and the Furious Five, Prince's "When Doves Cry," the Knack's "My Sharona," and John Lennon's surrealistic chanting in "Come Together."

Even in songs that aren't rhythmically driven overall, as in the work of the great Motown writers or early Beatles classics, we hear a definiteness and assuredness in the rhythmic phrasing of every line, and an alignment of phrasing across lines in the song. Sometimes, it's only in writing or revising that we come to appreciate the impact of even slight rhythmic alterations in making a song work. A hook line vague and unconvincing in one rhythmic setting may suddenly come alive—become memorable and believable—with a minute shift in rhythmic phrasing. The rhythmic magic may lie in the harmony or accompaniment as well. Two rhythmic variations turn a stock I IV I V chord progression into the anthemic, chordal motif tolling throughout Tom Petty's "Free Fallin'."

THE CHALLENGE OF RHYTHM IN SONGWRITING

Despite how vital and integral the element of rhythm is in songwriting, it often receives less attention than lyric, melody, or harmony. As you begin working with the four facets of the songwriter's compass, you may find one facet you're most familiar with and think about most readily—your "comfort zone" facet. Or you may discover a "shadow facet"—the facet that's *least* comfortable for you to work with and bring to conscious awareness. For me, and for many other writers, that shadow facet is rhythm.

Why would this be the case? Few songwriters are trained directly in percussion. Many songwriters can work ably with specific rhythmic idioms that characterize a given style or genre they know well, but would struggle to develop *novel* rhythmic ideas. For many performing songwriters, rhythm may be most active *as* an element of performance, used almost like dynamics, rather than built compositionally into the "bones" of the song.

Yet, there are deeper reasons for our difficulties in working with rhythm— reasons that lie in the relationship of rhythm to the other songwriting facets. In the context of a song, we encounter rhythmic elements intimately intertwined with other elements. Some rhythmic elements are embedded in the very "landscape" in which we compose, perform, and hear the song. We encounter these rhythmic elements directly, but not in a form easy to shift at will, especially as we're *writing* the song. In core *compositional* elements of the song, on the other hand, rhythmic aspects are primarily expressed *indirectly,* through other elements: lyric syllables, melodic pitches, chord changes. Here rhythms are difficult to shift, not because they're defined by the whole groove of the song, but because they're tied to the specific phrase.

Working with Rhythm

We face a variety of challenges in developing the skills to work independently with the rhythmic facet in songwriting:

- *Working arhythmically with lyrics, melody, and chords.* It's fairly easy to sing a wordless melody, to sing a melody without playing chords, or to speak lyrics without singing pitches. That allows us to experiment, sketching different lyrics or chords to that melody, or different melodies for a lyric line. But we *can't* easily speak words (and hear them as song lyrics), or sing a melody, or play chords, without speaking, singing, or playing them in some rhythm. Song seed material in each facet tends to arrive already infused with rhythmic impulses. These may or may not be the best rhythmic designs for the song to be. Yet, we often lack the skills to *vary the rhythmic settings* as we work with the material later.

- *Isolating rhythmic seed ideas.* Conversely, it's very challenging to work with rhythmic phrases and patterns separately from their embodiment in some combination of lyric, melodic, or harmonic material. We almost always experience and work with rhythmic patterns embedded in accompaniment grooves, spoken or sung lyrics, melodic or chordal phrases. Thus, we rarely start from a song seed captured in purely rhythmic form. This limits the expressiveness and complexity of the rhythmic ideas we can work with effectively, and our ability to interweave *independent* rhythmic patterns in the various facets.

Dimensions of Rhythm in the Song

We'll consider three distinct levels at which rhythm interacts with the song. Though the boundaries between these levels can be fluid with respect to any specific rhythm elements or effects, the distinctions are helpful in understanding how we work as songwriters in different ways with rhythmic material at each level:

1. *The temporal framework.* Certain global rhythmic aspects create an overall rhythmic "landscape" that potentially influences every element of the song. These include feel (strict to loose), pulse, time signature, and tempo. Arrangers, producers, performers, and band members are accustomed to establishing this landscape, and know how to shift it for a different feel or vibe when required. But when songwriters write songs, they *already* feel this temporal framework—and this intuitive rhythmic ground strongly influences and constrains compositional choices and phrasing in every facet and every part of the song. To work effectively with rhythm, songwriters need to be aware of the effects of elements of the temporal framework, and need the skills to experiment with and vary these parameters while writing the song.

2. *Accompaniment rhythm.* Within the context of the temporal framework, specific rhythmic patterns are built into the song accompaniment, as part of the overall groove, an ostinato rhythm or beat, or a production track. Rhythmic aspects of accompaniment textures may be stated by specific "rhythm instruments" like drums and percussion, as well as by chordal accompaniment such as particular strums on guitar, keyboard vamps, etc. A single pattern with minor variations may be repeated to form a groove. Distinctive rhythmic riffs and grooves mark songs stylistically as particular dance forms or genres.

   Like the temporal framework, creating a specific accompaniment rhythm is a large part of arrangement, production, and performance. Yet the accompaniment patterns we use in writing the song shape the rhythmic phrases we find and their effects for the listener. Accompaniment rhythm can also be even more integral in songs built around rhythmic riffs, or instrumental riffs with strong rhythmic components.

3. *The rhythmic phrase.* A rhythmic phrase is a series of rhythmic events occurring in multiple facets within the metrical framework of beats and phrases—the stream of time. The simplest way to think of the rhythmic phrase is in terms of lyrics: where each syllable lands in the metric stream of time. We'll explore various steps in moving lyric lines to fully realized *rhythmic lyrics* in the "Lyrics" chapter. But melodic contour also creates rhythmic events, not always locked to lyric rhythm, as we'll explore

in the "Melody" chapter. Finally, harmonic rhythm—where chords *change*—can also function as part of the overall rhythmic phrase, as we'll explore in the "Harmony" chapter. (In contrast, rhythmic *accents* on harmonic instruments, such as strums of the guitar, are primarily part of accompaniment rhythm. In some musical situations, though, even these rhythmic effects can become, effectively, part of rhythmic phrasing.)

We work with rhythmic phrases in interaction with the temporal framework and accompaniment levels. Shifting elements of the framework or accompaniment can shape the phrases we compose. At the same time, aligning all rhythmic phrases, expressed in each facet, with a common temporal and accompaniment framework helps ensure the unity and integrity of the song.

These respective challenges lay out the roadmap for the material we will cover in the sections that follow. First, we'll explore ways to capture rhythmic ideas in a more isolated form, separate from material in the other facets. Then we will explore techniques for working with the various elements of the temporal framework, accompaniment rhythm, and the rhythmic phrase in terms of "dry rhythms." This foundation will be essential to discuss interactions of rhythm with the other facets, in subsequent chapters.

RHYTHMIC SONG SEEDS

We'll call a rhythmic idea, captured without associated pitch or lyric information, a "dry rhythm" or *rhythmic seed* (though we can compose such "seeds" directly rather than catching them via the serendipitous "seed-catching" techniques). Rhythmic seeds might ultimately be embodied in accompaniment rhythm or rhythmic phrasing, or might contain aspects of both layers. In addition, rhythmic seeds might wind up shaping lyric, melodic, or chordal rhythm, or the interactions of all these in the overall rhythmic phrase.

Rhythmic seeds can be derived from a number of sources:

- *Rhythms from environmental sounds.* We can pull rhythmic ideas and patterns directly out of the realm of sensory experience: water drips, radiators rattling, rain falling on the roof, windshield wipers slapping.

- *Rhythms extracted from other seed material.* When you catch a melodic or lyric song seed, you may realize that the truly interesting thing about it is the rhythm; the specific melody or lyric is "filler." It can be great practice then to try to capture and notate that seed in purely rhythmic form.

- *Other music.* You can also catch fresh rhythmic ideas by extracting a distinctive rhythmic component from particular spots in existing songs. If you recognize a rhythmically compelling motif, try isolating and transcribing just the *rhythm* of the phrase, separating it from lyric, melody, and harmony. See if you can identify qualities that create intrinsic interest in the rhythmic phrase alone. You can use this "borrowed" or "lifted" rhythmic idea in your own work by modifying it and casting it into different lyric, melodic, and harmonic settings.

- *Rhythmic seed "catalogues."* Last but not least, the world of rhythmic theory and percussion offers countless "rhythmic repertoires" to work with as rhythmic source material. Think of these resources as rhythmic seed catalogues.

EXERCISE 3.1. COMPOSE A "DRY" RHYTHMIC PHRASE

You can develop your rhythmic ear by composing rhythmic material directly. Here, it's helpful to work with a simplified, stripped-down form of rhythm, excluding parameters of *dynamics* and *articulation*: a series of percussive events with little or no definite pitch or extended duration. Focus on the moment of attack for each beat. Minimize attention, at first, to dynamics, varying pitch, durations, or textural effects (rubbing vs. clapping, shuffling vs. stomping). This helps you isolate idealized or "dry" rhythmic patterns and phrases, not bound to lyric or melody. Of course, any real drum part is not just a sequence of abstract rhythmic hits. It has timbre, attack and sustain, dynamics that differentiate rhythmic hits, etc. But the stripped-down version lets us begin to discern distinctive or memorable qualities of particular rhythms, as they'll eventually interact with other elements of the song (as opposed to the music as a whole).

Develop a single rhythmic phrase intended to "take a lyric"—a lyric rhythm sans lyric. The phrase should be about the length of a lyric line—that is, two to four measures. To express the rhythms, use any of the following:

- *Mental imaging.* Try to hear the rhythm internally. At first, this will be hard to do without reinforcing the rhythm with some bodily gesture, even a minute one like clicking your teeth. (Careful of those dentist bills!) As you work with the other techniques below, keep coming back to this silent internally heard rhythm as a reference point.

- *Hand claps, finger taps, foot stomps.* Use your body to create rhythms via "hits," "taps," "claps," or "stomps." But notice: as you rub palms or slide feet, you begin to play not just with duration (intervals between hits), but duration vs. silence, dynamics, pitch, and timbre in the sounds of each rhythmic event. These contrasts begin to suggest lyric qualities. Sustained vs. shortened rhythmic beats suggest longer, more open vowels, nasal, or fricative vs. percussive (plosive) consonants. Similarly, differing dynamic levels in various hits begin to suggest melodic aspects.

- *Singing or speaking on a monotone pitch, use vocalized nonsense syllables ("doo-doot dooh… doot duh doodle doo…").* As you vary these syllables, you start to bring in elements such as sustain and dynamics, which again hint at lyrical or melodic aspects.

- *Play rhythms on a percussion instrument, or using percussive effects on a tonal instrumen*t.

Notating Rhythms: Woodblocks and Bagpipes

There are two complementary approaches to notating "dry rhythms"—rhythmic patterns stripped of lyrical or melodic associations, and not utilizing dynamics or timbral contrast. These approaches are supported by two contrasting styles of rhythmic notation, each involving a simplification or "temporal fiction" about the rhythmic materials involved:

- *Timeless hits*—"the rest is silence." Think of this approach as rhythm played on a woodblock. Here, you choose a single duration value for a rhythmic "hit"—e.g., an eighth note. No hit has duration longer than this value. Any duration is expressed as a hit followed by a rest or silence, until the next rhythmic event. You can include "triplets," though, that move faster than the basic duration value. This style includes, in essence, only attacks. In lyric associations, it tends to privilege *consonants*.

- *Cuts in the stream of time.* In the other approach to rhythmic notation, you pretend there's no such thing as silence. Think of it as rhythm played on a bagpipe—a constant drone. Imagine the phrase as a sustained stream momentarily or instantaneously "cut" by rhythmic events. Each rhythmic event is notated with the full value of the duration, sustained until the next hit, with no rests. (This is, if you like, the "restless" way to notate rhythm.) This style of notation, in terms of lyric associations, will tend to privilege *vowel sounds*.

These two notation styles are shown in figure 3.1 for the same rhythmic seed idea.

FIG. 3.1. Two Styles of Rhythmic Notation

When you hear a rhythmic pattern as a song seed, it usually embeds variations between these extremes. Even an abstracted "dry rhythm" contains lyric associations; before you've written lyrics, you'll hear lyric-like suggestions or tendencies in the rhythm. Shorter rhythmic values pull toward percussive consonants and short, closed vowel sounds. Longer durations invite fricative, sibilant, and nasal consonants, and long and open vowels. By attending to these aspects, you start to intuit a template for lyric choices from the rhythm.

EXERCISE 3.2. WRITE INTERLOCKING ACCOMPANIMENT AND VOCAL RHYTHMS

This progressive set of exercises takes you to the "rhythmic gym" in terms of work with rhythmic patterns for songwriting. This first series is a warm-up, highlighting connections of different kinds of lyric sounds to rhythm patterns (a look forward to the sonic aspects of lyrics we'll examine in detail in the "Lyrics" chapter).

1. Practice transforming a given rhythmic seed into *both* styles of notation—woodblock and bagpipe—in strict form. Try setting from each version to a lyric that feels natural with that rhythmic emphasis.

2. Mix the notation styles: play with different combinations of sustained vs. percussive durations for each rhythmic event in the pattern. Again, find a lyric that matches the pattern: you'll find increased freedom and flexibility in setting lyrics to the pattern.

3. Try going the other way. Generate a lyric matching to the overall shape of the rhythmic phrase: the right number of syllables with the right stresses. Set the lyric to a mixed version of the rhythmic pattern, finding the right varying durations for each syllable's rhythmic event.

Now we'll apply the two notation styles in tandem, as an aid to discovering differing qualities of accompaniment rhythm and vocal rhythm.

1. Compose two rhythmic patterns, in the woodblock and bagpipe style, that interlock as accompaniment and vocal rhythms respectively. (You can use the same approach to write interlocking vocal lines, but the desired textures are somewhat different.)

2. Try "hocketing" the rhythms: that is, avoid having the two rhythmic patterns coincide on any given beat. Figure 3.2 shows an example generated with this hocketing technique.

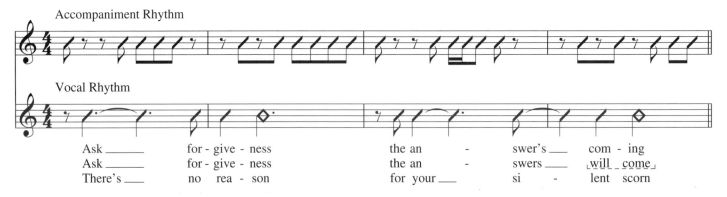

FIG. 3.2. Accompaniment Rhythm vs. Vocal Rhythm

This hocketing technique is an extreme textural option. In real writing, multiple voices will, of course, coincide at various points. The clearer the rhythm patterns in both rhythmic parts, the easier it is for listeners' ears to track the voices separately.

3. *Add lyrics.* To test out how well your vocal rhythmic phrase works, try setting a few different lyric lines against it. Fix any mis-set words, until your line matches the rhythmic phrase in a flowing way. (In figure 3.2, the first line mis-set "com-ING," and I fixed it with "the answers *will come.*")

These exercises highlight the often subtle interactions of rhythmic phrasing in songwriting, arranging, and performance. These techniques can also be directly useful in writing true "call and response" songs, where lead and background vocals are both integral to the song rather than just arrangement choices. Examples of such songs abound in old-time country or gospel songs, blues and R&B, Latin styles, or contrapuntal duets in musical theater.

Distinctions between accompaniment or instrumental rhythm and vocal rhythm are particularly fluid in genres such as rap and hip-hop, with lyric rhythm patterns far more intricate than those in genres driven by conventional melody/harmony textures. While some of the rhythmic techniques and rhythm/lyric connections discussed in this and the next chapter might be useful in these genres, the 360º songwriting framework does not encompass all artistic parameters relevant to these styles. For example, there's a strong melodic and pitch component, even in spoken rather than "sung" rap or hip-hop lyrics. This is *speech-tone* melody, however, not limited to diatonic or even chromatic scales.

THE TEMPORAL FRAMEWORK

In the following sections, we'll discuss several different attributes or parameters of the temporal framework. These include the relative strict or loose feel of the rhythm, the basic pulse, time signature, groove, and tempo.

The Flow of Musical Time

When we write a melody or chord progression, or even set a lyric rhythmically, we cross over into a musical perception of time: a *temporal framework* shared by the elements in each facet. This sense of an ongoing, *flowing stream of musical time* is the background structure or canvas against which all musical elements—melodic phrases, lyric lines, and harmonic movement—are heard and interpreted. Qualitative attributes of this flow of time vary from song to song, across genres, and for particular musicians.

Strict vs. Loose Time

The temporal foundation is broken into a stream of repeating units of musical time. As a backdrop to specific rhythmic events that may hit at irregular intervals, we experience this stream itself as a rolling, metronomic metrical beat that continues evenly and inexorably. This global attribute affects every facet of the song.

We can experience this flow of musical time as strict, measured, "metronomic" time, or as a more breathing, rubato, loose kind of time. Some classical music performance practice relies heavily on a "plasticity" in the flow of time. We judge performers and ensembles by their ability to stay synchronized amidst these breathing variations.

As songwriters, the relative strictness or looseness of the temporal feel of a song, determined largely by genre and style, influences what we write. A looser rhythmic feel might inspire more conversational lyrics; a stricter temporal sense more of a dance music feel. Composers and songwriters can cultivate the full range of this strict/loose continuum. Strict time keeps us "honest" and precise, for example, in committing to definite word-setting and phrasing decisions. Looseness in temporal feel gives us the freedom to let the phrasing "breathe," to try different rhythmic settings, and to experiment more boldly with elements like odd rhythms or extra bars at the ends of phrases. In an extreme form, a loose rhythmic feel can create a "plainchant" kind of compositional space, where rhythmic material is kept in the background and the focus is on elements such as lyric or melody.

Pulse

As soon as we start writing a song—whether from lyric, melody, chords, a groove, or track—we settle, consciously or unconsciously, into a particular *pulse*: a distinctive propulsive quality to the flow of the music. That pulse shapes every aspect of the song and unifies material in every facet. Pulse is intimately linked to the groove, yet embedded in every phrasing decision in the lyric, melody, and even harmonic structure of the song.

Awareness of pulse is particularly crucial when writing lyrics first. The presence of a consistent pulse differentiates spoken-word poetry, for example, from musical delivery of lyrics. However, when songwriters work lyric-first, they often employ an intermediate form of "spoken lyric" where there's a felt steady flow of time and pulse, but the specific rhythmic settings are still malleable.

The Pulse Continuum

When we write lyrics, the patterns embodied in syllabic stress reflect two main options for the primary *pulse* of the lyric:

- *Duple pulse* creates expectation for *one* unstressed syllable after each stressed syllable: DUM da or / ‿: "Talking over where we're going/Never question easy answers…" In this form of pulse, strong- and weak-stressed syllables have approximately equal duration, and so are differentiated by weight or metric emphasis.

- *Triple pulse* creates an expectation for two unstressed syllables or beats after the stressed beat: DUM da da or / ‿‿: "Wondering whether we're coming or going/Me never questioning, you never answering…" Beats are still approximately equal duration, with two (or possibly three) distinct levels of stress or weight.

Most working lyrics will mix these two pulse feels: "Wondering if we're ever going to answer the questions we're never asking…" (/ ‿‿ / ‿ / ‿ / ‿‿ / ‿‿ / ‿ ‿ / ‿ / ‿). Writing to a pulse will shape the song materials you generate but does not prescribe the rhythm exactly.

We can see duple and triple pulse as respective end points of a pulse *continuum*. In conventional musical parlance, this continuum describes the relative degree of *swing*. As the first beat of duple pulse lengthens relative to the second, we move from two even eighths toward dotted eighth/sixteenth, increasing the degree of swing as we go, eventually shifting from a duple to a triple feel. Alternately, as beats two and three of a triple pulse are shortened relative to the first beat, we move toward a "squarer" duple-pulse feel: eighth/sixteenth/sixteenth.

The duple/triple continuum notion can provide a unified way of looking at pulse, groove, and even time signature as critical components in the temporal framework of the song. To ensure integrity in your song, especially when working in fragmentary fashion, apply coherent and consistent pulse "pockets" to lyric and musical aspects of the song. Remember also that you can experiment with (and intentionally shift) pulse as an element during the development of the song. Explore revisions for a song whose pulse isn't quite locking in by shifting gradually from duple to triple pulse or vice versa. See how that changes energy and phrasing.

Time Signature and Tempo

Closely related to strict vs. loose time and pulse are factors of time signature and tempo. *Time signature* is a grouping of beats into larger metrical units, along with a hierarchy of felt stresses associated with each beat or metric position within the measure. *Tempo* is the speed of these metric beats in the temporal framework. Generally, the first beat of a four-beat structure gets the strongest stress, beat 3 the next strongest, and beats 2 and 4 weaker stress. Different genres and different songs may vary this "weight signature" in both subtle and dramatic ways. These weightings may be determined in part by the *groove*, a distinctive accompaniment texture incorporating pulse, time signature, and a range of tempos.

All these attributes have a degree of independence, yet influence each other in subtle ways. For example, as tempo accelerates, a loose, swinging triple-pulse feel, at a certain point, straightens out into duple pulse. This is a phenomenon well-known to jazz drummers, where the "ride cymbal" pattern at a slower swung groove shifts into a straighter 4/4 time as tempo increases. Many distinct rhythmic grooves can be laid down for a given pulse and tempo, while pulse and/or tempo could also be shifted for a given groove, changing its quality and effect—possibly in a dramatic way.

Working with the Temporal Framework

Aspects of the temporal framework can be manipulated independently of specific rhythmic material in various facets. However, there's a bit of a challenge here. Unless you're listening to a beat or track in a sequencer, the trace of changes to tempo, groove, time signature, etc. are expressed in audible changes to accompaniment rhythms or rhythmic phrases. From a songwriter's point of view, these changes are the important thing. If tempo didn't affect our writing, we could simply leave the ultimate choice of tempo to the arranger, producer, and performers. But the tempo at which we set a song will shape the song itself. It's useful to be aware of those effects, and to be able to change those parameters during writing when necessary. To experience these links and bring them to greater awareness and strategic control, practice intentionally shifting various parameters of the temporal framework as you write, noticing effects of these shifts on your creative results.

EXERCISE 3.3. SONGWRITE-IRAMA: TRANSFORM A RHYTHMIC IDEA BY ALTERING TEMPO

This is a songwriter's version of a technique used in Indonesian *gamelan* music, where different rhythmic/textural levels are known as *iramas*. Periodically, the entire ensemble slows down; various instrumental parts double the notes they're playing. Conversely, as the piece accelerates, faster-moving voices begin to drop out strategic notes. Several tempo levels can be played at each *irama* before the texture changes. While Western popular music doesn't employ this orchestral concept directly, songwriters can adapt it as a rhythmic exploration and revision technique.[5]

4. Write a two-bar rhythmic phrase, noting the original time signature and tempo at which you heard or composed the phrase.

5. Gradually *accelerate* the tempo. Note the tempo at which you begin to want to drop out beats. Transcribe the new, rhythmically "thinned" pattern and note the tempo.

6. Return to the original tempo and repeat the phrase to reestablish the initial feel.

7. Gradually *decelerate* the tempo. At certain points in deceleration, you'll begin to hear "ghost beats" or counter-beats emerge, where the slower tempo pulls new rhythmic impulses into the pattern. Add these beats explicitly into the pattern.

Figure 3.3. shows an example of the exercise:

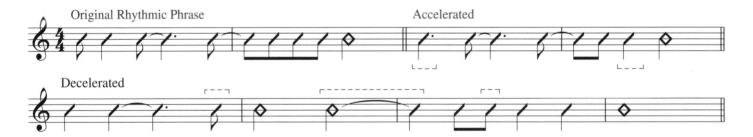

FIG. 3.3. Two-Bar Rhythmic Example, Set to Different Tempos

The original idea's eight rhythmic hits are thinned at the faster tempo: e.g., the initial eighth and quarter notes "coalesce" into the dotted quarter, while the two eighth notes in the second bar simplify to the quarter note (as shown with the dotted brackets). The accelerated tempo makes us "skim" over the rhythmic pattern, losing some hits in the process. The converse takes place with the decelerated version. Extra hits are added to propel the slower rhythm at key spots.

---

5. Spiller, Henry. *Focus: Gamelan Music of Indonesia (Focus on World Music Series)* 2nd edition. New York: Routledge, 2008.

In general, faster tempos make us want to drop beats out and to deemphasize contrasts in duration; slower tempos make us want to add beats and to exaggerate contrasts in duration. (Note: That's not always the case. In bar 2 of the decelerated version, where the anticipation of the original is "softened," a literal transformation would have dotted half/quarter, in accord with the slower pace.) With each change of tempo, the rhythmic figure takes on a different associative value, potentially matching to different kinds of lyrics. At certain thresholds, these qualitative and associative changes may prompt further compositional changes.

You can apply this exercise to each aspect of the temporal framework for any given rhythmic figure: time signature, pulse (duple to triple), loose vs. strict-time feel, etc. In each case, incrementally transform the figure. Then reflect on the varied affective and emotional qualities of the results. Notice where transformations suggest changes specific to the rhythmic figure itself.

ACCOMPANIMENT RHYTHM

When writers say they write "from rhythm first," they usually mean starting from an accompaniment rhythm in the sense described earlier. Whether starting from a hand slapping a knee or a fully produced hip-hop track, working "from rhythm" in this sense means composing things other than the rhythm: setting to melodies, lyrics, and/or chords (often in an improvisatory way) over the rhythmic accompaniment. The beat, groove, or produced track is used as a starting point to spark creativity. Working this way is a prominent strategy for writers in many genres, not only genres where rhythm is in the foreground in final production.

Writers who work from rhythmic ideas first often have preferred pathways for generating material from the rhythmic base. But accompaniment rhythm as source material can inspire matching rhythmic material in any facet. You can expand your writing in response to accompaniment rhythm by setting directly to material in any facet: lyric, melody, chords—even to a purely rhythmic phrase (as distinct from accompaniment). Listening to the beat or track, your next step might be to vocalize a wordless melody, chant lyric ideas rhythmically against the beat, or play chords in a specific harmonic rhythm.

As you generate this other material (in any facet), you create distinct rhythmic phrases against the rhythmic accompaniment. In casual improvisation, a first instinct is to mirror or imitate the accompaniment rhythm in the rhythmic phrase. The following exercises will help you explore richer, more independent relationships between accompaniment and rhythmic phrase, ideally achieving a contrapuntal freedom between these elements.

EXERCISE 3.4. CAST FROM A GROOVE TO A LYRIC, MELODY, CHORDS

Start from a rhythmic accompaniment. It can be a simple loop or drumbeat, or a fully realized and produced track. The more fully produced the track, the more timbre and other sonic aspects will play a role in your response, beyond the rhythmic patterns alone.

1. *Rhythmically speak* a lyric inspired by the beat or groove. You may want to think of imagery or scenes inspired by the groove, and use these as a basis for the lyric, or let the groove suggest lyric sounds. Notice where your rhythmic lyric *coincides* with rhythmic beats of the groove, where beats of the groove play without the lyric, where the lyric moves on rhythmic beats not articulated in the groove. You should be able to hear the instrumental track as a rhythmic part or "voice" distinct from the lyric syllables in their rhythmic setting.

2. Putting aside your lyric, try the same exercise, this time working from the groove or track to *wordless vocal melody*. For the most intensive version of this challenge, sing melodic contours only (oohs and aahs, with no articulated syllables or consonant sounds), so that pitch shifts are your primary rhythmic expression. (See the section on Melody/Lyric Connections, page 108, in the "Melody" chapter.)

3. Once again, putting aside your lyric and melodic experiments, at your instrument *lay down chord progressions against the beat or track*. (Note: Many produced tracks will have embedded harmonic progressions, if only simple cyclic progressions. It will obviously be harder to try this aspect of the exercise in these cases.) Once again, for the purest experience of this challenge, think about the rhythm of your chords as being the rhythm of chord *changes* rather than rhythmic patterns with which you perform them.

4. Lastly, try working from the accompaniment pattern or groove directly to a *rhythmic phrase* that you express in isolation from specific lyric, melodic, or chordal material. You can vocalize the rhythm, using nonsense syllables, play a single repeating melodic tone on an instrument, or tap the rhythm out. The key is maintaining awareness that you're generating a *rhythmic phrase* in counterpoint to the accompaniment.

Accompaniment rhythmic material used in earlier writing stages serves primarily as a creative stimulus for generating material in other facets. This material might or might not wind up as part of the final song, either in direct or re-orchestrated form. Even for rhythmically driven songs, rhythms you work with at first can be treated as scaffolding or filler, to be later swapped out during revision.

THE RHYTHMIC PHRASE

The rhythmic phrase is created by metrically placed lyric syllables vocalized with melody. Vocal melody is a union of rhythmic patterns expressed in lyrics and melody, with an additional layer of harmonic rhythm also playing a role. Rhythmic aspects of phrasing can be subject to interpretation and modification by individual performers. But to work with the greatest rhythmic freedom and assurance in our songwriting, we want to compose in terms of distinct rhythmic phrases, even before determining precisely how to map those phrases into lyric syllables and melodic contours.

Attributes of Lyric Rhythm

There's a vast universe of rhythmic patterns and beats, not all suited to lyrical settings. Some rhythms sound like a "lyric in waiting," others like an accompaniment pattern. There's no bright-line distinction between rhythmic patterns that lend themselves to instrumental vs. vocal roles. Vocal rhythms draw on speech cadences; they regularize and accentuate speech rhythms while generally exaggerating and intensifying rhythms of casual conversation. Merely setting spoken syllables to metrically regular beats (think of a rhythmic version of "Auto-Tune the News") would differentiate vocal or lyric rhythm from rhythms of casual speech. The more heightened the emotion to be conveyed, the less conversational and more dramatic and contrastive the rhythmic effects used. At a certain point, rhythmic effects cease to imitate or exaggerate speech rhythms and impose more instrumentally driven rhythms. We can speculate about a continuum ranging from conversational speech rhythms, to lyric rhythms conveying heightened emotion, to more instrumental or percussively oriented rhythmic patterns:

Speech Rhythm   **Sung Lyric Rhythm**   **Instrumental Rhythm**

FIG. 3.4. The Speech/Instrumental Rhythm Continuum

Let's consider some qualities of the lyric rhythms that occupy the middle ground of this continuum.

1. *Lyric pace.* A natural rhythmic pace lends itself to lyric rhythm and the rhythm of the vocal phrase. This pace bears close connection to rhythms and pace of natural speech, though of course, sung lyrics involve emotional heightening and thus might be delivered more quickly or slowly than conversational speech. There are natural limits to how much lyric syllables can be shortened or elongated. Song lyrics are sung by human singers with limited lung power and heard by human listeners with limited ears and attention span. By contrast, the pace of an instrumental rhythm might be much quicker than vocal pace. We generally don't sing syllables for every strum of the guitar!

2. *Speech rhythm proportions.* Just as important as overall pace is maintaining characteristic lyric *proportions* between shorter and longer durations in the rhythm. Since they're based on syllables and meter, lyric rhythms tend to cover a relatively small range of durations, modeled on those found in speech. Lyric rhythm tends to involve just a few durations clustered around a basic syllabic pace. Certain proportions between durations suggest qualities of spoken language; ratios of 1 to 2 or of 2 to 3 are basic proportions creating a sense of alternating strong vs. weak stresses. If you build rhythmic patterns out of mostly eighth notes, with some quarter notes for emphasis, some sixteenth notes as passing triplets, you're working with a "vocally friendly" range of durations.

However, these durations can be extended, even with very elongated syllables and held notes, or—to some degree—shortened as well. As long as the proportions among durations of syllables stay similar, the phrase can still retain aspects of spoken or sung speech. This is what allows us to use acceleration and deceleration, within or between song sections, for prosody or contrast. We can slow lyric pace and still have a natural-sounding, audible, and comprehensible lyric.

3. *Varying durations.* Speech involves successions of strong and weak stresses on syllables. In pure rhythm, sans the element of dynamics, metrical placement and duration are the primary ways to convey these stress variations. This means sequences of rhythmic events of *varying* durations have a more vocal or rather lyrical quality.

As we sing longer series of consecutive notes of similar duration, the rhythm begins to suggest an increasingly instrumental rather than lyrical effect. Even when moving at a comparable pace to lyrical or vocal rhythm, instrumental rhythms tend to be more uniform in terms of durations—for example, long series of regular eighth notes. As an interesting, possibly related phenomenon, as lyric pace slows or speeds up to extremes (relative to a pace approximating the cadences of natural speech), there's a tendency for syllables to converge toward notes of similar duration. In effect, vocal rhythm begins to be more imitative of instrumental rhythm.

4. *Pattern.* Lyric rhythm flirts with *pattern* as does instrumental rhythm. But *lyrical* patterns are typically loose; percussive or instrumental patterns are more strict. As a rhythmic pattern is repeated successively without variation, we move from lyrical toward more instrumental rhythmic effects.

5. *Breaths.* Vocal phrases end with a breath; lyric rhythms thus naturally break into *phrases*, punctuated by pauses or rests of some duration. By contrast, instrumental rhythms are often *cyclic.* They loop and dovetail with a forward-rolling momentum. When such cyclical rhythms are put into the context of vocal melody, the "join" may need to be handled with overlapping vocal parts, call-and-response lead and background vocals, or adjusted phrasing.

6. *Line endings.* Lyric lines end in distinctive ways, depending on whether the final syllable is stressed, unstressed, or a secondary stress. (These line endings may or may not coincide with breaths.) A rhythmic phrase that lends itself to a lyric setting will suggest a characteristic line-ending of this kind.

7. *Vocal interpretation.* Some interpretive freedom is intrinsic to lyric rhythm. Musical effects such as anticipations and delayed phrasing, syncopations, elongations, triplets, and other counter-rhythms or polyrhythms are characteristic of vocal delivery. Songwriters should articulate a clear foundation for the vocal melody, determining which rhythmic effects are structural to the lyric, and which are up to the discretion and interpretation of the vocalist. Hearing your song sung by an artist or demo singer quickly sensitizes you to these issues.

8. *Vocal imitation of instrumental rhythm.* In some styles and for some songs, lyric rhythm intentionally (or perhaps unintentionally) imitates instrumental effects. Lyrics can be set via so-called *wrenched stress*—phrasing forced into "riffy" rhythmic patterns or successions of notes of the same duration. Speak the following lines to a regular eighth-note rhythm:

> Where you going my baby where you goin' tonight?
> Can't you find some sweet time for me, the feeling's so right

In the example, "baby," "goin'," and "feeling" are all technically mis-set. In addition, pronouns like "my" and "you," and the all-important word "the" all get strong stresses set into the regular rhythmic pattern. Such effects are prevalent in contemporary pop styles, from mainstream country to hip-hop, neo-soul, and R&B. Though distortion of natural speech rhythm inevitably results, that distortion might be desired, creating pleasing effects for the ears of some writers and listeners. The effect certainly brings rhythmic patterns to foreground attention, and also strongly communicates a distinctive attitude and persona. This can be suitable for particular themes and lyrics, though possibly overpowering a lyric more dependent on narrative clarity and focus.

The following exercise helps you manage this range of textures and the creative tension between instrumental and vocal rhythms.

EXERCISE 3.5. REGULAR TO IRREGULAR LYRIC RHYTHM

Set a lyric line first to a succession of even eighth notes. Now incrementally transform the lyric line, shifting the rhythmic setting to bring out the emotion and meaning of the lyric. With each change, you should feel the rhythm make the lyric more expressive—more "lyrical." You can move toward a less energetic, more conversational lyric rhythm, or a more intense and emotionally charged setting. You may lengthen syllables at will, or change eighths to sixteenths. (But don't introduce shorter durations, or you'll go down the rabbit hole! If you start hearing both sixteenth and thirty-second notes, shift all durations to half time so that eighth notes become the norm again.)

The following example shows several transformations simultaneously. For yours, make them sequentially, and stop to evaluate each intermediate version.

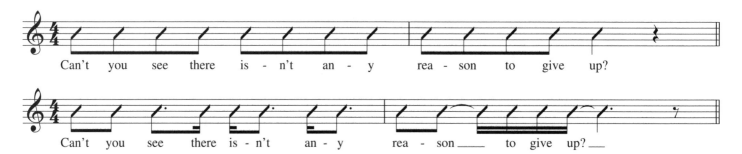

FIG. 3.5. Shifting Regular to Irregular Rhythmic Setting

In the transformed version, the remaining even successions of eighths ("Can't you...," "rea-son") take on different emotional tone in relation to the variations surrounding them. Anticipations ("up...") emphasize key words. The resulting setting conveys emphasis that, in ordinary speech, might be conveyed with other elements such as dynamics and pitch. Here, the different emphases of the notes are conveyed entirely through rhythmic variations.

Rhythmic Events

The rhythmic phrase threads together distinct rhythmic patterns in melody, lyric, and harmony. The rhythmic component is expressed differently in melody, harmony, and lyric respectively, and rhythmic elements of each of these can move independently. These layered rhythmic interactions, within and across facets, can be surprisingly complex, even in apparently simple musical textures. It's challenging work to manipulate these varied rhythms independently, even for percussionists, trained to hear and play highly sophisticated *instrumental* rhythms. The key in rhythm for songwriting is not complex rhythmic patterns for their own sake, but rhythms inherent to *vocal melody*, that complement emotion and meaning for the phrase or line as a whole.

In each facet, rhythmic *events* are created by *changes* in material in the stream of musical time. Any musical event (syllable, note, or chord), considered as a rhythmic event, has two attributes:

- *placement*: the event *lands* or *hits* on a given beat in the metrical framework
- *duration*: the event lasts or is held for a set amount of time

As we're working with it here, rhythm has an inherently metric or measured aspect—it's not free, *rubato*, breathing time. Both placement and duration are reckoned in terms of beats in the metric framework. A series of rhythmic events in a given facet is grouped into the sequences we can call *rhythmic phrases*. We can compose rhythmic phrases the same way we might compose a melodic phrase or a lyric line.

The rhythmic events that make up the separate threads of the rhythmic phrase are different in quality for each facet:

- In a lyric, rhythmic events or changes are created by *singing* a new *syllable*.
- In vocal melody, a rhythmic event is created by *moving* to a new *pitch*.
- In harmony, a rhythmic event is created by *moving* to a different *chord*.

We can even discern rhythmic aspects unfolding at larger hierarchical levels: phrase groupings and overall song form. As the temporal scale of rhythmic events stretches, we respond experientially more to perceptions of balance and expectations of form and structure than rhythm per se. Still, it can be helpful to view these larger structures in rhythmic terms.

Consider a song section with four four-bar phrases, then a concluding fifth phrase of six bars. The inherent instability in this structure can be attributed in part to a rhythmic effect, albeit one unfolding at a relatively slow temporal level. In a sense, one could call this level *phrasal rhythm*. We'll revisit this in the chapter on structure, in the context of *phrase structure*. We could speculate that surprising, asymmetric, or unbalanced temporal units highlight *rhythmic* aspects, while regular or symmetric groupings highlight *structural* aspects, at whatever hierarchical level of structure we are working.

This detailed view of lyric, melodic, harmonic, and even structural rhythm lets us work with rhythms in each facet as independent though interwoven aspects. It also helps to distinguish core or compositional aspects of rhythm, intrinsic to the song, from other functions of rhythm in the creative process and the final song. A rhythmic event in melody, harmony, or lyric is part of the core rhythmic material of the song, manifesting in the rhythmic phrase. Rhythmic groove, riff, and other accompaniment aspects can affect the writing *process*, and overall arrangement, production, and performance of the song, but are only indirectly part of the compositional core of the song. Similarly, changing aspects of the temporal framework such as tempo, groove, or beat can shape the melodies, lyrics, and chord progressions you write. But those changes are, in the end, inscribed in the rhythms of melody, lyrics, and harmony.

Rhythmic Pace

We've characterized rhythm as a stream of events of varying durations, occurring within an overall metrical framework that links syllabic placement, changes of melodic pitch, and chord changes. Rhythmic events land with varying durations. A sense of rhythmic *pace* is created when one duration value occurs most frequently within the phrase, creating an overall sense of flow and continuity.

Pace can be determined either by the duration occurring most frequently in a given rhythmic passage—the *norm*—or by the duration lying midway between the extremes (longest and shortest durations) occurring in the passage—the *mean*. Norm and mean are not always the same. In the first example of figure 3.6, the eighth notes establish pace as a norm, the most frequent duration heard. In the second example, durations range from sixteenth to whole notes. Though there are more occurrences of eighth-note durations (three) than of other durations, these don't dominate the texture by virtue of their frequency. A quarter-note pace better describes the feel, set by the mean.

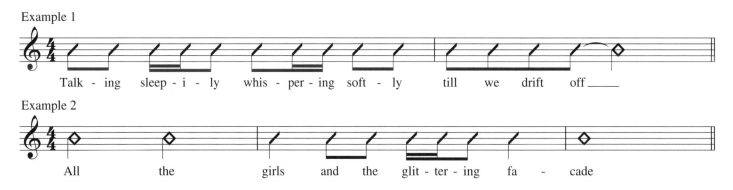

FIG. 3.6. Rhythmic Pace as Norm vs. Mean

In notation for songwriting, it's often convenient to set the basic *syllabic pace* as eighth-note durations, with triplets represented by sixteenth notes, and some syllables getting longer emphasis. This allows for showing both acceleration (faster triplet syllables) and deceleration (through extended durations), as variations pulling against the basic pace. Reserve a sixteenth-note pace for special-effect fast lyrics, like Gilbert and Sullivan–esque humorous rapid-patter songs, or rapidly delivered hip-hop. (Note that in such songs, the sixteenth-note pace is the norm—the most frequent duration—but not the mean.)

Pace is heard *in relation* to the metrical framework but is distinct from it. The metric framework rarely changes over the course of the song (unless we switch time signatures or between duple and triple pulse, for example). Pace can be shifted, especially for sectional contrast. We notice these shifts. When we feel the overall pace speed up, we get a feeling of *acceleration*; when it slows down, we get a feeling of *deceleration*. These rhythmic effects have emotional and energetic associations. But these impressions can be subtle and many-layered, since you can create simultaneous acceleration in one rhythmic aspect, deceleration in another.

Pace is key to *lyric rhythm*, since it's an attribute of natural spoken language. In most languages, conversation tends to settle on a particular pace of delivery for syllables, measured by the flow of both stressed and unstressed syllables. While unstressed syllables may take shorter durations than stressed syllables, the differences are not extreme. Of course, sung lyrics often evoke the rhythms not of casual conversation but of *emotionally heightened* speech. (The late Henry Gaffney liked to refer to lyric rhythm as "speech rhythm on steroids.") That heightening is conveyed in part through durational changes, both absolute (relative to the tempo of spoken conversation) and relative (proportions of short to long syllabic length within the phrase). Still, some lyric pace is established, though it may not be completely naturalistic in delivery.

Pace can *accelerate* or *decelerate*, usually at the sectional level. (If pace changes continually within a section, a pace is never established!) Material in different facets can establish different, even counterpointing paces in the same passage, phrase, or section. Melodic, lyric, and harmonic pace interact in a variety of subtle ways, as we'll explore in subsequent chapters.

Rhythmic Patterns

A *rhythmic pattern* is a regularly repeating sequence of rhythmic events and durations. A rhythmic phrase need not create a particularly distinct, repetitive rhythmic pattern. But our ears do seek out bits of order in the stream of rhythmic information. By "pattern," I generally mean something more marked than even successions of steady rhythmic values (as shown in pattern 1 of figure 3.7), though these definitely do sound "pattern-y" to our ears. In such highly repetitive passages, the underlying metric framework pokes through as rhythmic articulation.

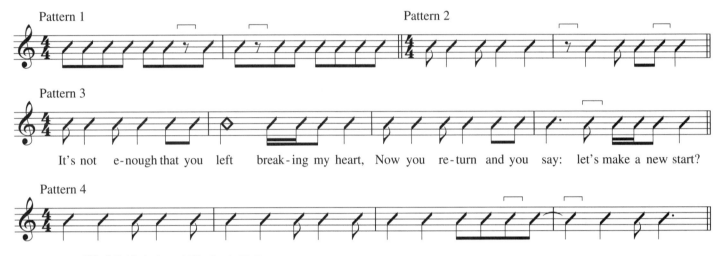

FIG. 3.7. Varieties of Rhythmic Patterns

More interesting patterns offer recognizable figures in the rhythmic stream—landmarks for our ears. Accompaniment rhythms usually rely strongly on a repertoire of such repeating patterns, often stylistic markers as well. Pattern 2 in figure 3.7 shows a two-bar pattern of this kind (vaguely suggestive of something tango-like). Skilled accompanists vary these in performance to create variety for the ear.

Vocal rhythm, on the other hand, must carry the narrative and sense of the line. Rhythmic patterns that "speak" to us tend to be longer, more irregular, and more expressive, relying on the qualities of vocal rhythm discussed earlier. As the pattern gets longer and less predictable, it moves in the direction of a unique rhythmic phrase—though skilled songwriters may exactly match the rhythmic phrasing of entire lines, from one line to another in a chorus, or across verses. An example of a rhythmic phrase used as a pattern for lyric matching in this way is shown in pattern 3. Other patterns are repeated figures heard more locally, within a line or phrase for example, as shown in pattern 4. Patterns set up powerful aural expectations in the listener's ear, allowing small variations to have dramatic effects. As shown in the bracketed moments in each example pattern, adding (ornamenting) or removing (thinning) even one rhythmic event in a repetition creates longer arcs and higher-level patterns. Patterns of such repetitions and variations become primary ways that rhythm participates in overall structural aspects of the song, as we'll explore in the "Structure" chapter.

Working with the Rhythmic Phrase

Our first versions of lyric, melodic, or harmonic ideas arrive with rhythmic settings already embedded in their first expressions. There are limits to how well placed or expressive these rhythmic phrases can be, especially when writing in an improvisational way. If we want rhythmic emphasis, we'll tend to repeat rhythmic patterns fairly literally throughout the phrase. If our focus is more on lyrics and melody, rhythmic phrasing will tend to be random and a bit scattered.

A simple but powerful writing and revision strategy is to experiment with or "sketch" different rhythmic settings for a lyric line or melodic phrase, before settling on one and locking it in through repeated performance. Rhythmic skills help you isolate and modify initial rhythmic settings, and experiment with setting lyrics, melodies, or chord progressions in varying rhythmic ways.

EXERCISE 3.6. WRITE A RHYTHMIC SONG SECTION

Write a song section consisting of four or five rhythmic phrases, each of about four bars in length, entirely as a *rhythmic template* only. Don't think about melody, chords, or lyrics—or subject matter or emotional tone of the emerging song. Don't repeat exactly the same rhythmic pattern four times; try to make rhythmic phrases outline and reinforce initial and cadential lines of the section.

You can think of the section as any structural section—verse, chorus, etc.— or you can choose not to worry about this. After writing the section, notice whether you've written it with a closed, balanced kind of cadence (typical of the verse of a verse/refrain song, or a chorus), or a more open, unstable kind of sectional cadence (more typical of a verse or prechorus leading to a chorus, or a bridge). Then write a second section, not connected to the first, that uses the *other* kind of closure.

CHAPTER 4

Lyrics

Lyrics—words in songs—have been written about (in words!) more than any other element of songwriting. Many lyric techniques and exercises have been adapted from creative writing fields, especially poetry and fiction, by teachers and authors including Sheila Davis, Pat Pattison, and others. A 360º approach to lyrics broadens this repertoire of techniques, with strategies that connect sound aspects of lyrics to rhythm, melody, and harmony.

We'll begin by looking at sound aspects of lyrics. We'll then explore strategies for setting from lyric material to rhythm, linking to the rhythmic facet explored in the last chapter. This will involve working from both sense and sound aspects of lyrics, initially to syllabic rhythm,[6] then to specific lyric rhythms. We'll then explore sonic constituents of syllables, consonants and vowels, and their connection to both rhythm and melody. This will provide a basis for specific techniques and strategies for moving from content or sense to lyrics, and from lyric seed material by sound to sense. Building on these techniques, we will finally tackle perhaps the most demanding of these strategies: setting from rhythm to lyric by sound.

SOUND ASPECTS OF LYRICS

Working with lyrics by sound is a time-honored approach for songwriters in many genres and styles—from Woody Guthrie to Lil' Wayne. The lyrics of many highly successful songs appear to fly in the face of general writing principles. Often the focus doesn't seem to be on lyrics at all—certainly not on deep, poetic, metaphorical, or narrative lyrics. The craft of such lyrics often relies, however, more on sound and rhythm than conventional or poetic meaning. Sonic aspects of lyrics are also critical in new settings for music consumption and exploitation of song material—synchronization placements in film, television, advertising, Web media, video games, and apps.

---

6. This section builds on seminal work by Pat Pattison, as detailed in books such as *Songwriting: Essential Guide to Rhyming* (2nd edition, Berklee Press, 2014) and *Writing Better Lyrics* (2nd edition, Writer's Digest Books, 2010).

Lyrics-by-sound techniques follow different linguistic and associative pathways than writing about themes or subjects already determined. Songwriters howl nonsense syllables at pianos at midnight, speak in tongues, stare out windows. Lyrics arrived at using these techniques are different in quality and subject matter. Yet becoming more skilled at working with sound aspects of lyrics will improve even lyrics driven by theme or subject. Lyrics that affect us deeply as listeners must sing and sound well, as well as speak honestly and truly.

Thought Phrase

Lyrics unfold at multiple hierarchical levels: line, sentence or phrase, word, syllable, and individual sonic elements (vowels and consonants). At the finest-grained hierarchical levels, we're most clearly in the realm of *sound* aspects; at broader levels, we address aspects of *sense* or meaning. These levels interweave, though, in many ways.

In lyrics, "thought phrases" have their own boundaries and cadences. Many lyrics do not roll out in complete grammatical sentences; yet, there are still distinct, audible groupings of thoughts. Boundaries of lyric thought phrases often coincide with phrases in vocal melody, but also may move independently in at least two ways. Using terminology carried over from poetics:

- A *caesura* is a pause in lyric flow in the middle of a line. A caesura generally reflects the sense or meaning boundary of the sentence or phrase.

> A pause for thought—a thought for paws
> My cat has got <> some wicked claws

  Here, the first caesura, indicated with the dash, reflects a natural break in the thought phrase. The second, indicated by the <>, does not. Too long a musical pause on "got," and the lyric setting will have "got" us into trouble.

- An *enjambment* carries over a sense or thought phrase, across a line boundary to the next line.

> If only this poor heart could find
> A little bit of piece of mind
> I fear that it may prove just too
> Much work to keep loving you.

  Here the first enjambment works because "find" dangles the listener enticingly, waiting for the completion of the thought. The second is unfortunate, as the listener will likely hear the confusing "prove just two."

In poetry, these concepts are defined relative to the layout of poetic lines on the page, with only indirect reference to how the poem might be read aloud. In song lyrics, the relevant boundary of the lyric line is tied closely to the vocal melody. The lyric thought phrase can move independently to this vocal-melodic line, as demonstrated in figure 4.1.

FIG 4.1. Shift of Lyric Phrases Against Musical Phrases

The first (two-bar) line has short, rhythmically echoing phrases, using the songwriting equivalent of caesuras. The second line intensifies this with even shorter phrases that still stand as complete grammatical statements. The third and fourth lyric lines carry a continuing thought across the musical phrases—enjambment in a song context.

Word Boundaries

Subtler lyric rhythms and textures are created by word boundaries and *junctures*—the juxtaposition of the vowel and consonant sounds ending one word or syllable and those that begin the next. We hear the contrasting effects of passages with short, one-syllable words vs. multisyllable words. An extended passage of one-syllable words will punch harder than one with lots of multi-syllable words: "Hit me with the love I need/Satisfy and intercede." These are not purely rhythmic effects; they lie at the boundary of sound and sense aspects of lyrics.

Syllabic Stress Patterns

Working with lyrics from sense (meaning), key units are thought phrases and lines to words. Working with lyrics as sound, *syllables* are the fundamental sonic and rhythmic units of lyric texture.

In English-language lyrics, we generally recognize three key levels of stress, which can be indicated with *scansion marks* borrowed from poetic analysis: primary stressed syllables ("/"); unstressed syllables ("‿"); and an intermediate level of stress called "secondary stress" (usually marked as "//"). Secondary stresses are necessary to deal with differential stresses in certain multisyllable words. For example, in "necessary" (/ ‿ // ‿), it's necessary that "nec-" receive a stronger stress than "-sar-," while both syllables are stressed more strongly than "-es-" or "-y." In "neces*sar*ily," on the other hand, "-sar-" must be stressed more strongly than "nec-"—yes, necessarily so.

We count line length as the number of *primary* stresses in the lyric line. For example, "Take me to the store" might be scanned as "/ ‿ / / /"; "I'm going to the market" as " ‿ / ‿ / ‿ / ‿." Both lines have a length of three stresses: the specific syllabic rhythm of the second line differs by an *upbeat* syllable at the start and an unstressed syllable at the end.

The stress pattern for a given line can be determined at several levels:

- Multisyllable words have stress patterns largely determined by language. In: "I'm *considering* going to the market," the word "considering" *must* receive " ‿ / ‿ //" as its stress pattern. Putting the primary stress on the last syllable "-ket" of market sounds wrong.

- Single-syllable words receive stress within the line by meaning or emphasis. I could choose to weight "I'm going to the store" with a secondary stress on the relatively unimportant connective "to": " ‿ / ‿ // ‿ /." But if I was responding to the question, "Have you been at the store?" the word "to" could get extra emphasis. Secondary stress levels are needed for multisyllable words, but can also suggest nuances of emphasis, tone of voice, and emotional intensity.

- It's also possible, as a special effect, to deliberately mis-stress lyrics with so-called "wrenched stress" emphasis. We might set: "Baby come party with me" to the pulsing rhythm "/ ‿ / ‿ / ‿ /," deliberately mis-setting "par-TY" to show how cool we are. Often, though, these are just mistakes resulting from sloppy word setting.[7]

For our purposes, a lyric line can begin on a stressed syllable or with one or more unstressed syllables (upbeat or anacrusis syllables). Then follow stressed syllables, each followed by one ("/ ‿"), two ("/ ‿ ‿"), or more unstressed syllables, or at times directly by another stressed syllable ("/ /"). Unless you're writing in a strict style matching specific syllabic rhythm in parallel lines, it's *line length* (the number of primary stresses), not the literal number of syllables, that ties things together. "A far cry from where we stand" and "Teach me kindly, dear friend" both feel like four-stress lines, though the first line is seven syllables, the second six, and the rhythmic patterns are different.

Song lyrics can freely vary the interchange of strong and weak stresses, rather than holding to regular patterns with occasional syncopations. If a strong/weak (/ ‿) pattern predominates, the line pulls toward an overall duple pulse or feel; a "/ ‿ ‿" pattern pulls toward a triple pulse. Consecutive strong stresses or a "/ /" pattern can reinforce either a duple or triple feel. A "/ /" pattern coinciding with a natural break in the "thought line" or phrase may split the line into being heard as two separate lyric lines—especially if reinforced with extra musical space between the lyric syllables, or if the second syllable is

---

7. In the prosodic analysis of poetry, patterns of stressed and unstressed syllables are grouped into complex systems of metric feet: iambs, trochees, anapests, dactyls, and many subtle variations. These derived originally from Greek, Latin, and later poetic forms that variously treated stress as created by intonation, emphasis, or length (that is, duration). In song lyrics, this kind of metric analysis is not as helpful. In a musical context, time signature, phrase structure, and even pulse or groove create metrical groupings against which the lyric is heard and felt.

aligned on the strong start of a musical phrase. In the examples below, speak the line and try to jot down the stress pattern you hear. Then compare with the stress marks indicated following the line.[8]

Tell me what you think I said	/ ˍ / ˍ / ˍ /	(duple)
Telling me just what you're thinking I'm saying	/ ˍˍ/ ˍˍ/ ˍˍ/ ˍ	(triple)
Tell me just what you think I'm getting at	/ ˍ / ˍˍ/ ˍ / ˍˍ	(mixed)
Tell me now. What am I saying?	/ ˍ / / ˍˍ/ ˍ	(two 2-stress lines)

This discussion of duple and triple stresses in lyrics should bring back to mind the discussion of the duple-triple pulse continuum in the "Rhythm" chapter. However, it's critical to note that even a predominant duple or triple feel in the lyric does *not* constrain the time signature, pulse, or groove chosen for the musical setting (or vice versa). Duple-pulse lyrics can be set to triple-time music, and vice versa. This flexibility is essential in mapping between *syllabic rhythm* of the lyric as text and final *lyrical rhythm*: setting the lyric to a specific rhythmic pattern, in the musical context of time signature and phrasing.

MAPPING LYRICS TO SYLLABIC RHYTHM

The inherent subjectivity in stress interpretations of lyric lines is a source of anxiety for writers learning to work with syllabic stress. As you consider multiple stress readings (or "hearings") for a line, you can worry you're doing it "wrong," or impatiently conclude that anything goes. But this seeming arbitrariness circumscribes a range of choices you make in setting the line. Of course, there will also be truly awkward, mis-stressed settings for a line.

Determining a lyric line's syllabic stress is an interpretation. There may be multiple ways to stress a given line, each technically correct (i.e., no mis-stressed syllables with respect to natural stress patterns) yet shifting nuances of meaning and associated emotion. Deftly exploring the space of these choices is key to flexibility in your lyric writing. Sometimes, it helps to lightly pound your fist on the table, as if it's a podium and you're declaiming the line as part of an impassioned speech. If you find yourself pounding on every word, you'll just annoy people. If you pound only at the end of the line, you lack the courage of your convictions!

We frequently generate lyrics by sense rather than sound and rhythm, such as in free writing in prose or spoken conversation. A lyric line conceived this way has its own rhythm, often prosaic or conversational in quality—a rhythm to which we tend to cling as we work with the line. If we're setting between lyric and musical facets (moving in either direction), that syllabic rhythm has only a

---

8. The prosodic system useful in song lyrics has points of similarity with simplified systems advocated by some poetic theorists, such as the "sprung rhythm" system developed by English poet Gerard Manley Hopkins.

vague chance of aligning with musical rhythms we're trying to match. A lyric line that flows well in its own syllabic rhythm may not match well to music with a different feel or phrasing. To challenge a first instinctive rhythmic setting for the line, a cornerstone lyric skill is hearing natural syllabic stress patterns and, more importantly, experimenting with alternate *well-set* variations of these patterns.

Syllabic Rhythm Example

Consider this fragment of a few contiguous lines from a song section, written lyric first:

> This isn't the way I was hoping things would turn out between us
> History repeating itself
> I start acting like somebody else

Here are alternate syllabic rhythm settings for just the first line.

Setting 1. 7-Stress Line

/   / ◡ ◡   / ◡ ◡ / ◡ /   ◡   /   ◡ ◡ /   ◡

This isn't the way I was hoping things would turn out between us

Setting 2. 6-Stress Line

◡   / ◡ ◡ /   ◡ ◡ / ◡ /   ◡   ◡ / ◡ /   ◡

This isn't the way I was hoping things would turn out between us

Setting 3. Over-Stressed Line

/   / ◡ ◡ / / ◡ / ◡ /   ◡   / / ◡ /   /

This isn't the way I was hoping things would turn out between us

FIG. 4.2. Three Stress Settings

- Setting 1 is a single 7-stress line. Of the seven stresses, three have triplet-rhythm (/◡◡) stresses, three have duple-rhythm (/◡) stresses, and one ("this") has no unstressed syllable, neutral between a duple and triple feel.

- In setting 2, the first syllable is treated as an upbeat or anacrusis syllable. The line is heard as a 6-stress line, again with a balanced triple/duple feel (T-T-D-T-D-D). Note the potential shift in meaning: we've stressed "out" rather than "turn"—or maybe it just turned out that way? (Or are we just stressing out?)

- Setting 3 moves toward over-stressing. Relatively unimportant words (this, out) are stressed. In addition, pronouns (I, us) receive a full stress. This could be felt as a 9- or even 10-stress line—too heavy for the line (but maybe not the situation?).

Songwriters have a tendency to overstress pronouns in lyric lines. A setting that leaves these unstressed is often just as clear to the listener and sings better. Sometimes pronouns can be removed entirely, such as an initial "I" at the start of a line: "I hope you'll come back" becomes "Hope you'll come back."[9]

So far, our example shows an initial iterative strategy, trying *different* syllabic rhythms for the lyric line. Syllabic rhythm is *not* yet in full musical time, i.e., within the metrical framework. Yet shifting stress emphasis changes sense aspects of the lyric, as well as rhythmic and other sonic aspects that will come into play in setting the lyric.

Let's look at similar issues in setting the second half of the lyric verse:

> History repeating itself
> I start acting like somebody else

Both lines contain three-syllable words, two of which require secondary stresses. ("Repeating" doesn't, with its primary stress in the middle, second syllable.) "History" is an example of a three-syllable word stress pattern (/ ‿ //) frequently mis-set in lyrics: words like "mystery," "harmony," etc. Often, these words end lines, and often our musical settings will end lines on full stresses. In strict terms, this often makes the final syllable of such words feel stronger than the first. The effect is not as striking as a mis-setting that inverts strong and weak stresses, but it adds a hint of affectedness. Such settings can be made more conversational by respecting the linguistically built-in secondary stress. In "somebody," the secondary is placed directly after the primary stress; this is an example of a word often set with deliberate mis-stressing or "wrenched stress" (some-BOD-y) for stylistic or idiomatic effect.

Since multisyllable words (with or without secondaries) force stress patterns, choices for a syllabic rhythm setting for these lines are almost—but not completely—determined. Figure 4.3 shows one setting possibility.

```
/    ‿//  ‿ /    ‿  ‿ /
History repeating itself

/ ‿    /  ‿   /    /    //    ‿ /
I start acting like somebody else
```

FIG. 4.3. Setting 1

Strictly speaking, the single-syllable words (I, start, like, else) are the only "wiggle room" here. Secondary stresses provide pivot points for selecting heavier or lighter stress readings of the line. You can *demote* a secondary to an unstressed syllable without violating the word's internal stress pattern. Or you can *promote* the secondary to a full stress, shifting its relationship to the surrounding context of the line—though in the final musical setting you should

9. I remember with some embarrassment my own lesson in this, when my friend and vocal coach Piper Heisig was helping me work on lyric phrasing for my album *Crazy Faith*. After listening to my demos, she gently told me in one session: "Have you noticed that whenever you get to the word 'I' or 'me' in one of your lines, you hang on to the word as long as you possibly can?"

still take care not to set it in a stronger metric position than its primary-stress sibling syllable. Setting 1 makes heavy-set choices for each of the secondary stresses.

Alternatively we could set these as 3-stress lines, as in figure 4.4.

/ ‿ ‿ ‿ / ‿ ‿ /
History repeating itself

‿ ‿ / ‿ ‿ / ‿ ‿ /
I start acting like somebody else

FIG. 4.4. Setting 2

In setting 2, we demote the secondary stresses to unstressed syllables. The couplet begins to have a triplet feel—with the exception of the "/ ‿ ‿ ‿ " pattern at the beginning. (This is a "secondary-shy" pattern; if prevalent, it indicates an under-stressed line.)

Still a third reading uses secondary stresses integrally to create a more regular syllabic rhythm pattern, and as a basis for rhythmic matching across the lines:

/ ‿ // ‿ / ‿ ‿ /
History repeating itself

‿ ‿ / ‿ // / ‿ ‿ /
I start acting like somebody else

FIG. 4.5. Setting 3

In setting 3, the two upbeat syllables in the second line are heard as a rhythmic variation in otherwise closely matched lines. "Like" is promoted to a secondary stress to match the last syllable of "history" in the preceding line. The secondary stress in "somebody" is demoted to an unstressed syllable to match the "-ing" in "repeating." The resulting feel is transitional: either a heavy 3-stress, or a light 4-stress line length. In an alternate, weightier reading, we can align these as matching 4-stress lines:

/ ‿ / ‿ / ‿ ‿ /
History repeating itself

/ ‿ / ‿ ‿ / ‿ ‿ /
I start acting like somebody else

FIG. 4.6. Setting 4

This matching is accomplished by promoting the secondary stress of "history" to a full stress—effectively changing the line length—while again demoting the secondary stress in "somebody." Not only do perceived line lengths now match, but the variation in the duple (D)/triple (T) syllabic rhythm of the lines make a pleasing pattern:

D D T D

D T̲ T D

A triplet pattern feels like a relative acceleration of a duple pattern, so this rhythmic pattern mostly matches, while the shift from duple to triple in the rhythm builds intensity.

EXERCISE 4.1. DEVELOP ALTERNATE SYLLABIC RHYTHMIC SETTINGS FOR A LYRIC LINE

1. Start with a new lyric line. Avoid a line from a song you've written or someone else's song. You want your thinking free of influences from settings you've already heard.

2. Find a first, intuitive syllabic rhythm for the line. Speak the line conversationally, but *as if you mean it.* "Speak-sing" if you like, but avoid binding to a specific melody or letting melody distract from the rhythmic emphasis. Now, slightly slow down the spoken version; speak it with more deliberate emphasis, feeling the weight each syllable seeks. Transcribe that pattern and make sure you've accounted for each syllable.

3. Generate several (at least three) *alternative* syllabic rhythmic settings for the line. Multisyllable words will constrain you by in-built linguistic stress to a specific rhythmic setting for those words. Single-syllable words allow you more freedom to play with stresses to shift meaning. Try some settings that make only subtle shifts in rhythm (introducing just one change), others that are more radically different. Test each alternative. Avoid the temptation to intentionally mis-set words. The purpose of the exercise is to find many well-set alternatives for a line, and explore their nuances of meaning.

4. Multisyllable words may also introduce secondary stresses. Other than these, you might start by avoiding extensive use of secondary stress markings in your experiments. These often confuse writers who are first learning about how to work with stress patterns and syllabic rhythm.

5. Select the syllabic rhythm that best suits the line as you want to use it. Notice the decisions you've made in that setting and why it works best for you. That will give you extra information about how to develop the line further in the context of the song.

The skill of experimenting with alternate syllabic rhythms is essential, whether casting from idea to lyric, framing from lyric to idea, or setting between lyric and musical elements. Casting from idea into lyric, the theme is determined. Playing with alternative rhythmic settings helps you choose the setting that best matches the desired meaning and emotion, and can shed new light on alternate shades of meaning. Experimentation with stress placement can also be critical for alternate *framing*, especially of lyric seeds driven by sound.

Heightened ability to work independently with syllabic rhythm also enables us to use a lyric line as a rhythmic template, to find our way to new lyric material. Setting from lyrics to lyrics by sound (specifically, by syllablic rhythm) is illustrated in the following exercise, complementary to the preceding exercise 4.1.

EXERCISE 4.2. PIVOT: LYRIC LINE → SYLLABIC SETTING → NEW LINE

Work from a lyric line to a syllabic rhythm pattern, then back to a new lyric line, using just the syllabic rhythm pattern as a template. You're not trying to match the lines, either thematically or in terms of rhyme or sonic matching. The line doesn't need to make sense, either!

/ ‿ // ‿ /   ‿ ‿ /
History repeating itself

/   ‿ // ‿ /   ‿ ‿ /
There's a serenade in my mind

Strike the very courage you feel

Falling unforeseen to your end

These examples show additional ways you can work with patterns involving secondary stresses. We've matched the secondary stress of *history* into different positions of two multisyllable words (*serenade* and *unforeseen*) with a different stress pattern (// ‿ /). In the second line, we've matched the secondary stress by emphasis to a subsidiary word (*very*).

SYLLABIC RHYTHM TO LYRIC RHYTHM

When a lyric is set to rhythm, *syllabic rhythm* is mapped to a more specific *lyric rhythm*: placing each syllable on a specific beat of a specific duration in a musical context. We start with a *dry lyric*: without a melodic setting but with syllabic rhythm determined. Our job is to place each syllable in a specific spot in the metrical context (repeating measures in a given time signature) of a musical phrase.

We've seen that a given lyric line can be set to multiple possible syllabic rhythms. In turn, there are alternatives for setting syllabic rhythm to lyric rhythm. Some settings may feel forced relative to the meaning of the line, but there should be multiple settings that respect the natural rhythms and cadences of the language. Working only instinctively, we're likely to try just a few of these, and to pass over settings that shift the meaning of the line in intriguing ways. Through push-and-pull encounters with musical elements, we discover or decide what we really intend our lyrics to say. This is important to clarify, since music is far from a neutral medium for carrying lyrics. Once set into the texture of the song, a lyric line is shadowed and buffeted by myriad musical effects that either reinforce or obscure meaning and emotion. With precise attention to syllabic rhythm, and then lyric rhythm, we increase the chances of our words coming through believably as musically set lyrics. In this regard, even the humble secondary stress plays a critical role, linking purely rhythmic and more contoured melodic settings for the lyric.

Some ways of varying lyric rhythm respond to possible shifts at the level of the temporal framework and overall arrangement of the song.

- *Set the line as a whole at a different tempo or pace.* For example, as the tempo slows, you can add more anticipations and syncopations to the rhythm to "activate" the line.

- *Extend the rhythmic setting to different phrase lengths* (number of beats, number of measures).

- *Set the lyric line in different time signatures* (4/4, 3/4, 6/8). For an extra challenge, try working with an odd-meter time signature such as 7/8 or 5/4. Sometimes adding or extending the breath or pause at the line end effectively creates an irregular measure, odd-bar phrase, or compound time signature.

Other changes can be made holding the basic phrase structure and temporal framework constant:

- *Change rhythmic proportions within the line*, either minimizing or exaggerating the stress contrasts with durations of greater or lesser contrast. The extreme form of minimizing stress contrasts via duration is a line where syllables are set to notes of all equal durations. In this case, only skilled metric placement in musical context will preserve natural stress-patterns. Mis-settings are frequent with this texture. Still, it can work well over a constant repeating rhythm ostinato or riff.

- *Vary where the lyric line begins* relative to the downbeat of the measure or phrase: on an upbeat, directly on the downbeat, or a delayed-entry (or back-heavy) setting.

- *Spotlight particular words or phrases* using elongation (hold a syllable for a longer duration), pauses or rests after a syllable, or repetition of lyric fragments.

We'll show an example of setting from syllabic to lyric rhythm later, in the "Melody" chapter.

ANATOMY OF A SYLLABLE

We've now bridged from syllabic stress to specific lyric rhythms. Beyond rhythmic aspects of syllabic stress, sonic formants of syllables form a "sound color" aspect of lyric language. As we will see, sonic characteristics of specific vowels and consonants have implications for rhythm, as well as connections to melody.

Sound Color Aspects

Exploring this aspect requires us to dive inside the "atom" of the syllable to find the "particles" of specific sound elements: a spectrum of sounds roughly classified into two tribes (with occasional inter-marriages and raiding parties):

- *vowels:* sustained, pitch-carrying sounds of language differentiated by where and how we form the tones

- *consonants:* relatively discrete sounds with characteristic qualities of attack and release

At this level, we can truly talk about the "music"—not just the rhythm—of the lyrics. It's a complex repertoire of sounds to draw from. The element of pitch resolves, in diatonic and tonal music, into a relatively small group of discrete tones (seven to twelve, with some blues bends and microtonal quavers thrown in). The sense aspect of lyrics—the vocabulary available to us for song lyrics—is practically infinite. The sonic palette of lyric language lies between these extremes. It's a richer palette than tones, yet with a structural aspect we can quickly lose sight of when focusing on meaning and the outer-world sense reference of words.

When combining only a few different sonic values, patterns created by lyric sounds tend to be more rhythmic in effect. In close proximity and especially within an individual line, rhythmic spotlights are created by sonic connections such as *assonance* (agreement of vowel sounds) and *consonance* (agreement of consonant sounds, including alliteration as a word-boundary sensitive special case). These rhythmic spotlights form a secondary rhythmic texture in the lyric, overlaying the ground rhythm of levelled syllabic stresses.

As the number of distinct tone colors increase, we get more contour-like effects. Unlike melodic or pitch contours, these are "color" or timbral contours: *vowel contours, consonant contours,* or composites of both elements. If syllabic stress connects lyrics most strongly to the facet of rhythm, sonic contours might be considered the "melodic" aspect of lyrics.

Additional Rhythmic Aspects

There are also *rhythmic* implications of lyric sounds that go beyond the metric stress patterns already considered as part of syllabic rhythm. Skilled songwriters know how to choose vowel and consonant sounds that sing well in varied rhythmic contexts. Songwriters need to understand these attributes, as do vocalists, producers, engineers, and arrangers. Some of this knowledge is intuitive to strong vocalists. Other songwriters acquire it through the painful experience of writing unsingable lines.

At whatever pace the lyric rhythm is moving, spoken language and its intensified form in sung lyrics involves interplay of quicker and slower, longer and shorter syllables. Here are a few tendencies (not hard and fast rules) to keep in mind.

- Longer vs. shorter durations seem to invite different word sounds. Roughly, vowels seek longer durations, consonants shorter durations. The more strongly rhythmic the pattern, the more associated word-sounds will favor consonants over vowels.

- Within the palette of consonant sounds, *unvoiced* consonants (such as "k" or "t") tend to move more quickly than voiced consonants (like "g" and "d," spoken with an accompanying glottal hum or "grunt"). Unvoiced consonants are "drier," more percussive in effect, while voiced consonants are slower and softer. Compare "tuck" vs. "tug." The "k" sound, an unvoiced plosive, is stronger in dynamics and can be delivered vocally more rapidly than its voiced partner sound, the hard "g." Similarly, compare:

  > Enough is enough; death is my judge.
  > Give me your love; breathe in the beige.

The first line uses primarily unvoiced consonants, the second uses the associated voiced "partner" sounds: "v" for "f," soft "th" for hard "th," soft "j" for hard "j." You should feel the first line singing more quickly than the second.

- Different consonant families are associated with varying rhythmic durations:

  - *Plosives* (k, p, t unvoiced; j, g, b, d voiced) move most quickly
  - *Fricatives* (f, sh, s unvoiced; v, zh, z voiced) move more slowly
  - *Nasals* (m, n, ng), along with l and r, move the most slowly
  - *Letters y and w* are borderline, sharing some attributes of vowels and some of consonants.

- *Consonant clusters:* The more adjacent consonants in a syllable, the slower it will sing and the more time the singer needs to clearly enunciate the words. So, "sock" will sing faster than "socked" or "sparked."

- Vowels also have differences in intensity and velocity. Shorter vowels sing more quickly than longer vowels, closed vowels more quickly than open: "I bet you can't see me" vs. "I beat you unfairly."

- Closely related to consonant clusters at the start or end of syllables, *junctures* between syllables (connections between consonants at the end of a syllable and those at the start of the next) also affect how well they will sing. Junctures can affect flow and tempo through awkward combinations. The lyric "cruel family" will sing slower than "cruel time" because the fricative "f" is slower than the plosive "t" sound. When vowels adjoin (like "way out"), the tempo is generally faster. The singer may need to use a glottal to put a distinguishing "edge" on the second vowel sound. This is more necessary the more similar the vowel sounds are.

- Junctures involving the same consonant or vowel sound may allow for eliding of syllables, speeding the pace. However, you can pay a price in comprehensibility: e.g., "dark crystal" sounds like "darkrystal." To avoid this, the singer must enunciate by placing a pause between the two sounds, or a glottal in the case of similar vowels. This robs time, counting almost as much as (or perhaps more than) an additional consonant (or in extreme cases, an additional syllable).

SENSE/SOUND LYRIC STRATEGIES

We've now looked in detail at strategies for taking a lyric line that began with speech or conversational rhythm, and mapping it first to a definite syllabic rhythm, then to a specific lyric rhythm. We'll now consider strategies focusing on lyric material itself, including both sense-to-sound and sound-to-sense techniques, and techniques for generating new lyric material from existing lyrics. We'll employ these techniques in the final strategy described, moving from rhythm to lyric.

The essence of a *sense-to-sound* lyric strategy is simple: figure out what you're trying to say, then how to say it. An equally powerful strategy is *sound to sense*: figure out the sound of what you want to say, then let this lead you to what you want to say. Each of these strategies can be effective in a range of situations, and each has potential limitations and risks. In project-driven songwriting, where theme or subject matter is a given or very constrained, working sense to sound makes sense. In inspiration-based writing, with no predetermined subject that you must write about, moving from sound to sense may be a sound strategy.

Lyric Sense to Sound: Paraphrasing

Paraphrasing is a more disciplined version of an informal technique used all the time in songwriting. The idea is simple: Get the sense first, and then work toward the sound. First, write the line that says *exactly* what you mean to say. Don't try to get the *sound* of the words right in this first step; don't worry about rhyme, rhythm, line length, or even clever language and metaphor. Then you can gradually transform the "bald statement" version into a line that sounds and sings better. Referring back to our old woman on the bus from the Seeds chapter:

An old woman on the bus carrying too many shopping bags	—	original concept seed
Old woman on the bus / *Too* many bags in her hand	—	four-stress / five-stress couplet
Old *wo*man on the bus / Too many *bags* in her hand	—	two three-stress lines

This technique works (when it does) in part by momentarily relaxing and releasing your mental pressure to find "lyrical" words. It's a great way to develop the knack of saying things in a simple and straightforward way.

Co-writers practice a simple version of this technique with the "What I'm really saying is…" trick. One writer paraphrases what's intended to be conveyed by the problem line, speaking in ordinary conversational language. The other writer acts as scribe and captures a specific line or turn of phrase the speaking writer might not have thought to include in the song. A related paraphrasing strategy is the "Write the Letter" technique, part of the folklore of Nashville songwriters. Instead of writing lyrics directly, you write a letter from the singer (in the world of the song) to the "sung-to." Writing the letter gives you permission to use direct, emotional language. This technique works particularly well in direct-address, situational songs, with a clear emotional declaration involved.

Paraphrasing techniques can help generate lyric material couched in ordinary, everyday language. It's not necessarily a great way of discovering surprising metaphors rather than clichés, or poetic language in general. Occasionally, some lines might make it directly into the song, often in the chorus or bridge—sections supporting a sudden, direct statement of emotions. But the primary value of the technique is as a process step, clarifying or reminding yourself what you're really trying to say. This requires keeping clear that the first paraphrase line is *not* the final lyric.

Once you have your paraphrase line and it says what you want it to say, transform it as many ways as you can—grammatically, rhythmically, with synonyms—until you find a way that *sounds* right. You can do small successive transformations—change the line, then change the change, etc.—or go back to the original, trying different possibilities. Roll around a lyric phrase until it has the right rhythm, vowel and consonant quality, or placement in the musical phrase. Don't settle until it sounds right.

Lyric Sound to Sense

In paraphrasing, you reach for the sense while not trying to get the *sound* of the lyrics right in the first pass. To work skillfully with lyrics by sound requires precisely the opposite skill: an ability to untether your rational mind and be led by sounds, without worrying about what the line means. Lyric "by sound" techniques are particularly useful when working from music. But we use the same skills when generating new lyrics in response to existing lines. Thus, you can develop and practice lyric-by-sound techniques working with lyrical material alone; such isolation practice will give you more confidence to find compelling word-sounds when working from and to music.

Lorem Ipsum: Dummies for Dummies

Filler material (as discussed in the "Song Seeds" chapter) is stock or cliché material, weaker than the seed it accompanies. Unless we work with it carefully, it gets mixed in with the seed material, making the whole fragment harder to work with. In later development of the song, however, intermediary prototype or placeholder material can be an essential tool. *Dummy* material is provisional material you generate *intentionally* to help build out structure. Unlike filler, you know it's provisional as you generate it. Often, dummy lines are intentionally silly and off the cuff, to help reinforce their temporary status. But that's not why they're called "dummy" lines. I believe the word "dummy" used in this context is a borrowing from the printing world. Printers and typesetters use nonsense Latin phrases like the ubiquitous "lorem ipsum" for visual mock-ups of page layout before final text is ready.

Smart songwriters learn to work skillfully with dummy lines. Dummy material is essentially a *prototype* of the final lyric. Dummies can also serve as rhythmic and sonic approximations of the eventual desired line. You can also work with dummy material in any facet: dummy chords, melodies, even rhythms. In other facets, little but your level of dissatisfaction distinguishes dummy from keeper material. Dummy lyrics have a distinctive quality: ideally, they sound so ridiculous we're not likely to mistake them for keeper lines. A dummy does no harm until you put it in the driver's seat.

Sense vs. Sound Approximations

Dummy lines and paraphrase lines are complementary techniques. Dummy lines provide templates for desired *sound* attributes of the line you want; paraphrase lines approximate the *sense* of the line you're targeting. An alternative to a dummy line is a simple "placeholder" marking that shows the desired stress pattern or end-rhyme sound desired for the line. You can use the strategies in tandem, *iterating* and/or *triangulating* (our strategy friends from chapter 2) by generating several possible dummy and/or paraphrase lines for a given line or bit of music to match, to get closer to both sound and sense aspects.

Here's an example of a practical process distinction between an inadvertent or off-the-cuff filler line, in comparison to using dummy, placeholder, and paraphrase lines techniques.

- *I never thought I'd see the light.* Seed lyric line. It sounds good and suggests meaning as well.

- *I never thought I'd say good night.* Typical "filler line" generated as an off-the-cuff couplet (an "off-the-cuff-let"?). It includes literal repetition and "chases the rhyme" as well, with a predictable rhyme and cliché. But it presents as an attempt at a "real" line, and thus might easily get lodged in the working version of the song, despite its improvised origins.

- *Magenta cow that zips up tight.* A "self-declaring" dummy line, catching rhythm and rhyme sounds with no attempt to match the line by sense. This will be easier to work with later.

- *Da dum da dum da dum da* <-ite>. A placeholder template for the line-to-be. This stress template (or "stress-o-gram") uses the stress-marking techniques discussed earlier to lay out line length and even the specific syllabic rhythm, with a marker for the desired rhyme sound, while not committing to even a dummy line as a prototype.

- *Or get a second chance to hold you tight.* A paraphrase line that follows the sense of the first line. It still "chases the rhyme," and strays from the desired rhythm to be matched, but approximates the desired meaning.

- *A second chance at second sight.* A potential "keeper line" that matches the rhyme sound, the rhythm, and the content of the first line in a fresh way. It's great if you stumble onto such a line, but you're more likely to get there by triangulating between paraphrase and dummy lines.

Paraphrase lines, dummy lines, and placeholders allow you to work with song structure in a more flexible, nonlinear way. Instead of stopping in your tracks until you get the perfect line, you put something there and move on. (Often, there's no way to get to that perfect line until you come back later anyway.) In the end, we want our lyrics to mean what we mean to say, and sound right and sing well, as well. But we often stumble when we try to get sense and sound aspects right in one fell swoop. We can divide and conquer rather than fight both battles simultaneously.

The Gibberish Scale: Seven Levels of Nonsense

Dummy lines are gibberish. But some gibberish lines are more gibber-ish than others. Paradoxically, working with lyrics as sound produces disappointing results if we allow our rational, sense-based filtering mind to intervene at the wrong point in the process, and don't let our sound-based searcher's ear do its work. But it's actually quite a difficult skill to generate truly nonsensical lyric lines, especially by casual free association. Lyrical song seeds are rarely in this form; they're typically coherent lyric fragments lifted out of context in part because of sonic aspects—very different from a true line of gibberish.

You can practice and develop lyric-by-sound skills, just like any other aspect of songwriting or musicianship. To do this, we need to make a more intentional technique out of what great songwriters are doing intuitively as they roll their eyes to the ceiling and spill out seemingly random word-sounds. As a starting point, I've distinguished a seven-level "scale" of gibberish, that moves progressively from lines mixing sense and sound aspects towards purer lyric sound-music. This list is by no means exhaustive or all that systematic. I've tried to list the different styles of nonsense in order of increasing "nonsensicality," since I believe it takes increasing skill to be bolder with these sound aspects of your lyrics. There are various routes into these kinds of lyric experiments. I'll illustrate with a rhythmic source, generating successive nonsensical matches to the syllabic rhythm "/ / ⏑ / ⏑ / ⏑⏑ / / ⏑ /."

1. *Nonsense.* Real words put together in surprising, nonsensical ways. "You've got a harem litany skewed by a string."

2. *Wonder-puddleful.* Words put together in ways that jumble grammatical categories. (Apologies to the poet E.E. Cummings, who was famous for lines like these, as in his poem that begins "in Just- spring …") How about: "Green as the always turning to angrying night."

3. *The neologist twist.* Made-up words that sound like words that mean something. These are more convincing if they appear in grammatically familiar contexts. "I'm talking candalicious if you'll swoodle too."

4. *Faux-foreign.* Singing in a faux impression of a foreign language you don't speak. (Go watch old Danny Kaye movies to see a master of "faux-foreign" speaking and lyric-spouting at work.) "A lora della piccola bon bella bon."

5. *Word buds.* Think of this as speaking in something that sounds like a language, but you don't even know what language it is! The syllabic sounds may not even sound like plausible words, but are made up of consonants and vowels with the right textural feel for the line. Here's some faux-Klingon: "Jak tultu cha-deh kitana forl paka tran."

6. *Syllable buds.* Word buds stretched until you're not even sure where word boundaries would fall. Syllable buds can include vowel contours, consonant contours, and combinations of these. "Fa ne do ka ne dinala yo va ne sa."

7. *The howl, the mumble, songwriter satori.* Where you open your mouth and let sounds spill out in a free improvisational stream. (You try it!)

As you move through the Seven Levels of Nonsense, results may at first sound very funny. We associate nonsense lyrics with humor, and that's not a bad instinct. Humor is not an emotion in and of itself, but actually a way to stay loose, to avoid preemptive commitment to one specific emotion. The French philosopher Henrí Bergson, in his book *Laughter,* points out that for us to find something funny, we need at least a brief moment of emotional detachment. If we feel sorry for the clown who does the pratfall, we won't allow ourselves to laugh at him. Allowing yourself to generate humorous lyrics is a temporary distancing—a way to keep the emotional content of your final lyric open and malleable. Remember, nonsense lyrics are dummies, so you need not wind up with humorous lyrics at the end.

Make no mistake, though: this is potentially powerful work. Take your nonsense seriously. You're accessing the unconscious mind's greater wisdom, to get to lyrics you'd be far less likely to find with a more "rational" process.

EXERCISE 4.3. LYRIC-BY-SOUND STRATEGIES

Here are ways of working with Songwriter Gibberish and the Seven Levels of Nonsense.

- Practice moving seamlessly through these levels of nonsense. The examples above and on page 82 are rhythmically but not sonically related. However, the technique is probably most useful when each level serves as a sonic approximation for the next, honing in on vowel and consonant sounds as well as rhythm. You might start at the gibberish end and work your way toward the sense lines. Alternatively, you could start from a meaningful dummy line that's still not the right line, deconstruct it into its sonic nonsense version, then pivot back to a new sense line.

- Generate lyric sounds in response to material in another facet: rhythmic, melodic, and/or chordal material. In working this way, it's often most effective to begin at the "formless" end of the nonsense spectrum. For example, in setting from a rhythmic pattern to a lyric, begin with a vowel or consonant contour, move to syllable buds and then word buds, and finally to real words and dummy lines.

- Use an existing, sense-based lyric line as a template for associative generation of new lyric lines. Here again, practice extracting vowel or consonant contours, or a combination of the two. You can try generating response lines linked thematically (sound + sense), or connected only sonically.

- Create lyric syllable-bud *patterns* using structural templates. This is more a skill-building technique than a specific writing strategy, unless you plan to incorporate nonsense lyrics directly in the song. You can apply one pattern for leading consonant sounds, another for vowels.

> Gah Tay Low Goo
> Sah Nay Koh Noo
> Tie Lie Nee Kee
> Tah Lay No Koo

Patterns may be reminiscent of musical or other forms including: scat singing, Gaelic mouth-music, auctioneer lingo, nursery rhymes, nonsense refrains of folk songs, even speaking in tongues or glossolalia, the cooing of babies and those smitten with them, and last but not least, the raving of lunatics (or the Nashville version, "former hit songwriters who lost their publishing deal").

Sonic Contours

Just as we used a lyric line as a rhythmic model or template and pivoted back to new lines (see exercise 4.2), we can also derive sonic contours from existing lines, matching one or more aspects of these contours in new lines. End rhyme and internal rhyme are special cases of this kind of sonic contour matching. Note, though, that exact rhyme relies for its effect, not only on matching syllabic sounds—vowels plus consonant sound(s) at the *end* of the rhymed syllables—but also on *contrast* or nonmatching of the respective *initial* consonant(s) of rhymed syllables. (Without this latter condition, we get identity or false rhyme: e.g., "lease" and "police.")

The sonic contour of the line as a whole can be worked with as a template to be imitated, strictly or loosely, in subsequent lines, using sonic matching, free association, and thematic focus. In theory, you could even work from an abstract vowel or consonant contour, but these patterns are so sonically complex that we generally need to model from contours of a real line. Some hip-hop lyricists develop considerable skills in creating new lines that match the rhythmic and especially sonic contours of lines—even improvising such matching lines in real-time free-styling:

> Talk about guessin' there's a real mess ahead of us
> We keep messin'—the wheel toss will skid the bus
> Oedipus, Sisyphus, octopus omnibus...

(This is why aging former classic civilization majors like me shouldn't try to rap....) Note there are *four* internal rhymes in the first two lines (guessin'/ messin', real/wheel, mess/toss, head/skid). This sonic matching is impressive and can also produce surprising and fresh results. But it's best treated as a special effect technique for the purposes of general songwriting skills.

In old-school songwriting, with lyrics set throughout to vocalized melody, we often build up the song by setting from starting lyrics to new lyric material. In this scenario, the close matching of the sonic contour for the whole line as described on page 84 is actually too close for our purposes. (I've seen accomplished hip-hop lyricists struggle with just this problem; their ears are trained to build too many sonic connections to adjacent lines.) Instead, in conventional song form, when we generate a second verse from a first verse as "template," we want to match lyric rhythm (more or less closely, depending on genre) and the rhyme *scheme*—while *not* repeating the specific lyric sounds used in that first verse. Tighter sonic matching would tie our hands too much, both sonically and in terms of theme and subject matter. Still, songwriters in all styles can benefit from the lyrical skills to isolate rhythmic and other sonic aspects of an existing lyric line, and to pivot from these as templates back to *new* lyric lines.

EXERCISE 4.4. MATCH A LYRIC LINE'S SONIC CONTOUR

Starting with a model line, identify key vowel and consonant sounds of the line. Use these contours to generate new lyric lines, sonically matching the original in terms of the selected contour. As with the earlier lyric generation in exercise 4.2, resulting words need not relate to the original line. You can try this with vowel contours or consonant contours derived from the model line. There is, however, a curious asymmetry in how intuitively we can hear and imitate vowel vs. consonant contours. Vowel contours seem to be easier to hear; consonant contours require more intense mental effort, and more quickly depart rhythmically from the model line.

You can use this exercise starting from any "model" line of a song that delights you. Using a familiar or even famous line (as in the example below) isn't a drawback. You'll quickly leave behind the familiar associations. For a bit of extra fun, try this with a partner or in a group setting. Pick a lyric line secretly and see if your partner/the group can guess it from the sonic contour! For example, consider the following vowel contour:

AH – EE – I – IH – AH – AY – UH – OO   (Recognize it?)

(Luckily, as of this writing, songwriters cannot actually copyright sequences of vowel sounds, so Dolly won't be comin' for ya any time soon!)

As you work back from the selected vowel contour to new lines, try different qualities of consonants: more plosive and harsh, to more sibilant and liquid. Dive in boldly, or sound your way along the Seven Levels of Nonsense scale toward sense lines:

Lyrics	Nonsense Type
Cry is all they assume	dummy line: real words but weak sense
Dais wall clay from room	you'll tend to start rhyming with iterations...
Ply this stall say some brew	even looser: phrases disappear, individual words
Trying call freedom soon	moving toward sense lines...
Try we'll call it freedom soon	intrusion of thought line on sound, pull back...
Cry—a cold freedom's rule	liberties taken with vowels but shape remains

FIG. 4.7. Nonsense Types

As you try iterative attempts, you can gradually loosen your commitment to the exact original contour sounds, especially as you get a promising idea for a real line. But be careful for spots where the thought takes over and pulls you too much from the flow of the vowel or consonant contour you are writing to.

Sonic contours are also a way to set from a lyric line to a melody and/or rhythm, or from other facets to lyric. Vowel contours tend to suggest melody, consonant contours rhythm (though again, these correspondences are still somewhat speculative).

SETTING FROM RHYTHM TO LYRIC

We first made use of sonic constituents of lyrics—syllabic rhythm, vowel and consonant sounds, and contours—in setting *from* a lyric *to* rhythm. Here, our main challenge was cultivating rhythmic *flexibility* in hearing a given lyric line in different rhythmic ways. We've also looked at techniques for moving between lyrics by sense and by sound, and for matching lyric lines. We will rely on the same intuitive connections going the other way: setting *from* a rhythmic phrase *to* a lyric.

We deal more rarely with pure rhythmic song seeds than lyric ideas. We also follow this path—*from* rhythm *to* lyric—when we align *new lyric* material with material already written, and want that alignment rhythmically tight. This could be, for example, a chorus of rhythmically matched lines, or—if writing in a strict phrasing and sectional matching style— a later verse matching the lyric rhythm of a "template" first verse.

In these cases, you generate and match new lyrical material to a rhythm that was itself derived from a lyrical line. The new lyric must match rhythm but not specific lyric sounds such as rhyme. The match is more satisfying to the ear, and creates better sectional differentiation, with contrasting lyrical sounds. By abstracting rhythms from the source lyric to generate the new lyric, we can be less influenced by either lyric sounds or meaning aspects of the source lines.

Rhythm to Lyric by Sound

In principle, we can set from a rhythmic pattern to a lyric via alternate paths: by sense or by sound. Generating a lyric from a rhythmic phrase strictly by sense would involve, in effect, first *framing* the rhythmic phrase. While lyric rhythms alone can carry associative meanings, in practice, we rarely frame from rhythmic material only. The pull toward the "by-sound" route is much stronger. Rhythm provides so much structure directly suggestive of lyric *sounds* that these connections tend to dominate. The more strongly patterned the rhythmic aspect, the more it invites exploration by sound.

Setting from rhythm to lyric by sound is also challenging. You'll be tempted to fall back on familiar words and phrases, cliché lines, or free association and memory for scraps of coherent lyric, *whether these fit the rhythm or not.* These words will have their own innate rhythm, more often than not mismatching to the source rhythm in slight or extreme ways. Ironically, this process produces both many poorly set lyrics, and many thematically unfocused lyrics.

To avoid these pitfalls in setting from rhythm to lyric by sound, give yourself creative permission to generate lyric-like sounds that are *not yet* actual lyrics or even words. However, the critical skill is to hold yourself to rigorously *honoring the exact source rhythm.* Even if you catch yourself in moments of fear-based searching or clinging for referent meaning, keep returning to that source rhythm and its sound associations.

The following example shows some—admittedly speculative—stages in exploring this "proto-lyric" space. Our goal is to pull a lyric "out of the air" suggested by or at least matching well to a rhythmic phrase. Here's where you'll need those Songwriter Gibberish skills! Ready to sound temporarily ridiculous?

We'll start with a simple rhythmic phrase for a single lyric line, beginning on an upbeat syllable, shown in figure 4.8 as a "dry rhythm" (as described in the "Rhythm" chapter). Note that in working from a rhythmic phrase rather than a groove or accompaniment rhythm, we're already working from a rhythmic pattern captured as seed material, or composed, to potentially "take a lyric." (The example shows the sustained rhythmic durations of the "bagpipe" vs. "woodblock" style of rhythmic notation.)

FIG. 4.8. Rhythmic Phrase to Be Set to Lyric

ENERGY CONTOUR OF A RHYTHMIC PHRASE

As you vocalize the rhythm, hear it in your mind's ear, or tap it out, you can start to sense an implied *energy contour*. In any given rhythmic phrase, any articulated beat or "strike" can be felt to receive a relative weight or "energy": through interactions of pulse, its metric position and duration (or, in the case of a durationless "woodblock" pattern, the amount of space before and after it), and emergent figures and patterns surrounding it in the phrase. In a sense, this technique reverses the process by which we obtained a "dry" rhythmic phrase, which required suppressing dynamic information. We're now listening specifically for dynamics of a kind, in order to move toward a lyric setting.

What does your ear tell you about the relative strengths or weights of the individual hits? This is *not* a formula or an objective mapping; different writers might interpret a given rhythmic phrase with different contours. In figure 4.9, we see two successive refinements of an energy contour for the rhythmic phrase of figure 4.8.

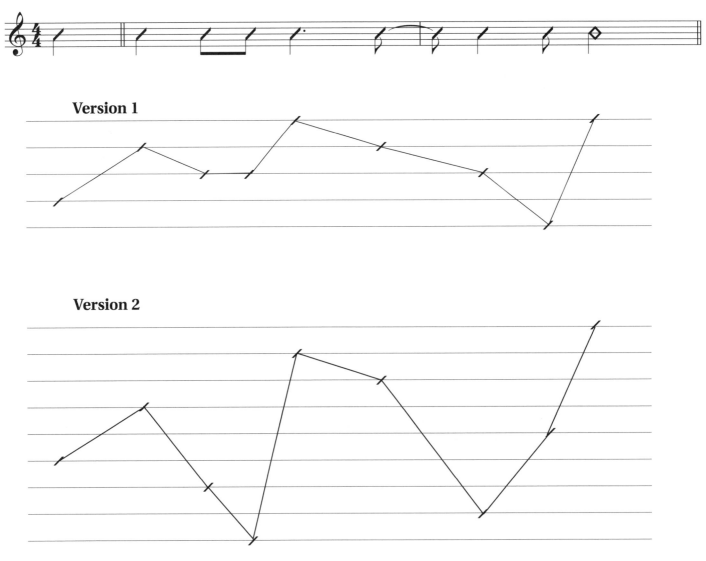

FIG. 4.9. Rhythmic Phrase with Two Energy Contours

It's easier to hear relative weight differences of *adjacent* rhythmic hits, which tend to cluster into units. In version 1 (drawn on a five-line "differential energy staff"!), the first two hits are clearly in a "weak-strong" relationship; the next two hits are felt at the same level; the next hit is felt as "as strong" as the final hit. Version 2 refines the contour, and the "staff" now has a line for each hit in the phrase. Now the last hit is felt as strongest, the hit before it no longer the weakest. With each iteration, you might shift relative weights. Continue refining the contour until you can discern contrasts in energy between *any two* rhythmic events in the phrase.

The energy contour *might* imitate or echo performance aspects of the rhythm, if you're working from a fully realized rhythmic track or beat as your inspiration. But it's not *determined* by such extra-compositional aspects. If you do your songwriter's work well, creative information flows the other way: rhythm, lyric, melody, and chords can shape performance aspects, providing cues for arranger, player, vocalist, engineer, and producer to bring out the essence of the phrase—and of the song.

Vowel and Consonant Contours

The energy contour technique can be used for different setting pathways: mapping to lyric sounds, or leading to pitch contour and thence to melody. Here, we'll continue working from rhythm to lyric, mapping the energy contour specifically to lyric sounds: including the *vowel* and *consonant contours* described previously, as well as potential match or "chiming" points for assonance, consonance, and rhyme.

Let the energy contour, the pattern of longer and shorter, heavier and lighter stresses, begin to blur in your mind and suggest verbal sounds—a kind of songwriter's scat singing or mouth music. Approach this with purposeful use of "peripheral attention." Get the rhythm set, recite it to yourself a number of times; then go off and do something else, letting it percolate and simmer in your mind. When you next pay attention, you'll find that—like pale mushrooms in your mind's basement—little lyrical buds will have attached themselves to the rhythmic hits.

As in working from a model lyric line to a new line, you can work via either vowel or consonant sounds, or combine them. Here, we demonstrate a "vowel-led" approach. Picture yourself as a toothless old man or woman trying to order food in a restaurant, or a gagged hostage trying to tell a rescuer where the keys to the handcuffs are.

FIG. 4.10. Mapping a Rhythmic Phrase to a Vowel Contour

Unlike lyric-to-lyric transformations, here you're doing an arguably more difficult or more abstract creative task: letting differentials in the energy contour suggest contrasts between long and short, open and closed vowels—to create a vowel contour. Again, while this is not an arbitrary process, it's also not a deterministic "word painting by numbers." There are no definitively "right" or "wrong" transformations. That said, certain transformations should sound "righter" to you than others. In general, shorter vowel sounds (ih, eh, uh) flow better on quicker beats; longer vowel sounds (ay, oo, oh) work better on longer held syllables. Listen for quick passages that feel rushed or crowded, slower sections that feel less natural, less *singable*. Spend time experiencing these effects for a given rhythm and vowel contour. You'll know you have developed the skill when you can distinguish vowel settings that work for you from ones that don't.

Vowel Buds, Consonant Buds

If howling toothlessly is a little intense for you, put a *leading consonant* in front of the vowels—turning the vowel contour into vowel *buds*. Buds are more than a contour, less than full syllables. Our vowel contour in figure 4.10 would become: doo-dow-doo-dah-dih, etc. *Voiced plosive* sounds like "d" or "b" are helpful here. Being plosive (unlike "r" for example), they're percussive and provide rhythmic definition. Being voiced (unlike "t" or "p" for example), they're softer and flow better. Nevertheless, these are placeholders only, helping to articulate the rhythm as you listen to the vowels: the sequence is still a vowel contour, with "helper" consonants.

You can also work the other way, from a consonant contour to consonant buds. Syllables can have consonants at both start and end, but it's helpful to think of your consonant contour as uniformly *leading* consonants, vocalized again with a single helper or placeholder vowel like "ah" following each consonant. Again, let the energy contour of the rhythm suggest differences in the consonants. In the example in figure 4.11, I let plosive sounds match higher points of energy (ta, da) and choose contrasting sounds at match points (ta, la; ga, da).

FIG. 4.11. Consonant "Bud" Contour. Consonants with "helper" vowel.

Syllable Buds to Words to Lyrics

By generating vowel and consonant contours, then buds, independently, we're again applying the strategy of *triangulation* (first introduced in chapter 2, "The Songwriter's Compass"). We can now coalesce or synthesize separate vowel and consonant contours and buds toward more complete *syllable buds*. These are still nonsense sounds rather than sensible words, much less phrases. You can work from one contour or the other, or mix and match. You can refine sounds directly repeated in a contour (perhaps in analogous rather than adjacent spots) with subtly contrasting sounds (dih – dih -> dih – dee). You can alternate helper sounds in the vowel contour (doo dow doo dah dih -> doo bow doo bah dih …) or consonant contour (ba da ga – bah dee gah). As this experimenting proceeds, you start clustering the flow of vowels and consonants into full syllables—syllable buds.

Good songwriters, like detectives, *think backwards*, surprising themselves into drawing from an infinite pool of possibilities. You're *still* not trying for meaningful words, but sounds that *sound like words*. We're heading *towards lyrics*. The words are already there; we just don't know what they are yet! One advantage of all "by sound" techniques—dummy lyrics, placeholders, vowel and consonant contours, syllable buds, nonsense words—is that you get less attached to sonic experiments than to hastily extemporized lyrics.

Coming down the homestretch.... It's time to replace our studiously built nonsense sounds with real words:

Goo dow doo mah bit	Duh suh kee sit
Go now to mud pit!	Dumbstruck he spit

At each stage, listen for how well the line sits rhythmically, and beware of preemptive intrusions from "by-sense" lyrical instincts. In the line above, "mud…" sounds unnaturally crowded on a weak stress, especially with the juncture "d / p" that follows. Where did I get "mud pit"? Likely, from free association by *sense* instead of sound. Fix it: *Go now to the pit!*

Checking for rhythmic and sonic fit at each point, you can progress in incremental stages or faster, intuitive leaps: from syllable buds, to syllables, to word buds, to words, to nonsense lines, to lyric lines that reveal an unexpected kind of sense or story:

- *Nonsense words:* slow down choodaw glit; some sub fah git

- *Nonsense phrases* (real rather than made-up words, but not in grammatical sentences): slow down chew law fit; some shrug to set

- *Ambiguous lines:* Grammatically correct phrases that still don't necessarily make sense: slow down to forget; some hover yet

Throughout this process, you may desperately want the comfort of a content frame, to know "what the song is about." But if you are willing to go out of your comfort zone and stay with the "by sound" process, you may wind up with sonically compelling, rhythmically well set, singable and surprising *meaningful* lines you'd never find via a "by sense" strategy. For example, the following line was quite unexpected to me until I wrote it:

Slow   down   to   for - get,   Thoughts __ hov - er   yet

FIG. 4.12. Lyric Line "By Sound." Discovered from a rhythmic phrase.

A Few Small Repairs

Once you've worked to a complete real lyric line, there will always be adjusting to do. You may need to adjust the lyric to make better sense: in the last transformation above I changed "some" to "thoughts." As I reach for words I need to change to make the line make a new kind of sense, I change the sounds; that may in turn change the line's fit to the source beats. The new line might ask me to change the original rhythm, e.g., to shift a beat forward or backward. The rhythmic shift we need to better express the meaning and emotion of this line (especially to set the word "hover") is indicated with the bracketed passage in figure 4.13.

Slow   down   to   for - get,   Thoughts __ hov - er   yet

FIG. 4.13. Lyric Line Reshaping the Rhythmic Phrase

By shifting the rhythm after all, haven't we just broken the rules of the rhythm-to-lyric "game" we set out to play? In the world of songwriting strategies, breaking rules is always an option—at the right point in the process, and for the right reasons. This is an example of a *pivoting* strategy: i.e., we work from a rhythm to a lyric, then work our way back to an altered rhythm. Paradoxically, for this transformation to be effective, we need to maintain focus by holding the rhythm firm in our minds in the first part of the work. Once we have a result we like, we can let that result reshape our starting material in turn.

Such back-and-forth adjustments are part of the natural ebb and flow of real songwriting or other creative work. Especially in solo writing—where "you alone control the rhythmical, you control the lyrical..."—you're free to adjust material on either side as you go. By practicing "massaging" rhythmic patterns on their own, and exactly matching lyrics to a given rhythm, you'll develop the skills to make these adjustments more confidently, rapidly, and to better expressive effect. This greater control of rhythmic and lyric interactions will also stand you in good stead in co-writing or project writing, where you will *not* necessarily control all aspects of the creative work. In the words of my editor (which I immediately grabbed as a song seed), sometimes we're called to do our best work when "we're not in charge." Trust the sounds of the lyrics, and meaning will come. Slow down to forget—the thoughts will hover yet.

CHAPTER 5

Melody

Finding a great melody is like Harry Potter catching the Golden Snitch—the big win, enticing yet elusive. It's easy to throw together an off-the-cuff "filler" melody for a lyric, but surprisingly hard to find a melody that's memorable yet novel, fresh yet accessible, satisfying to sing and to hear. Music theorists have confidently systematized many aspects of harmony. Yet melody has often been treated with superstitious reverence, as somehow the province of divine inspiration. There is a rich tradition of pedagogy for melodic writing in the discipline of counterpoint, as well as in newer fields such as jazz improvisation. We're concerned here with melody from the songwriter's perspective, a context that offers particular challenges.

Since songwriters are writing vocal, not instrumental melodies, interactions with lyrics in the musical texture and qualities of the human vocal range shape the melodies we write. In this chapter, we'll focus first on techniques for working with melodic material in isolation, with some degree of *independence* from harmonic, rhythmic, and lyric aspects. This includes working with melody as shape and contour; and exercises in melodic memory and transformation. Then, we'll explore strategies for melody writing in relation to the facets we've already examined: rhythm and lyric. After the chapter on chords, we'll look more deeply at melody–harmony connections.

EXERCISE 5.1: A CAPPELLA, RUBATO MELODY (A SLOW AIR)

Working *away from* an instrument, write a *vocal* melody for a single song section (lyrics to come later). Beyond the initial absence of lyrics, don't worry about what the song will be "about"—theme or content, or even emotional quality. To minimize sectional structure concerns, think of the melody as destined for a verse/refrain song with no chorus—that is, a single repeating musical section to be set to successive through-written lyric sections. Write the melody *without using* notation or recording as an aid to memory.

The melody should have a tonal center (you can write over a tonic drone as a reference point). But do your best not to think of (or hear in your mind's ear) specific chords, or to build the melody around expected chord movement. Similarly, you can strive to make the melody arhythmic: not locked to a defined metric pulse, or even, necessarily, a definite time signature. It will help to make the melody fairly slow (so you can think carefully and distinctly about each note), and rubato or rhythmically free in feel. As much as possible, let the melody do all the work.

CHALLENGES IN MELODY WRITING

As you work on this a cappella melody exercise, you may discover that it's hard to hold a melody distinctly in mind, absent lyrics, chords, or rhythmic accompaniment. In fact, when we write songs we're usually blending these elements.

Most of us can easily sing a melody without lyrics—that's why we have "la la la." You can put "dry lyrics" on the page before committing to a melody. Still, songwriters usually try to develop lyrics and melody together. Similarly, even when we claim a song begins as a "melodic" idea, the genesis is often a riff or chord progression, over which we improvise melodic phrases until a few stick. For many writers, melodies also need the support of embedded rhythmic effects to generate sufficient interest.

Curiously, in writing strong melodies, vocal or instrumental chops can work both for you and against you—helping but also possibly hindering your melodic skills. Vocalists can often readily invent and sing a cappella melodies, yet their melodies often also depend on melodic idioms characteristic of their genre, or on vocal performance effects. They may be great vocal improvisers and yet struggle to zero in on a stable, memorable core melody. Strong instrumentalists have other advantages in hearing and composing melodies. You get a very specific sense of a melody by playing it on your instrument. Even writing away from your instrument, in your mind's ear, you can imagine playing the melody in a tactile, embodied way. You *feel* the melody move. But an instrumental orientation can also limit your melody writing. Songwriters aim to create great *vocal* melodies; vocal melodies move differently from instrumental melodies. Your melodies may have detailed angles and curlicues that vocalists would be hard-pressed to invent. Vocalists may also find them hard or unintuitive to sing. You'll encounter these differences if you try to set words to a previously written instrumental melody.

Thinking Melody

Even if you're *not* a diva vocalist or a blazing melodic soloist, you can learn to write great song melodies, by developing a *compositional* sense of melody. This means focusing on the *essential melody* of the song—separate from improvisatory flourishes, or even from too close a bond to your own voice, with its characteristic range, tone, strengths, and limitations (which can hold back both weak and strong vocalists). We can learn to "think melody."

Once you can hold a melody distinctly in your mind's ear, and transform it in flexible ways, it's easier to not settle for the first melody that pops into mind, but sketch, refine, and polish until the melody matches the song's desired meaning and emotion, and interweaves in compelling ways with lyric, rhythm, and chords.

Your goal need not be the ability to write every conceivable kind of melody. By spending time on melodic seed catching—both original melodic seeds, and magic melodic moments you catch in other peoples' songs—you'll begin to develop a distinctive melodic vocabulary: a sense for the kinds of melodic shapes and movements that delight your unique listener's and songwriter's ear, and the emotions, imagery, and stories they evoke. Over time, you'll expand this melodic "signature style," cultivating skills to move melodies in more mobile ways. But the goal is always to find your melodic "voice" (not just your singing voice!). Along the shores of melody's infinite ocean of possibilities, we all have our own harbors to fish.

Melodic Memory

As you get more attuned to the nature of melodic ideas, you can begin to work explicitly on *melodic memory:* your ability to recreate and retain a melody in your mind without changing it inadvertently. In addition, you want to be able to conceive or catch a melody away from an instrument, without words or chords to reinforce memory of the melody.

Practice conceiving of melodies as shapes or gestures—any visual imagery or metaphor that helps you retain and not inadvertently change the melody. As you sing the melody, move your hand in the air in front of you, letting height from the ground indicate shifts of pitch, with greater or smaller melodic intervals reflected or exaggerated by your movements.

Our song seed catching was preparation for this work, where I encouraged you to practice grabbing/isolating pure melodic seeds. Seeds are "discovered" material pulled out of context. The next step is to work with that seed material in active ways, and to be able to create new melodic material at will. Practice making up little melodies without words. Find ways to jot these down or record them to cross-check yourself. Gradually train your ability to hang on to those melodies.

EXERCISE 5.2. STRENGTHENING MELODIC MEMORY

Here are two simple ways to strengthen melodic memory: one a daily practice, and one more of a "game" you can play solo, with a partner, or in a group.

- *Morning Tune.* Start with a melodic idea at the start of your day, and try to remember it at the end of the day. Upon awakening, create a small melodic seed: your "tunelet" for the day. It can be a melodic seed you wake up with (perhaps remembered out of a dream?), an already-captured seed, a fragment drawn from someone else's music, or a melodic idea you invent for the exercise. Run over the melody in your mind a few times to get it set, then make a reference recording or notation of the melody (so you can check your work later). Then go about your day, making no particular effort to keep the seed idea in mind. At the end of the day, before going to sleep, try to recall your tunelet, as precisely as possible. Check your remembered version against the reference. Notice what you were able to retain and what you changed inadvertently.

As you devise your melodies for succeeding days, and as your melodic memory gets stronger, you can challenge yourself with longer, more intricate, or more stylistically unfamiliar types of material. Practiced over time, this exercise should improve both your melodic memory and the quality and coherence of your melodic ideas.

- *"Tunesmith Telephone."* This is a game I devised working with groups, modeled on the familiar game of "Telephone" (passing a whispered message around a circle to see how it changes), but using melodies instead of words, and with each "pass" audible to all participants. You can also play it in solo fashion—as a kind of "songwriter solitaire"—or passing melodies back and forth with a partner. In the first "calibration" pass, your aim is to pass the melody *unchanged* (harder than you'd think!). In the second pass, with each iteration, you change the melody by *just one note—* easiest at the end, then the beginning, hardest in the middle.

  The game is simple in principle, but can be made as arbitrarily and fiendishly challenging as you like by working with progressively longer and more complex melodic material. At "melodic grandmaster" level, see if you can remember the entire chain of one-note transformations from the original! You can also adapt the game to working with rhythms, lyric lines, and even chord progressions.

MELODIC DESIGN

To write strong melodies, you need a sense for *melodic design:* an intuitive grasp, almost visual or gestural in quality, of how melody moves as shape, form, and contour. We'll work first with a relatively loose notion of melodic contour, containing vestiges of rhythmic and lyrical elements. Then, we'll articulate a more precise notion of melodic contour, which facilitates working more independently with melodic material in relation to rhythm, lyric, and harmony.

Melodic Contour

Melodic design involves an interplay between two complementary kinds of melodic sense, each of which can take on metaphorical qualities important for melody's role in songwriting. At its most essential, a melody is a *contour*—a figure or shape—heard in the context of a *pitch space:* a set of distinct pitches arranged in characteristic patterns of varying interval sizes, establishing a tonal center and quality for a scale or mode.

As listeners, we might experience melodic contour temporally or dynamically, evoking gestures of human movement—an arm reaching out, a step or a leap in air. Or we might form more spatial associations and imagery: visualizing the contour as an ascending or descending arc, a stair step or zigzag, like a curving shoreline or a distant undulating ridge (see exercise 5.3).

We hear the curves of melodic shapes moving within a pitch space "curved" or featured in its own right—by typically irregular intervals of the underlying scale or mode. But we experience this curve more as a "landscape" over which notes of melodic shapes pass—as shadowed outlines of clouds might move across hills and valleys. Melodic design requires an ability to retain these different impressions, both separately and together—to hold them constant, and to transform them at will. We want to be able to change a melodic figure at its given spot in the landscape, move it within that landscape—or recolor the figure by changing the landscape itself, for example, by shifting the scale or mode.

Melodic Shape: Scales, Arpeggios, and Figures

Let's dive more deeply into the specific shapes that make up melodic contour. A melody moves by *intervals* (pitch changes from note to note), characterized in terms of *direction* (up or down, higher or lower in pitch) and *size* (movement by a second, a third, etc.). In general, it's *easier* to sing melodies with smaller intervals, but can be more *dramatic* and *expressive* to sing larger skips and leaps. But the shape of the melodic curve—the *sequence* of intervals—also influences the quality, vocal ease, and effect of the melody, especially in harmonic implications. The following example shows four canonic contour types arising from varying combinations of interval *direction* and *size*. These features of melodic contour "in the small" strongly affect our experience of melody:

Line or Slope   Sawtooth   Bend   Hook

FIG. 5.1. Melodic Contour Types. Labeled in terms of direction and size of successive intervallic motion.

- *Measure 1: Line or Slope.* Moving the *same interval* (size) successively in the *same direction* produces *scalar* (by seconds) or *arpeggiated* triads (by thirds) motion. Scalar motion mirrors the underlying scale or mode: figure recedes to landscape. Movement by thirds tends to link more strongly to a harmonic region. (In 4/4 time, scalar motion also tends to outline harmonic regions, with alternating chord tones and passing non-chord tones.) Wider, less vocal-friendly patterns (e.g., 1, 4, ♭7, as shown, evocative of the original *Star Trek* theme) may avoid these obvious scalar or chordal effects, but also tend to weaken the sense of tonal center. Thus, the more we move in the same direction in uniform intervals, the less detailed the melodic *shape* we hear.

- *Measure 2: Sawtooth.* Moving the *same interval* successively in *different directions* creates a sawtooth move: a dip down or bump up. The move can be to an adjacent (neighbor) tone or by a wider interval. If continued, this sawtooth pattern of melodic motion pulls toward *rhythmic melody*, where a few tones function as high and low drumbeat tones, or pitch contrasts in stressed vs. unstressed syllables of intensified, forceful speech. These rhythmic effects can be effective, as in the Motown classic "I Heard It through the Grapevine." But often this contour is not strongly conceived melodic movement: the alternating notes are used to create surface activity in an otherwise slow-moving and static melodic contour.

- *Measure 3: Bend.* Moving *different intervals* in the *same direction*, such as a step of a second followed by a skip of a third, creates more intrinsic shape and variety in the contour. It can also (though need not) avoid strong harmonic implications, with a degree of harmonic independence, implying a chord shift, a melodic tension, or chordal ambiguity.

- *Measure 4: Hook.* Moving consecutively by *different intervals* in *different directions* form quintessential cells of melodic shape: little melodic elbows and turns that satisfy the ear through variety in both intervallic direction and size. In small steps and skips, such figures tend to shift out of a single chordal area. They can lock into such areas, though, executed in larger skips. Many ostinato patterns are based on these types of movements, as the last arpeggiated figure shown in the example.

As you review various melodies that attract your ear, begin to notice regions that fall back on scalar, arpeggiated, or patterned effects, and more *figural* regions with potent melodic shapes. The key is to balance a pleasing variety in both direction and intervals of movement, to create distinct melodic figures and "imagery." As we'll see later in our exploration of melodic/harmonic connections, melodic figures with irregular contour tend toward more independence of harmonic and rhythmic interpretations.

EXERCISE 5.3. WRITE A MELODIC "RIDGELINE"

Write a four-bar vocal melodic phrase that uses a variety of the types of intervallic motion described on page 100; in particular, avoid extended passages of only scalar or arpeggiated motion (lines and slopes). Analyze your melody in terms of direction and size of motion, and annotate occurrences of the contour types discussed above. Strive for a variety of specific interval sizes and directions used, and to use most of the tones in the diatonic scale or mode of choice. The melody can be in an authentic or plagal range (i.e., with the tonal center toward the bottom or toward the middle of the range). Where scalar, arpeggiated, or sawtooth figures do occur, try disguising them with rhythmic effects, or by staggering or displacing them across metric boundaries such as bar lines. As you work with these melodic design principles, you should feel as if your melody takes on a distinctive shape, like the ridgeline of a hill seen from a distance.

Not every melody satisfying these contour principles needs to sound like a pentatonic bagpipe tune or a Hindemith exercise! You can try sticking to a strict pentatonic scale, but it's more instructive to integrate a gapped semi-pentatonic feel with other kinds of melodic motion.

FIG. 5.2. "Ridgeline" Melody. This avoids extended scalar or arpeggiated passages.

The range is a plagal octave (D to D, with tonal center G). It's a hexatonic rather than strictly pentatonic pitch set; all diatonic notes in the range are used except E (or E-flat, making the melody ambiguously Dorian or Aeolian in mode). Intervals used (in order of occurrence) include ascending fifth, second, third, and fourth (with a strongly suggested minor sixth in outline as well), and descending second and third. There are some implied or outlined chords (e.g., measure 3, an arpeggiated B♭ major and a descending D minor with a passing tone), yet the tune is far from chord-driven. There's also some rhythmic interest in the phrase. Durations include eighths (15 occurrences), quarters (3), dotted quarters (2), and half + eighth (1). This establishes an eighth-note melodic pace, likely to align with the eventual lyric's syllabic pace. But no rhythmic pattern is repeated throughout. Rather, rhythmic variation is used to break up passages of otherwise uninterrupted scalar motion (e.g., the descending D, C, B♭, A and B♭, A, G, F figures), as well as some of the sawtooth figures.

The brackets indicate where different types of melodic contour appear: slopes (in this case, almost all descending lines of a second), sawtooth figures (again, all downward dips of a second or third), bends, and hooks. The more "pattern-y" figures are broken up with rhythmic effects or metric displacement. The hooks occur at the start of the phrase and the second measure, acting as an initial landmark or anchor for the tune. The bends vary in intervallic size and direction, echoing each other with devices such as sequence and intervallic augmentation.

The Power of Pentatonics

Not coincidentally, *pentatonic* modes have intervallic variety built in. These modes are found in vocal melody in genres and styles around the planet, from Celtic to Motown to country to blues to African music. Even regular movement in a strict pentatonic scale still varies intervallic size after more than two steps from any tone in any direction, breaking up scalar or arpeggio patterns. The human voice seems to naturally fit around pentatonic tones and melodic sequences. We might speculate that intonation patterns of natural spoken language lend themselves to pentatonic realizations. For example, while the interval of a fifth reinforces the lower tone in terms of the overtone series, the interval of a fourth seems to lend itself to vocalization. (It may not be coincidental that many cultures with tonal languages, such as some Asiatic languages, also have strongly pentatonic musical traditions.)[10]

Melodic Transformations

As you listen and pay new attention to the shapes of melodies, and get better at accurately remembering melodies, you can begin to experiment with *changing melodies at will*, transforming melodic shapes in various ways. Practice making *small*, *discrete* changes, leaving the rest of the melodic idea undisturbed, aspiring to an *object permanence* of the melodic idea in your mind. This is hard work. You'll try to change just one note, and the melody notes around the changed note will dissolve into a vague cloud—the melodic equivalent of trying to lift just your ring finger.

Working with melodic contours as shape and gesture opens up a rich repertoire of melodic operations and transformations: sequence, inversion, retrograde, truncation and extension, etc. Many of these devices have been discussed extensively in the context of ear training, composition, counterpoint, and melodic improvisation. These melodic devices have distinctive value to songwriters, though. This reflects characteristics of *vocal* as distinct from instrumental melody. Many attributes of melodic figures and shapes that make them work well as vocal melodies are *preserved* across transformations such as inversion, retrograde, sequence, etc. These devices can thus take us from familiar vocal lines to fresh, interesting melodic figures—perhaps not the first we'd instinctively sing, but eminently *singable* once discovered.

For most operations, the listener's ear hears similarity in the derived shapes, and thus gets a sense of repeated melodic information. Transforming melodic motives, and then using both the original and transformed versions in a song

---

10. Of course, continued too long, even pentatonic motion can become pattern-y as the pentatonic spine becomes too audible. For example, the memorable riff from Stevie Wonder's "Sir Duke" uses a modified version of such extended linear pentatonic motion as a special effect (though this example goes beyond vocal melody in the strict sense referenced here).

section, is thus a primary means for creating melodic structure and phrasing. The technique yields melodies that combine the variety of transformations with the unity of their audible derivation from common material ("shared nativity" as opposed to common fate?).

FIG. 5.3. Melody reflecting motivic transformations

Sounding as if created by transforming just a few shapes or gestures, such melodies are *memorable* as well. Patterns and transformations can also overlap. The same melodic material can participate in multiple perceived shape relationships or transformations. Melodies that appear deceptively simple on the surface may conceal layers of such echoes and resonances, so that the listener hears them differently each time.

Even when they don't wind up in the final melody, these gestures and transformations are tools for developing, refining, and revising songs. The richer your toolset, the better chance you have of tinkering with that starting idea until a pretty good melodic setting suddenly turns to a magical one.

Shifting Figure and Field

We've discussed how a melodic contour is created by a succession of specific pitches in the context of a key or tonal center and a scale or mode. We can picture a contour statically or dynamically—as shape, vs. as movement or gesture—against the backdrop of a pitch space: figure and field. Viewed this way, we can identify two complementary transformations of contour in relation to pitch space, of particular importance in songwriting:

- Melodic *sequence.* Shift the contour as a whole to a different spot in the space—that is, starting at different scale-degree positions within a key. This is a distinct operation from *transposing* or modulating to a new key. In a sequence, each note shifts, along with its relation to the tonal center and, in a harmonic context, to the chord of the moment. But intervallic or *contour* relationships between notes are preserved, to varying degrees. Since sequence shifts the shape within a diatonic scale, sizes of intervals shift in accord with the particular scale's structure: e.g., minor seconds become major seconds, and vice versa. Sequence operations do particularly cool things in modal scales—even more so when applied to *pentatonic* scales, where major seconds can shift to minor thirds, and vice versa.

- *Modal interchange.* You can also transform a melodic contour, keeping it at the same scale degree (relative to tonal center) but shifting *the space itself,* changing the scale or mode—the landscape over which the contour is overlaid or articulated.

Both types of transformation change the contour's shape, and thus, its emotional and narrative resonances: sensory and image associations, lyric associations, etc. Specific intervals can shift through intervallic augmentation (increased size) or diminution. What's preserved in each case is the pattern of *directional moves* in the contour. You need the skills to hear melodic contour preserved through these transformations, as well as an ability to respond to the changes and their associative qualities. It's like looking at your hand in the water, refracted through the ripples. It's still a hand—just a wet one!

Melodic Range

Sequence is a particularly important tool for the songwriter due to the aspect of vocal range. For *popular* songs, we want melodies that listeners can identify with and maybe even sing along with, not just admire from afar as pyrotechnic feats. We want compelling melodies that move in interesting ways within reasonable vocal limits. Even holding to about an octave plus a fifth in range, we can shift range in relation to the *tonal center* in different ways: with the tonal center at or near the *bottom* of the register, or nearer the mid-point of the range (i.e., the primary octave of the range stretching from the fifth *below* to the fifth *above* the tonic).[11]

You can use this technique as a process tool, for exploring different range possibilities for a given section. A powerful exploration technique is simply to take a first version of a melody for a given song section and shift it—via sequence—a full fourth or fifth from its starting point—that is, from authentic to plagal range or vice versa. You'll feel as if you're replacing the initial melody with a harmony line, but since the interval of sequence is a fourth (or fifth), this will not be an obvious close harmony (i.e., tracking in thirds). Though you should try to preserve main outlines of the contour, adjustments will need to be made; even where the contour is preserved, the harmonic and therefore emotional and narrative implications will be quite different.[12]

Range is also essential in creating sectional contrast. For example, you might write the lower verse section in a plagal range (to the fifth below the tonic), saving the upper part of the authentic range for the chorus and/or bridge. Reversing this, you could let the chorus ascend to an octave and fifth above the low point of the range.

---

11. These range types are suggestive of *authentic vs. plagal* ranges in traditional vocal and part writing. The usage here is not completely consistent with these formal definitions.

12. This technique is different from a melodic formula prevalent in current pop writing, where a first verse is sung softly in a lower octave, and then later verses "power" the melody up a full octave. This is more a registral and arrangement-level effect than a compositional melodic change.

MELODY/RHYTHM CONNECTIONS

We've looked at several aspects of melodic design in isolation. Let's turn now to various connections between melody and the other facets examined so far: rhythm and lyric. We'll look first at melody/rhythm connections, then at connections of melody to lyrics, in terms of both sound and sense aspects. In the final section we'll tackle the more complex interactions between melodic contour and lyric rhythm (a lyric set to a rhythmic phrase). (We'll discuss connections between melody and chordal harmony in a separate chapter following the "Harmony" chapter.)

The Melody/Rhythm Continuum

We can conceive the melody/rhythm connection as a kind of continuum or spectrum. We can gradually transform given melodic or rhythmic material along this continuum, bending and shaping it at will. Here, *transformation* refers not to the types of motivic operations on melody discussed earlier, but an incremental shape-shifting or "morphing" of material. We can gradually transform a rhythmic phrase *in the direction of* melody, or go the other way, gradually increasing the *rhythmic* emphasis of a melodic contour.

Rhythm to Melody

We've defined an idealized concept of a rhythmic phrase as a succession of "pitchless" rhythmic events—hits, beats, strikes of varying durations. As soon as we articulate such a rhythm within a metric framework, we promote certain hits to more prominence. These differentials might follow expected metric weights set by time signature and groove, or syncopate against these, intensifying certain hits on metrically weak beats. In principle, listeners' anticipations are enough for them to experience this hierarchy of different weights, different levels of intensity. But we also employ dynamics, timbre, articulation, or percussive effect. For example, we can contrast short hits of quick duration and quick decay, followed by silence, with sustained tones that fill their allotted duration.

Quickly, we can turn also to *pitch* to signal these varying emphases. We might turn a rhythmic phrase, by degrees, into a melodically articulated phrase, first with a two-pitch rhythmic pattern, as used in many drum patterns, gradually extending to three or more pitches. This process is similar to the technique, described in the "Lyrics" chapter, of finding the energetic contour of a rhythmic phrase. In setting from rhythm to lyric, this contour was used as a basis for mapping from rhythm to *lyric sounds*. Alternatively, one can use this same intuitive "weighting" to set from a rhythmic phrase to a *melodic* contour.

Figure 5.4 shows an example of a rhythmically driven melody,

FIG. 5.4. A Rhythmically Driven Melody

This melody has an intrinsic rhythmic quality, exclusive of any rhythmic emphasis in performance, due to characteristic features of the rhythmic patterns and melodic contours.

Rhythmic aspects:

- Shorter rhythmic values (a predominant eighth-note pace in the example), with longer durations occurring mostly at initial or cadential spots in phrases.

- Regular successions of repeated rhythmic values (e.g., the six successive eighth notes in measure 3).

- Repeated rhythmic figures (e.g., the B♭ G B♭ figures repeated in measures 1 and 2). Such figures often attract sonic connections in lyric syllables such as assonance, consonance, or internal rhyme.

- Syncopations and anticipations (e.g., the anticipated downbeats of measures 2, 3, and 4). Delayed attacks can also add rhythmic emphasis, though with a differing energetic quality.

Melodic contour aspects:

- Smaller melodic *range* (example range is just a fourth).

- Smaller *pitch set*, the number of distinct pitches employed (the example has just three).

- Gapped-scale or pentatonic-derived as opposed to scalar or arpeggiated chordal movement. (The example is built around a *filled tetrachord:* G B♭ C.)

Following these principles, we could begin to "melodize" a given rhythmic phrase in a straightforward, if perhaps mechanistic way: assigning higher pitches to beats of greater metric weight. We could gradually extend this to simple two-note contours or a three-note "filled tetrachord" (as in the example), or extend the range further. This is not the only way to transform a rhythmic phrase to a melody, but it provides a starting "prototype" melodic version you can then play with further.

Melody to Rhythm

We can also go the other way, "rhythmicizing" a given melody. This could involve incrementally restricting melodic range, shifting from a full diatonic to a more angular (e.g., pentatonic) version, or introducing rhythmic effects such as anticipations and delays, consecutive notes of the same duration, or repeating rhythmic patterns.

We can also reverse each of these transformations, for example, revising a *too* rhythmic melody in the direction of more flowing "lyrical" melodic form. In the right stylistic setting and for the right kind of song, rhythmic melodies can be highly effective and infectious. But often, such rhythmic effects are artifacts of a first-version "filler" melody, and don't necessarily serve prosodic needs of the song. Working melody first, a heavily rhythmic setting might also overly constrain lyric choices later in the writing process. Figure 5.5 shows an example lyric we might write to the rhythmic melody of figure 5.4:

FIG. 5.5. Lyric Line Set to Rhythmically Driven Melody

As the example in figure 5.5 suggests, associated lyrics for rhythmically driven melodies tend to have these attributes:

- shorter vs. longer, closed vs. open vowel sounds
- use of plosive (rather than fricative or sibilant) consonants at the start of syllables, for percussive effect
- more staccato attacks than sustained durations of notes
- syncopations (anticipations, delays, off-beats) and wrenched-stress syllables
- a tendency for matched rhythmic figures to attract sonic effects like rhyme (baby/maybe)

Figure 5.6 shows a possible revision of figure 5.5's rhythmic melody. This more flowing melody contour would be a better response to, or alternately a prompt for, the accompanying more "lyrical" lyric:

FIG. 5.6. Revised Melody. A more lyrical direction, with altered lyric.

We've expanded range both below and above the original fourth, added "softening" diatonic notes, and muted some repetitions of rhythmic figures. We've added a peak in melodic contour, on a weak metric beat (the high F in bar 3). This emphasizes not just the peak note itself (and associated lyric) but also *succeeding* notes; the C B♭ figure, a repetition of a figure heard several times preceding, now sounds fresh approached via the descending fourth. We've also retained just one anticipation ("love" at the start of bar 2), while introducing a balancing delay (on "heart" in bar 4).

Principle: *Anticipations "push" rhythmic pace; delayed notes "pull" it.* Balance the factors of push and pull in a melody to make it feel less *driven* by and more responsive to the melody's rhythmic aspects.

MELODY/LYRIC CONNECTIONS

As with melody and rhythm, we can define an axis or continuum between melody and lyric. Sometimes, we want the melody to do little more than carry the lyric and leave it in the foreground. Other times, lyrics effectively accompany the melody. Each texture can be used artfully and effectively, or to poor effect.

At a broad level, lyric *content* can influence the types of melodies we set to lyrics, while conversely, certain types of melodies seem to invite different types of lyric content and tone. The texture of lyric language can be viewed as a polarity, ranging from direct sensory description to more abstract "thought and feeling" language. Metaphor creates an intermediate texture, often linking sensory images with an associated emotion or abstract quality. Certain melodic/lyric textures bring melody to the foreground; other textures set lyrics (with their content or referential connotations) into more prominence. Some songwriters have speculated that lyrics conveying will and energy "ask for" more rhythmic melodies, while lyrics full of imagery and metaphor are complemented by flowing melodic lines.

Lyric Sounds and Melody

The sounds of lyrics are intimately connected to melody. Interactions of lyric and melody include shaping vowels and consonants to melodic range and contour, and matching melodic contour to intonation patterns in spoken and sung speech. These factors play into the more detailed rhythmic interactions of melody and lyric we'll examine next.

One set of concerns is fairly pragmatic, from a vocalist's perspective, involving placement of vowel and consonant combinations relatively high or low in the vocal register. Vowels are a main focus in these interactions. In broad terms, notes at extremes of the vocal range, or held for longer durations, take open and long vowels in preference to closed and short vowels.

Often these concerns arise because of trouble spots and the fixes and revisions they require. The more demanding the vocal melody in range or speed of delivery, the more critical these considerations become. An anecdote reflecting these concerns involves lyricist Yip Harburg and composer Harold Arlen's timeless classic, "Over the Rainbow." Yip's original "song seed" or thematic prompt to Arlen for the song was the title phrase: "I Want to Get on the Other Side of the Rainbow." After Arlen wrote the soaring melody, with its signature upward octave leap at the start of the verse, Harburg (after some resistance) agreed to rewrite the lyric. He decided he needed a long "O" vowel sound at the top of the melodic curve, came up with "over," then worked backward to "somewhere," which suited the octave leap perfectly. In this case, theme and imagery shaped melody, which in turn shaped specific word choices in the lyric. If Arlen and Harburg could do it—why oh why can't we?[13]

Natural Intonation and Speech Melody

There are also implied melodic aspects of natural intonation patterns in speech. We've seen that lyricists heighten and regularize natural rhythms in speech into formal stress levels and syllabic rhythm patterns, and then further refine these into the musical framework of the song's lyric rhythm. We can also use the natural rise and fall of vocal intonation in speech as a basis for melodic ideas. In fact, there's a close connection between lyric rhythm and melodic contour. Pitch is one way to indicate stress emphasis, along with dynamics, duration, and other aspects of intonation. Pitch contours implied in speech intonation also communicate emotional cues. Casual, conversational speech tends to use smaller pitch contours; more animated, impassioned speech involves higher placement of tones in the range and wider overall range.

EXERCISE 5.4. "THE WELL." TRANSFORM A SPOKEN LINE TO VOCAL MELODY

This exercise demonstrates in a dramatic way the mapping from conversational speech to melodic contour. The goal is to discover a melodic setting that closely matches a natural intonation pattern and cadence for a given lyric line. I've facilitated this many times as a live group exercise, employing the playful metaphor of "The Well." Here, I present a modified version you can try in solo writing, or adapt for work with a partner.

To find a melody for our lyric, we must inquire of the Tune Genie who lives at the bottom of a well. When we throw a spoken lyric line down the well, the echo that comes back will have been turned into pitches!

1. Begin with a spoken lyric line, with a distinct syllabic rhythm. It should be long enough to feel like a complete phrase, but short enough to remember without too much effort. Here's an apropos example line: *"I'm calling to the genie at the bottom of the Well."*

   Repeat the line multiple times, settling into a consistent way of speaking it. Speak a bit like a radio announcer, with enough animation to create a good range of speech tones.

---

13. Meyerson, Harold and Ernie Harburg. *Who Put the Rainbow in* The Wizard of Oz? *Yip Harburg, Lyricist.* Ann Arbor, MI: University of Michigan Press, 1995.

2. Continue to repeat the line, but gradually *take away the consonants*. In technical terms, this step transforms the lyric into a *vowel contour* with intonation. In practice? Pretend you're drunk and slurring your words. Or imagine you're a dog at a dinner party, listening to the humans chatter, waiting to hear your name:

> *I'm calling to the genie at the bottom of the Well*
> *EYE AH-EE OO UH EE-NIE A UH AH-UH UH UH EH*

3. With succeeding repetitions, let even the vowel differentiation melt away, until all that remains are implied pitches of the vocal *inflection*. As you let the articulation go, you may start to sound like a patient in the dentist's chair. (Hopefully at this point you're having more fun with this particular "drill.")

   A pivotal "crossover point" is reached when the spoken, inflected tones audibly transform into steady-pitch musical tones. Slow the tempo slightly, and hear the speech tones, with their wavering rise and fall of pitch, turn into held tones at a constant pitch. (In a group setting, this is truly a magical moment—when it works right!)

4. Once you've locked in on a stable melody, sung with vowels only, sing the original lyric to your newfound melody. Your first version of the melody is likely to be an approximation you will want to refine a bit with repetition. Watch for repeated pitches at peaks or valleys in the melodic contour that could be differentiated in pitch, or simple scalar patterns or repeating figures that could be varied to better set the line. Figure 5.7 shows a possible melody derived from the example line using the technique, along with a slight adjustment of the contour with repeated notes (Gen-*ie at* the).

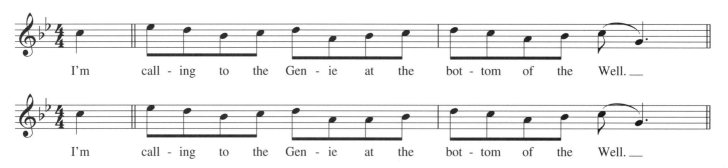

FIG. 5.7. Melody Derived from the "Well" Example

Melodies arrived at with this technique tend to be quite singable, often with a modal or pentatonic flavor. They follow natural speaking cadences, but are less likely to be innovative or attention-grabbing. This naturalness is useful when melody must support comprehension and absorption of a dense or complex lyric. Musical theater writers and opera composers working on *recitative* (as opposed to arias) may intuitively use variants of this technique when coming up with the effortless, translucent melodic settings needed for complex, nuanced lyrics.

LYRIC RHYTHM AND MELODIC CONTOUR

We've seen that melodies can move in more rhythmic or more flowing "lyrical" ways (the latter referencing conventional, informal connotations of "lyrical" as a descriptive term). We've seen also that in melody/lyric relationships, at times, we'd like the melodic line in the foreground of attention; at other times, we want the melody to recede, bringing the lyric to the forefront.

Here, we'll build on the description of setting between lyric and rhythm given at the end of the "Lyrics" chapter. The result of this setting work is a lyric set to a specific rhythmic phrase—what I'll call here, for convenience, a *rhythmic lyric*. To work with melody and lyric in a full 360° songwriting sense, we also want to be able to set between this rhythmic lyric and a melodic contour with its inherent rhythm—again, in either direction.

Control of these elements and effects depends on interactions between *lyric rhythm* and rhythms embedded in the *melodic contour*—and specifically in possibilities of moving these at different paces, to create different lyric/ melodic textures. We need this control to experiment with varied lyric/melodic textures in writing and revision. In particular, we want to be able to vary lyric and melodic rhythm *independently*. This will be a *lot* easier to explain with a specific example to clarify the various steps involved.[14]

Review of Syllabic and Lyric Rhythm

Let's start with an example lyric line:

Talk to me gently, hold my aching head in your lap

As we've seen, we can explore multiple *syllabic rhythm* settings of the line, reflecting in-built linguistic stress patterns, stress by emphasis decisions, etc.

/	‿ ‿ / ‿ //	‿ / ‿ /	‿ ‿	/
/	‿ ‿ / ‿ /	‿ // ‿ /	‿ //	/
Talk	*to me gently, hold*	*my aching head*	*in your*	*lap*

FIG. 5.8. Alternate Syllabic Rhythm Settings for the Example Lyric

---

14. I say **lyric rhythm** because I'm describing these mappings in a *songwriting* context. For general composition, including instrumental writing, we'd need to consider mappings between melodic contour and any arbitrary rhythmic pattern. Here, though, we're specifically interested in rhythmic phrases that carry a lyric. These already represent a placement of a lyric line, a string of syllables, into rhythmic form. This narrows our scope, but also makes the definitions a bit more tricky!

The lyric with its preferred syllabic rhythm is then set to a *lyric rhythm*: each syllable set to a beat and duration within the song's metrical framework.

Talk to me gen - tly, Hold my ach - ing head _ in your lap.

FIG. 5.9. Lyric and Syllabic Rhythm to Lyric Rhythm

Given a lyric and syllabic rhythm, different lyric rhythms can be developed, still with no necessary reference yet to melody:

Talk _ to me gen - tly, hold my ach - ing head _ in your __ lap. __

FIG. 5.10. Alternate Lyric Rhythm Setting. Back-heavy phrasing, shifted emphasis.

Melismas and Chanting Tones

So far, so good. Now: how does melody enter into the picture? How do we set *from* this rhythmic lyric to a vocal melody? Each rhythmic placement of a syllable must be set to some melodic pitch. However, that pitch can be a new or changing pitch, or a pitch held over from the previous syllable. Conversely, each pitch is sung to a syllable. That can be a new syllable articulated on that pitch, or a syllable held over from a previous pitch. This independence of rhythm in syllabic placements and melodic contour respectively yields three distinct kinds of lyric/melodic texture.

1. In the simplest texture, each syllable is sung on one melodic pitch. You can write extended passages in this texture, where melodic pitches and syllables change in tandem.

2. We can also sing *one* syllable on a series of notes at successive *changing* pitches—*melisma*. Strictly, *melisma* means simply singing more than one note on a syllable. As an adjective, "melismatic" is also used to describe an overall highly ornamented singing style (i.e., one with lots of melismas). I'll refer to even short runs of notes as melismas, though the overall texture of the song or the passage may not be melismatic in style.

3. We can also sing successive syllables on notes at the same pitch. Melisma is "singing multiple notes (changing pitches) on a single syllable." This is the converse: "singing multiple syllables on a single note (pitch)."

In the case of this third texture, we confront a curious lacuna in music theory vocabulary. Melisma is a standard musical term; surprisingly, I've found no readily known term for this converse effect. Given this lack of a standard term, I'll call the effect *chanting tones:* a passage or portion of a melodic phrase where multiple successive syllables are sounded on one pitch. Despite the lack of a term for the texture, chanting tone texture is anything but an obscure musical technique: singing a sequence of syllables on *one repeating melodic* pitch is ubiquitous in music of all styles. Like melisma, chanting tone textures also have specific effects and even emotional associations. Melisma and chanting tone textures are thus mirror image effects:

- melisma = many tones on one syllable

- chanting tones = many syllables on one tone

Most practical settings blend these textural options, as in figure 5.11 (working from the first rhythmic setting, in figure 5.9).

Talk to me gen - tly   Hold _____ my __ ach - ing   head _ in your _ lap.

FIG. 5.11. Setting from Rhythmic Lyric to Melody

Option 1, the one-syllable/one-pitch texture, is used on words like "gently" and "aching." Here, we only keep that locked-in pace for a few syllables at a time.

Option 2, melismatic texture, is indicated with slurs.[15] The extended melodic figure on "hold" is a typical melismatic flourish, with clear emotional and dramatic affect on the lyric setting. Other melismas marked in the example are short, even just two notes. These shorter melismatic figures have prosodic effects as well, albeit more subtle.

Option 3, "chanting tone" texture, is used in this example as well, as indicated with the dotted brackets over phrases like: "Talk to me..." and "[ach] – ing head in..." As with melismatic figures, some chanting tone passages in this example are just two notes long, and others are a bit longer. In one spot, melismatic and chanting tone effects overlap, on the words "your lap."

Lyric Pace and Melodic Pace

If our goal is to learn how to use the full range of melodic/rhythmic textures in lyric setting, we do want the skill and finesse to make small revisions in the interplay of melodic contour and lyric rhythm. However, our small example might leave you with the impression that we make compositional decisions about lyric/melodic textures as a series of separate, minute, phrase-by-phrase decisions. This isn't how it works in most practical songwriting.

We generally sustain a given lyric/melodic texture throughout a phrase, sometimes for a whole section or a whole song. This involves the concept of pace, introduced in our earlier discussion of rhythm. In any rhythmic phrase, in any facet, whether highly patterned and repetitive or through-written, pace is a durational *norm*, a durational value more frequent than others in the phrase.

---

15. Don't confuse these *melismatic slurs* with ties: visually similar notation that connects notes on the same pitch, tied across bar lines or other major metric boundaries.

In melody/lyric setting, the *lyric pace* is established by the basic tempo and duration at which *unstressed syllables* land in the rhythmic lyric. In vocal melody, lyrical pace matches our intuitive sense for the flow of natural speaking. Conversational speech rhythm establishes a lyric pace and tends not to make extreme departures from that pace. In more impassioned speech rhythms, the pace itself may change as well as the range of different durations employed. Pace can also be strongly influenced by tempo; a given pace may not be sustainable as tempo shifts dramatically. In notation of vocal melody, it's usually convenient to transcribe this basic pace as eighth notes. Quarter notes feel "held" a little longer and often receive stressed syllables. Sixteenth notes represent quicker "triplet" delivery of syllables.

Redefining Melodic Rhythm

Against lyric rhythm and lyric pace, we want to be able to sense and work actively with independent patterns of *melodic rhythm* and the pace these establish. However, just as we ran into a gap in standard music terminology to describe chanting tone textures, here we stumble over our understanding of melodic rhythm in relation to melodic contour. The problem: within melodic rhythm as conventionally understood is a hidden dependency on rhythmic patterns that are intimately tied to lyric rhythm.

The conventional definition of melody is simply a series of notes or pitches moving in rhythm. Melodic contour, understood this way, includes changes of pitch as well as sequences of notes *on the same pitch*. Melodic rhythm is then simply the rhythm of these successive melody notes, whether sung on the same pitches or at different pitches.

This conventional definition of melodic rhythm misses a critical distinction between instrumental vs. vocal melody. In instrumental melody, consecutive notes can be performed on the same pitch with *instrumental articulation*: initiating a new bow stroke, plucking the string again, interrupting the flow of air with tongue or throat. It's different in vocal melody. When we sing, there's only one way to articulate a new note on the same pitch: *sing a new syllable*. Here, we make the simplifying assumption about our vocal melody that multiple notes on one syllable will be true melisma—*changing pitches*. This excludes vocal effects like Buddy Holly-esque glottal stutters that break up vowels, e.g., turning "way" into "weh-eh-eh-ay." These effects do create a percussive effect of separate notes on the same syllable and same pitch, but for our purposes, it's cheating! So, way, but no "weh-eh-eh-ay."

Since each syllable creates at least one note, a melodic contour that contains repeated notes implicitly embeds *rhythmic constraints on the lyric*. Instead of being able to freely work between lyric rhythm and melodic contour, assumptions about lyric placement are now present in *both rhythmic and melodic aspects*. You can see this in figure 5.12, which shows a melodic setting for the first of our two lyric rhythm settings (shown again on the second staff).

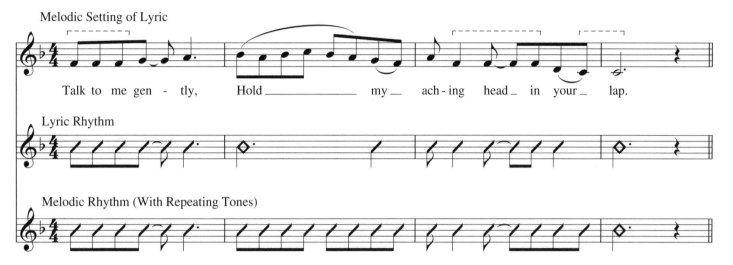

FIG. 5.12. Lyric Rhythm Contained in (Conventional) Melodic Rhythm

The first line shows the interwoven lyrical rhythm and melodic contour in our setting (melismas and chanting tones indicated as before). The second line repeats the lyric rhythm we worked from. Since this is a *lyric rhythm*, each rhythmic hit has a syllable, each syllable a rhythmic hit. The third line shows melodic rhythm as conventionally defined. Note that this rhythm has a hit for every hit in the lyric rhythm—and then a few more. Defined this way, melodic rhythm would *always* embed lyric rhythm completely, then possibly elaborate it. Melodic rhythm could be *busier* or more active than lyric rhythm alone (with melisma), but never *simpler*.

In process terms, here's the consequence. Setting *from* lyric rhythm to melody, when I get to a longer duration, I can set to a *single* melodic note and hold it longer, or break up that duration with several melodic notes as melisma. Setting in the other direction, from melody *to* a lyric—especially if I'm *creating the lyric in response to the melody*—I don't have the same freedom. *Where repeated notes occur in the melodic contour, I **must**—by definition—set a separate syllable on each note.* Drat!

The culprit is the presence of *repeated notes* (our chanting tone friends) in the melodic contour. The remedy is simple: take them out! Let's herewith redefine melodic contour as consisting only of *changing tones*. The melodic rhythm we're interested in, the rhythm we're overlaying with the lyric rhythm, is the rhythm of *this* melodic contour—the rhythm of *melodic changes*. Here's what that looks like for our example:

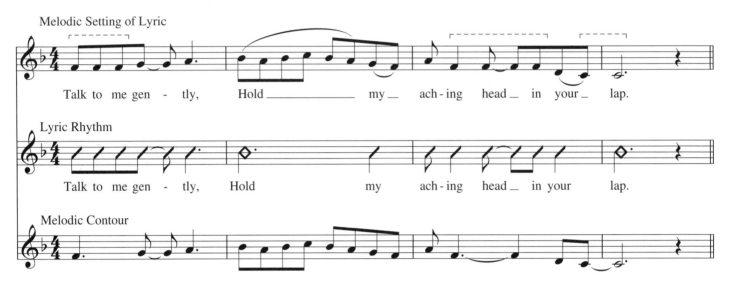

FIG. 5.13. Lyric Rhythm and Melodic Contour Moving Independently

The third line now shows the (revised) melodic contour with its rhythmic values. Repeated notes have now been "coalesced" into single durations in the melodic contour.

In this alternate view of melodic rhythm (I could say "melodic *contour* rhythm"), a rhythmic event is created *only* when a note changes pitch from its predecessor. There's still a rhythmic phrase defined, since notes are held for different durations, but consecutive repeated pitches are distilled to a single equivalent duration. Visualize this contour as a landscape or ridgeline, but with only hills and valleys, *no plateaus*.

This might seem like a nit-picking distinction. Yet, with this refined definition of melodic contour, we gain a new freedom of motion between melody and lyric. It's in the rhythmic interplay of *this* contour with lyric rhythm where all the interesting stuff happens. We are dealing with two interlocking rhythms: the rhythm of where syllables fall (lyric rhythm), and the rhythm of the melodic *contour*, where the melody *changes pitches*. Although untrained listeners couldn't articulate these separate rhythms for you, I truly believe they hear and respond to them. As songwriters, we also sense these rhythms intuitively. By learning to hear them more distinctly, we also learn to vary them independently when experimenting and revising. We could draw an analogy to pulses in medicine. Where Western medicine measures the pulse as a single rhythm in the human body, Eastern medicine recognizes multiple subtle pulses.

EFFECTS AND USES OF MELODIC TEXTURES

Melismatic and chanting tone textures are each useful in different lyric setting situations; we want the full spectrum of textures at our command. One strong contrast in the effects of melismatic vs. chanting tone textures lies in ways they move lyric or melodic aspects respectively to foreground or background.

- Chanting tone textures simplify and quiet melodic movement, and thus bring the lyric to the foreground and melody to the background. In particular, chanting tones spotlight *sense* aspects of the lyric as narrative. This can be particularly effective for relatively dense, complex lyrics that require more thought and focused attention from the listener.

- Melismatic textures spotlight *sound* aspects of the lyric (vowels and consonants) and bring the melodic curve itself into more prominence. This still spotlights the lyric, but draws greater prominence to individual words (through the slowed pace of lyric delivery) and particularly to the *sound* of the lyrics. (It can also draw more attention to the vocal *performance* itself.) On the other hand, meaning or referential aspects of the lyric move to the background.

Process Considerations

We work differently with these textures depending on the specific process or pathway we're following. When setting *from* a rhythmic lyric to a melody, we must choose how to handle syllables held for longer durations. We can simply hold the note, or add melismatic turns and twiddles; the effects are distinct. Melisma intensifies emphasis on a word or syllable differently than simple extended duration (holding the note longer).

Working from lyric rhythm, syllables with longer durations can eventually be set to held notes, melismas, or combinations thereof. When setting from a melodic contour *to* a lyric, the process is inverted. Here we have a melodic contour (in our special sense), and we're deciding whether to punctuate a given extended melodic tone with one or more *syllables:* that is, between a held note and *chanting tones*. As we're writing the lyric, we can "drop" more or fewer syllables against the contour. This symmetry and independence of lyrical rhythm and melodic contour (in the sense defined above) supports our overall goal of being able to write *in any direction:* allowing us to work ambidextrously (ambi-facetedly?) from melody to lyric or lyric to melody.

Melismas and Chanting Tones in Revision

Awareness of melodic contour and lyric rhythm as separable elements allows for a valuable level of precision in experimentation and revision. Returning to our example line on page 116, we can keep melodic contour unchanged but change lyric rhythm to a steadier quarter-note pace:

Talk to me _____ gen - tly _ hold _ my _ ach - ing head in your lap.

FIG. 5.14. Changing Lyric Rhythm, Holding Melodic Contour

Changing the lyric rhythm also changed implied "thought lines" and caesuras. "Talk to me gently… hold my aching head…" becomes "Talk to me… gently hold my aching head…" This in turn changes meaning and emotion. For better or worse? Do you want to be talked to gently or gently held? That's the writer's decision. What's remarkable is the way substantive questions about content, theme, and emotion can be sparked by what begin as purely musical transformations, miniscule ones at that.

Understanding the emotional and prosodic effect of different kinds of melodic movement is the best antidote to a kind of lazy or prototype melodic writing that is almost inevitable in creative work. Here's another example, showing how chanting tones and melismas naturally co-occur in a semi-improvised melody.

Chanting Tones | Melisma

I thought that there was all the time __ in the world __ for us _____ ba - by.

FIG. 5.15. Melodic Setting of a Lyric Line. Ad hoc use of chanting tones and melismas.

In revision, we reshape contiguous chanting tone or melismatic passages, sometimes for reasons of melodic design, but always serving the prosody desired. We may strengthen chanting tone or melismatic effects into more decisive statements in phrasing. The more delicate polishing work is pulling extreme chanting tone or melismatic effects towards a steadier matched pace of syllabic rhythm and melodic contour. Revision may require very small changes, such as breaking up chanting tone passages with single neighbor-tone moves, but small changes can have big effects.

Our example line references memory, thoughts, and feelings, and so, it could support a more flowing melodic contour. We might choose to better spotlight the word "all," a bit buried in the chanting tone passage, and could do this in various ways, some shown in figure 5.16.

FIG. 5.16. Four Ways to Reshape a Chanting Tone Passage

In doing this experimentation, reflect on what works and doesn't in the different trials. This will rapidly build your skills and insights into effects, while getting you to a better melodic line.

Our first versions of melodies, whether composed vocally while playing or just in our minds' ears, will always be full of convenient sloppy approximations. In learning to recognize these passages, notation can be a ruthless ally. Dutifully transcribing long passages of inadvertent chanting tone melodies will quickly reveal the differences between thrown-together and artfully sculpted melodic contours. Creative writers like to say writing is rewriting. To apply this to your melody writing, you need strong melodic memory and transformation skills, and an ability to hear the stories your melodies are singing. It's also wise to know when to stop revising.

Melodic and Lyric Pace Relationships

Overall melismatic and chanting tone textures arise from relationships between lyric and melodic pace. We could say in melisma, melodic pace moves *faster* than lyric pace, or alternately, that the lyric moves slower than the melody—if you're a glass-half-full, lyrics-half-fast kind of writer. (But who wants to write half-fast lyrics?) If lyric pace is generally faster than melodic pace, you get more chanting tone passages. When lyric and melodic pace are relatively matched, you'll tend to get one syllable per note as the norm, with a few variations thrown in of chanting tones and melismas.

EXERCISE 5.5. INDEPENDENCE IN LYRIC AND MELODIC PACE

Take a lyric line set to a melody with matching pace—that is, a norm of about one melodic note (changing pitch) per lyric syllable. Gradually, transform the line bringing melodic pace faster *relative to the lyric pace*. To do this and maintain the same overall phrase length, you must either (1) truncate the lyric or (2) accelerate the melodic pace in real duration (e.g., shift quarter notes to eighth notes). Alternatively, you can (3) keep the absolute melodic pace constant, extend the phrase, and *slow* the delivery of the lyric. Return to the original and gradually transform the line, this time increasing lyric pace relative to melodic pace, using complementary versions of the three options above.

Comfort Zones in Melodic/Lyric Pace

Many writers have habits or "comfort zones" in terms of where their melodies and lyrics sit in relation to each other. Lyric-driven writers, or writers who prefer to improvise melody and lyric "in one fell swoop," tend to settle by default into long chanting tone passages. The lyric focus outstrips the capacity to "think melody." Melodic shapes aren't supple enough to keep up with the lyric, and the melodic contour slows relative to the syllabic pace. The resulting chanting tone effects may or may not serve the expressive needs of the lyric and the song.

Vocally oriented writers may err in the other direction, overusing melismatic effects not just in performance but in the essential song melody. Melismatic flourishes might sound great but can obscure the clarity, meaning, even the audibility and comprehensibility of the lyric by over-emphasizing unimportant words, or shifting stresses in unnatural ways. In addition, because melismatic texture has prosodic effect, this can add an emotionally heightened layer that may ring thematically or narratively false or overwrought to the listener. To get flexible control over these textures, we need to be able to separately shift melodic and lyric *pace*.

Phrasing Templates

Chanting tone and melismatic textures are frequently intermixed, even within a single phrase. A common template or pattern is to contrast chanting tone passages (also often rhythmically regular) with melismatic emphasis, either at the start or the end of phrases. A template of this sort is usually mirrored in matching lines. These spotlighting techniques should complement the line's meaning and emotion, and shifts between textures should make thematic sense. The Beatles were masters at constructing melodic lines this way (e.g., the bridge or "middle eight" of "Girl" from *Rubber Soul*.)

The same principles can be applied at the higher level of overall sectional form. Varying melodic texture is a powerful means for creating sectional contrast—for example, using chanting tones for a descriptive, narrative verse, and then slowing lyric pace in the chorus through melisma, holding syllables for longer durations, or adding space around key words and syllables.

EXERCISE 5.6. PHRASING TEMPLATES

Here's an exercise, with an example (not quite up to the Fab Four's standards):

Construct a lyric phrase with chanting tones at the beginning, concluding with a word spotlighted by melismas. In the example, lyrics on chanting tones use internal rhyme, percussive consonants, and short vowels for quick, punchy delivery. The word "cryin'" uses melisma to shift toward more direct expression of emotion.

You just want some fun and you keep my mo-tor run-nin' but I'm cry' - in' for you. ____

FIG. 5.17. "Cryin' for You." Chanting tone followed by melismas.

Now try reversing the pattern with the melismatic title at the *start* of the phrase:

You left me cry - in'. I hope you get just what you de-serve. _

____ You left me cry - in'. Yeah, I hope you go deaf from the slap back re-verb.

FIG. 5.18. "Slap-Back Reverb." Melismas followed by chanting tones.

As the example suggests, chanting tone passages tend to co-occur with rhythmically driven melodies. The smaller contour moves rhythmic patterns in the delivery of lyric syllables to the foreground, and we move toward a rhythmically dominated texture. Our first melodic settings from strong *rhythmic* song seeds are likely to be chanting tone heavy. Chanting tones tend to invite even-duration, "motoric" kinds of rhythmic "dit-dit-dit" textures, but can also be set to more speechlike rhythms.

This can present a risk: too much of either rhythmic monotony *(mono-rhythm)* or rhythmic patterning can start to work against the lyric spotlighting effect of a chanting tone melodic contour. Consider revising chanting tone melodic textures as much by varying rhythmic patterns as by widening their melodic range and contour. The following exercise helps build these skills.

EXERCISE 5.7. ALTERING THE RHYTHM OF A CHANTING-TONE MELODY

Set a lyric line to a chanting tone or small-contour melody. Begin with a "mono-rhythmic" setting—that is, a passage of notes all of the same duration. Gradually transform this to a rhythmically patterned setting with a repeating rhythmic motive within the phrase. Next—either by breaking up and varying the repetitive rhythmic patterns, or starting fresh—work toward a rhythmically free-flowing setting that follows lyric phrasing more closely.

CHAPTER 6

Harmony

As we've toured through the songwriter's compass, we've discovered *sound* vs. *sense* polarities active for each facet. Lyrics connect intimately to rhythm and melody, through sonic aspects as well as referential meaning. While lyrics are the most obvious carriers of meaning and emotion, rhythms and melodies not only support lyrics, but also bring their own intrinsic and direct kinds of thematic and emotional meaning to the song.

A similar sound/sense polarity is at work in harmony-led writing. In this chapter, we'll explore the harmonic facet in terms of this sound/sense polarity. We'll look at techniques for discovering and working from chordal "seeds" as sound-led discoveries, especially techniques at your instrument. We'll also look at techniques for developing chordal ideas *away from* an instrument, generally a more challenging creative task for most writers. Then we'll look at various "sense" or meaning aspects of chords and chord progressions, complementary to those addressed in traditional discussions of harmonic relations: intervallic motion in chord roots; harmonic rhythm; and cyclic, narrative, and motivic progressions. In this discussion, the term "chords" will sometimes be used to encompass both individual chords and progressions. "Harmony" will refer to the facet as a whole, in relation to rhythm, lyrics, and melody.

SOUND AND SENSE IN CHORDS

Harmony springs from multiple pitches sounding together: a chord. Harmonic progressions are sequences of chords flowing according to a particular logic or design. Musicians, especially those with formal training in harmony, are accustomed to thinking of the meaning—the *sense*—of chords and progressions in terms of a particular harmonic vocabulary (major/minor tonality or functional harmony). But in songwriting, we sometimes work directly with *sound* aspects of chords, and of progressions—either holding in abeyance or at times even leaving behind a harmonic interpretation of the chordal material. Every part of the song "means," and has a story to tell—including the harmony.

Sound Aspects of Harmony

The sonority of chords, even of an individual chord, may be a primary source of inspiration for songwriting, especially when writing at your instrument. Through exploration, accident, or just messing around, you can get to chordal material where you have no conscious notion of the chord's role in a functional progression, or even what the root of the chord is. You can even use seed-catching techniques at your instrument that rely on *aleatoric* (by chance) discoveries for intriguing and suggestive sounds, voicings, and registral effects. In effect, your instrument becomes "the World," and you can let it surprise you with unexpected effects and sonic discoveries.

In such sound-led strategies for chordal writing, you want to defer functional interpretations of the found chords and progressions as long as possible. Also typical of this kind of writing is emotional *ambiguity* of the material. While chords can evoke imagery, memory, and association, you may not be able to easily categorize these reactions in emotional terms. It's a glorious act of discovery to throw your hands down and hear a chord you couldn't have imagined without playing it, and that you can't name or immediately fathom in terms of harmonic function—yet respond to it with powerful emotional or narrative associations.

These exploratory, sound-based, experiential practices of working with chords are used by songwriters spanning widely varying levels of technical knowledge. Technical knowledge can even—temporarily—get in the way when employing these techniques. It's almost better if you *don't* know what you're playing when you find the chord. More technically advanced musicians therefore sometimes rely on specific *disorientation* strategies to get themselves into unfamiliar chordal territory. They might put their guitar in new tunings, or try to write on an instrument they don't play. (The Jackson Pollock exercise described later in this chapter is a useful aleatoric and disorientation technique of this kind.) After the song's written, of course, it never hurts to expand your knowledge by going back and figuring out what the heck you played!

Sense Aspects of Harmony

A complementary style of harmonic writing emphasizes the sense or meaning of chords and progressions. Here, there's an interesting reversal of the sound/sense polarity as compared to lyrics, where sense aspects involve referential connotations—words as description of the world. Sense or meaning in chords and progressions lie primarily in their *musical* meaning: the very systems of internal, self-referential relationships we denote with the term "harmony."

In some usages, "harmony" might imply a particular vocabulary—i.e., functional harmony in the context of major/minor tonality. Knowledge of this specific harmonic theory and practice is, of course, an advantage to any musician and especially to songwriters. But just as songwriters often work from chords as sonorities, they often create progressions in exploratory ways, not necessarily following conventional voice-leading paths or progressions.

Some chord sequences are cyclical, creating a sense of mood and landscape. Some are more through-composed, creating a narrative—a story of a kind. But where standard progressions create their sense of narrative in the context of a key, tonal center, and progression through tonic, subdominant, and dominant functions, there are alternate ways that chords can move in progressions, to create emotion, meaning, and narrative.

Here, I don't mean particularly those ornery, contrived progressions that make weird moves for their shock-value effect. Though many a progressive metalcore band has built their sound out of such harmonic experimentation, an "anti-harmonic" aesthetic could still be said, ironically, to reference standard harmony in its very act of rebellion. Rather, to expand the harmonic resources available to us as songwriters, we want our repertoire also to include chord sequences that work—"function"—in musical terms, but in ways less typical of "functional-harmonic" progressions. Some of these alternative harmonic vocabularies draw on the rich body of influences and confluences that have shaped contemporary popular music, reflecting the interchange of Western European harmonic practice with African-American, Celtic, Anglo-American, and diverse other cultural sources. Other progressions can be discovered through experimentation, both at or away from your instrument. By understanding different ways chords and progressions can tell a story, we gain powerful new strategies for getting to distinctive thematic material through harmony.

Process Considerations

Some songwriters report that in their experience, melody and chords always come "simultaneously." While "all at once" is always a strategy option, the focus of this chapter is about gaining extra facility by being able to work independently with the facet of harmony.

The term "harmony" here might be interpreted more narrowly than intended, implying a particular ordering of creative steps—specifically, "harmonizing" in the sense of adding chords to an already present melody. For the full power of the 360° songwriting approach, we want the agility to move in any direction: starting from melody and harmonizing, or possibly starting from harmony—chords and chord progressions—and then "melodizing." Other pathways are also possible, such as adding rhythmic lyrics to a chord progression even *before* moving to melody.

It's particularly powerful to try working from chords *before* you have melody, lyrics, or any preconceived theme or subject matter for the song. You're thus *framing* from the harmony as you'd frame from an ambiguous lyric title. Surprisingly vivid imagery, stories, memories, thoughts, and even themes and issues can arise as you listen to chords and progressions alone, attending to the associations they spark. Conversely, you might *cast*, searching for chords to fit a song's theme and story already in progress. Whatever direction you're working, songwriters must focus as listeners on what the chords evoke, always asking how they complement the overall imagery, narrative, and emotional aspects of the song.

JAMMING

Many writers who might describe their process informally as beginning "from chords" are using a technique I'd simply call *jamming:* improvising vocal melody or lyrics against a backdrop of familiar chords, riffs, and progressions. A time-honored technique, especially when writing on chording instruments such as guitar or piano, jamming has no doubt been the genesis of many great songs. However, in jamming, the chords are generally not the focus of attention, and therefore tend to be simple, repeating stock progressions. They thus serve as a creative aid—a sonic "pad" inducing a relaxed state of almost-trance, to inspire imagery and language, or a scaffolding for generating fresh melodic or lyric material. In 360° songwriting terms, the songwriter is "seed catching" from lyric or melodic material improvised over the chords. In contrast, when working from *chordal seeds*, the chords themselves—voicings, transitions, or progressions— become the *first object* of creative attention and compositional focus.

While jamming rarely produces innovative chordal discoveries, that's not generally the goal. Many musical genres are not dependent on original, distinctive chord progressions, but are based on stock or cliché chord riffs and cyclic progressions. Listeners in these genres are oriented to these idiomatic progressions, rather than expecting innovative chords and moves. (This is even reflected in copyright law, which makes it difficult to protect a chord progression alone, without at least an associated melody and possibly a lyric.)

In principle, even in styles where harmonic innovation is desired, jamming doesn't compel us to keep the initial chords. Once melody and lyrics are in place, we could rethink and revise our progressions. Surprisingly often, though, we don't bother. Our scaffolding chords become "the chords." If these initial chords suit the final song's theme, style, and emotion, this can work fine. But when lyrics and melody might be better served by new chords, the progression at that point may be baked into the writer's ear, and into track production. To use jamming most effectively as a strategy, it's best to treat the chords as, in effect, "filler" material to be revisited and reconsidered later in development of the song. Of course, jamming can also be a way of stumbling across true chordal seeds. Once such a seed is discovered, however, the nature and quality of the creative work shifts.

I believe misuse or over-reliance on "jamming" as a de facto writing strategy has contributed to a kind of chord-lazy writing, widespread now in many genres—resulting in overuse of cliché progressions that thereby lose potency and meaning. In track-driven mainstream pop writing, progressions can sometimes get lost in a no-man's-land between beat composer, track producer, and top-line writer(s) responsible for lyric and melody. But the problem is just as prevalent in mainstream country or among acoustic singer-songwriters. I've been at Nashville "guitar pulls" where playing a song with non-obvious chords that you can't instantly follow on first listen is treated as a kind of antisocial behavior. Singer-songwriters may put intense focus on poetic lyrics, while treating their chords and progressions neglectfully. We seem to have lost, or weakened, the notion of sparking a song from a unique, fresh voicing or chord progression.

Regardless of the genres you write in, a limited vocabulary of chordal ideas limits in turn the themes and emotional tones you can tackle. You might expect that working with familiar progressions, which you can play without much thought, would at least leave your creative mind freer to focus on generating strong melodic or lyric ideas. But in practice, habitual progressions also seem to invite concessions in other, at least musical, aspects of the song.

CHORDAL SONG SEEDS

A chordal song seed is a specific chord or voicing, a chord move or transition, or a progression that has a fresh, distinctive, original aspect—to you, at least. "As Tears Go By," the first song completed by Mick Jagger and Keith Richards, is built around a central chordal idea: moving from a II major *straight* to a IV chord. I'd call that a chord seed—though I can't vouch for whether that move, strummed on guitar, was their actual starting point in writing the song. I believe the idea felt fresh to them at the time, and was also a relatively fresh sound in pop music.

Yet, if we required our chordal seeds to be chordal phenomena never before experienced by humankind, we'd be setting the bar a little high for songwriters! So, if *you've* never written a song with a major/minor seventh chord, never started a song on the IV chord, never moved from a VI minor straight to a I chord, these might serve as chordal seeds for you. The process distinction is, as with all seed catching, that some aspect of the *chords themselves* draws your interest in writing. This fresh, surprising content sparks associative creation of other elements of the song—melody, lyrics, theme—in response.

There are significant challenges in catching true harmonic song seeds, rather than just jamming over familiar riffs. In the sections that follow, we'll examine a variety of harmonic strategies, including: working both *at* and *away* from your instrument; working with harmonic material by *sound* and by *sense*; and working with individual chords and progressions.

Chords as Sound, Shape, and Feel

An individual chord, taken as a vertical sonority or combination of tones, has powerful acoustic sound and touch associations. Composers, instrumental players, and singers have a sense for affective qualities of specific keys and chords (e.g., C major vs. F♯ major). This is conditioned by many factors: pitch memory; natural resonances of specific keys on instruments, in acoustic spaces, or relative to human vocal range; for players, ways chords fall on the instrument and the motor memory this invokes; the sound of open vs. stopped strings in certain keys (e.g., A vs. E♭ tunes for fiddlers).

These qualitative aspects can dramatically shape our writing process as well as the final listener's experience. Harmonic considerations blend with timbre, orchestration, and dynamics. The *feel* of a chord as a gesture of the hand on the instrument can affect us, as can *placement* and *voicing* of the chord relative to our vocal range. Each key, and each chord, sits in a distinctive spot relative to that range and creates a distinct connection to our melodic and lyric sense. Playing a progression without accompanying vocal melody, we might still respond to the chords by silently vocalizing melodies and lyrics.

Chords at Your Instrument

When writing at our instrument (or with instrument in hand), we'll often play chords and progressions we already know. But we can also discover unexpected, accidental sounds at the keyboard or on guitar, and catch these surprises as chordal seed ideas. Keep your seed-catcher's ear perked amidst other musical activities, both purposive and drifting: practicing, noodling, daydreaming, playing songs, and making chance mistakes.

EXERCISE 6.1. JACKSON POLLOCK

The abstract artist Jackson Pollock became known for splashing paint directly on huge canvases laid on the floor, making art out of the (only apparently) random splashes that resulted. Parallel developments in music can be seen in John Cage's concept of *aleatoric* or chance music and the "found sounds" of musique concrète or hip-hop beat composing. This "Jackson Pollock" exercise works with musical sounds on an instrument in a similar way to Pollock's approach with paint. I originally developed it for guitar-playing songwriters; it can be applied to keyboard instruments, or any chordal instrument.

Let your hands fall onto your instrument as if "splashing paint" on canvas. Let your fingers fall onto the strings (or keyboard, etc.) *at random*, striving *to not control* your hand movements. The goal is to land in an unfamiliar shape and position, one where you genuinely don't know how the chord will sound at the time you grab the shape. This will be disorienting, and maybe a little scary. If you tense up, you'll tend to play shapes you already know, but this will not get you to fresh chordal seed material. You might need to do this a number of times before you stumble on a sound with the right qualities. Between attempts, shake out your hand and release all tension from your fingers, and then try again.

Almost every chord is known to *someone* (especially when you teach at Berklee!). The important thing is that the resulting shape should be unknown *to you*: a chordal sound you haven't played before, certainly one you haven't used in a song—ideally, a sound not immediately familiar to you. The chord should also not immediately remind you of an already written song. Stealing cool chord "snippets" from existing songs is a different exercise! If the seed does remind you so strongly of a song that it locks down your way of hearing it, "catch and release," and try again.

The point is not to play complex chords with lots of different tones, or fiendishly difficult chords involving awkward stretches. The emphasis is on the sound. On guitar, the chord should involve at least two, no more than four fretted notes; at least one open string, but not necessarily all strings; overall, a four- to six-note chord. Open and fretted strings can be interspersed. On piano, try two to three notes with each hand.

Don't be put off by a sound that elicits a comical reaction. Often this exercise yields music reminiscent of cartoon or horror film music. Humor is a natural response to unfamiliar juxtapositions. What first strikes us as funny can eventually become material we use more seriously, once the initial shock of surprise wears off.

The chordal sound you stumble on can be *ugly* (though deliberately trying for as ugly a sound as possible is yet another exercise… "Ugly Chords and Learning to Love Them…"!). Or it can just be cool, weird, harmonically ambiguous, evocative. You might need to try several times until you hit something intriguing.

This exercise takes practice. Happily, you can practice it no matter *what* your current level of technical skill on the instrument. In fact, beginners have an advantage over more experienced players, *if* they can overcome inhibitions and fear, and manage the physical challenges. Their hands are less likely to grab automatically for known chords, because they know fewer chords! More experienced players may need to use additional "disorienting" techniques: e.g., put your guitar in an unfamiliar tuning, or turn it around and play left-handed.

The Jackson Pollock technique also doesn't rely on a particular level of harmonic knowledge. Theory helps, but at times, can also hinder. Of course, there's no harm in figuring out what you played *after* the first creative unfolding from the seed.

Jackson Pollock Example

Here's an example Jackson Pollock seed idea at the piano, with first steps of working the idea. The original "hand-throw" was a six-note chord: three notes in left and right hands respectively. Note that the two three-note clusterings are rough (not exact) intervallic mirrors—typical of a voicing found by hand and feel rather than by ear (though the ear must assess the results, of course). The second voicing (bar 2) was derived from the first by noticing a prominent dissonance (low E against the F) and swapping the notes, again, with no prior certainty of the resulting sound. The starting seed idea is now a two-chord riff or cycle, but with a far-from-cliché sound:

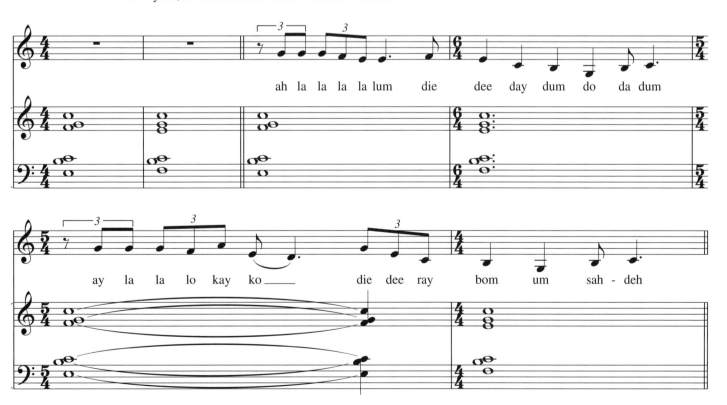

FIG. 6.1. Jackson Pollock Example. With initial working of the seed idea.

Because the chords are unusual and harmonically ambiguous, a melody set against these chords is also likely to take us out of our comfort zone. I illustrate a first melodic development step in figure 6.1. The initial phrase begins and ends on tones found in the voicing (G and C). The second phrase seeks out and emphasizes a note *not* in the voicing (D). The cadences form a question-and-answer phrase structure, with a start at lyric exploration via syllabic sounds. A slow rubato tempo and pulse allows phrase durations to breathe. This encourages experimenting with shifts to odd-bar timing, alternative phrasing, and metric positions. This irregular timing may or may not persist into the final song.

Other "At Your Instrument" Strategies

Here are related strategies for discovering chordal seeds at your instrument:

- *Seeds from technical practice.* As you practice scales, new chords and combinations, and physical patterns, seed fragments naturally leap out at you: sounds, voicings, and progressions that are fresh to your ear. If you're stirred by a particular chord sound, even if it doesn't immediately suggest clear emotional associations, capture it as a seed. (Then keep practicing!)

- *Seeds from exploration.* Related to disciplined practice of repertoire or technical exercises is more free-form *exploration*: playing in a new tuning, or experimenting with new shapes, patterns, and sounds. Though also technical work, this is more self-guided discovery than practice and drill. Fresh harmonic ideas or chordal textures often arise from such sessions that you'll want to capture as seed material.

- *Seeds from mistakes.* Songwriters practice differently than performers. When we make a mistake, the mistake itself sometimes suggests cool creative material. Be attentive for serendipitous sounds you stumble across when you get a chord shape spatially switched around, or when your hand slips. Accidents are sometimes songs waiting to happen. ("Don't waste that mistake!" says my student Ellie Buckland.)

- *Seeds from repertoire: In Search of the Lost Chord.* As you listen to or learn to play existing repertoire music, be attentive for particular chordal "magic moments" that move you and delight your ear. While this isn't exclusively an "at your instrument" strategy, it helps to be learning how to play the song when you make the discovery.

  The Beatles often worked this way, creatively "borrowing" isolated fragments from other songs. For example, the classic Motown hit song "I Heard It Through the Grapevine" (written by Norman Whitfield and Barrett Strong, and a signature song for Marvin Gaye) makes an unusual harmonic move in the transition from verse to prechorus—from the IV7 chord of a minor blues key to the VI minor. The prechorus thus contrasts harmonically to the starting key before returning home to the blues-based tonic on the chorus. Reputedly, John Lennon borrowed this distinctive chord idea for "Come Together," where the same move is used to spotlight a move to the refrain line. (Listen to the two songs and see if you can hear the borrowing.)

Using Your Chord Seeds

To write interesting and evocative full progressions, we need more than just novel chord sounds and voicings as starting points. If these are our primary source of innovation, we can easily wind up with stock progressions peppered by a few chordal "special effects."

When working from a fragmentary chordal song seed—typically the kind of material obtained at your instrument—consider carefully where to use this bit of harmonic novelty. Unusual chords or novel chord transitions draw attention as a landmark. One or two such chordal seeds can provide a signature moment for a song, while stringing successive weird chord moves dilutes impact of the individual ideas. Try using just one seed (from a given facet) or "surprising move" per section. Don't crowd seeds in the planter!

In addition, don't assume you must lead off with the seed at the start of your song or section. Seed-based writing is inherently *asequential* with respect to structure and flow of the final song. The strong or fresh idea—your starting point *in process*—might be best placed at a transition point or a spotlight position, for a primary bridge, or as just an intro, interlude, or coda.

Suppose I'm playing in the key of D and—whether by accident, experiment or a self-challenge—stumble on the B♭– chord. This is a ♭VI– in the key of D major—an unusual chord, and one I've never used in a song. To use it in a section, I'll spotlight the chord by surrounding it with less surprising material, and by transitioning to and from the chord in a plausible way, making the surprise of using the chord even more effective. In figure 6.2, I show an example progression written around this chord seed. I decide to get to the ♭VI– via a "rocking" motion from and back to the less startling ♭III chord (F):

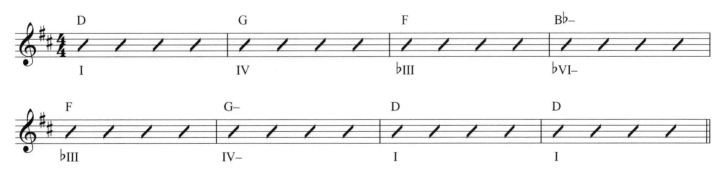

FIG. 6.2. Using a Chord Seed in a Sectional Context

Chord Seeds Away from Your Instrument

For most writers, chordal seeds are hard to hear away from an instrument. Song seeds typically come amidst everyday activity: a lyric title, or a bit of melody that pops into your head. Chords or progressions that "come to mind" this way are sometimes remembered fragments of already existing music. It's harder to find novel chordal ideas away from your instrument, "in your head." Exceptions are strong instrumentalists and/or those with extensive compositional training and inclination.

Picture an inspired composer walking through the Alpine hills, hearing entire symphonies in his mind's ear. Beethoven could reputedly "hear" his music even after he was almost completely deaf. The great French composer, organist, and ornithologist Olivier Messiaen was a synaesthete ("heard" colors, "saw" harmonies) who notated the rushing of waterfalls and transcribed landscapes of natural sounds (wind, bird calls) into dense orchestral textures.

For us mere mortals, hearing chordal ideas away from an instrument involves dual challenges: complexity and originality. Though many musicians (and nonmusicians) can silently conjure the *memory* of existing music, it's challenging to conceive, hear, and capture *novel* harmonic material in this way. It's particularly hard to hear complex, many-voiced harmonic textures without benefit of the external sound of an instrument. Here are three strategies that, taken progressively, can move you toward greater ability to hear and "think" harmony away from your instrument: (1) recording technology, (2) notation, and (3) cultivating your harmonic "mind's ear."

Recording Technology

Recording technology can be a valuable tool for songwriters very early in the writing process. Although you use it initially when playing at your instrument, it provides a bridge toward working more independently. By using recording technology, you can be freed from having to *play* your instrument while trying to compose related material at the same time. Compose your chord progression, and record it. Then listen back as you generate related melodies, lyrics, or even wordless lyric rhythms—in separate 360° style passes, if you prefer. An advantage of this simple strategy is that you can write to chordal ideas that are at the leading edge of your instrumental ability—stuff you *can* play, but only when focusing almost entirely on executing the chords. If you can manage to play it and then record it, you're now in "hands free" mode! It's safer to drive that way, and a lot more productive to write this way. It expands your writing options and scope, while also motivating you to expand your instrumental technique and knowledge. You more quickly see these skills translate to direct creative material for your songs.

Notation

A complementary strategy to recording technology is using *notation* to build ideas for your progressions. This can be especially helpful if you're *not* confident as a player of a harmonic instrument (guitar, piano), and feel your writing is held back by the limited progressions you can easily play. It can also be liberating for more experienced players, who may tend to rely on familiar licks or to overwrite progressions working at their instrument. You can get to *more* interesting places—and more *interesting* places—when not constrained by what's easy for you to play (whatever your current level of skill).

A common misconception is that recording technology makes notation unnecessary, even an annoyance. This misses the critical role notation plays, not just in *communicating* to players and singers, but as a mnemonic and visual aid in the creative work of composing itself. When you improvise musical ideas and record them, you are not necessarily forced to crystallize them and give them definite shape. The act of notating your own work helps you hear it and understand it in a different way. (This applies, not just to chordal notation, but to melodic and rhythmic notation as well. Even being meticulous about writing out "fair copy" lyrics can be revealing—lyric sheets are a notation as well!)

Notation enables you to write beyond not only what you can physically play, but also what you could *remember* to play, in live performance. *Composing* in notation, you're free to design the progression outside of performance "real time." Relieved of the pressure of remembering and executing the progression in performance, you can think about what you want the progression to do—as a story or narrative. This also helps you visually organize *longer* sequences and structures than you'd be able to retain in memory playing live, and to see parallels and correspondences that would be hard to hear and attend to in real time. As you write and recognize these longer-arc patterns, you get better at hearing them as well, and eventually, playing them. Skills of notation and live, extemporaneous play thus play off against each other in a "virtuous spiral."

Notation can support both sound and sense connections to chords. For example, working with a chord seed on guitar—grabbing a shape you've never grabbed before—you might want a chord diagram capturing the *shape* and *position* of the chord, without analyzing or interpreting it. If you've stumbled on an interesting voicing on piano, write down the (exact) individual notes before asking what functional type of chord it is, or even what the root is (implicit in the interpretive act of "naming" the chord). On the other hand, it's also great to start "thinking in progressions." You might be playing guitar as you write the progression, but you're thinking about the *function* of the chord in the key, not that it's a G chord in particular. I find this kind of harmonic thinking is facilitated by using notation that is pitch-independent but functional in nature, such as the Nashville number system (see the sidebar "Nashville Notation for Songwriters" on page 134). And functional notation is particularly helpful when working "notation first" as discussed on the next page—writing the progression as if you were writing a stanza of poetry.

134   CHAPTER 6

NASHVILLE NOTATION FOR SONGWRITERS

I *love* the Nashville number system for songwriting. This system evolved in Nashville studio recording environments, where session players often had to write charts from songwriter worktapes on first listen, and determine vocal keys for singers on the fly. Like the Roman numeral notation style used most often in harmonic analysis, Nashville notation is a key-independent or "instantly transposing" notation, in which chords are written in terms of scale degree relative to the tonal center, but in "plain-dirt" (Arabic) numbers (1, 2, 5) instead of Roman numerals (I, II, V). The notation is well-suited for the simple harmonic vocabulary of most country songs, and diatonic songs in many genres. The notation hits limitations for songs with ambiguous or shifting key or tonal center, rapid modulation, or very specific chord voicings.

Nashville notation is sometimes thought of as primarily a tool for performers and session musicians. I find the notation's simplicity and visual clarity is also a great aid for songwriting, particularly in "thinking chords" and progressions. Here's a Nashville chart of the section from figure 6.2, with some modified rhythms, to show rhythmic conventions:

$$
\begin{array}{llll}
& \overset{<}{} & & \overset{<}{} \\
1 & 4 & \flat 3 & \flat 6- \\
\flat 3 & \underline{\flat 3\ 4-} & 1 & \backslash
\end{array}
$$

Chart writers tend to write Nashville notation in phrases set on separate lines, helping to outline phrase structure and sectional form. The notation also provides cues for harmonic rhythm as well as the chord changes. Underlining of chords represents "split bars" or doubled pace; for this chart, at a pace of one chord (number) per bar, underlining switches whole-note to half-note durations. The "\" symbol, a personal notational preference of mine, indicates a "continuation" chord. Some session players might prefer an explicit chord for every bar; I like the visual reinforcement of seeing the varying durations on chords. The "<" marks represent anticipations or "pushes" of certain chords. While these marks begin to involve aspects of accompaniment rhythm or arrangement, they can also be integral for some songs at the compositional level. These conventions facilitate considerations of phrasing, harmonic rhythm, and even motivic aspects in composing and revising progressions. Here, for example, the visual layout draws the eye to the sequence 4 $\flat$3 in the first line, recurring in retrograde sequence in the second line.

Roman numeral notation is often used in functional analysis of existing music, and can indicate functional interpretation or "harmonic intent," e.g., with slash notation for secondary dominant relations like V/V. Nashville notation doesn't readily support this analytical function. But songwriters and musicians familiar with Nashville notation for session work would benefit from greater awareness of the notation's power as a songwriter's tool. I find the notation particularly powerful with notation-first techniques such as those discussed in the text.

Working Notation First

Notation is primarily useful as an *adjunct* to composing via live performance, or working with recorded material. However, there is a powerful if unusual strategy you can use as well—working *notation first*. In this strategy, you use the notation as your primary "performance" vehicle for generating the ideas. You compose *directly* in the notation itself.

There are inherent risks with a notation-first strategy. The first few times you try writing a progression "notation-first," it may seem unnatural, awkward, artificial, and contrived. You won't necessarily hear the progression in your mind's ear; the notation will be doing too much of the work for you, and may lead you down some dead ends. Write the progression, then play it back. (You may want to use a tool like an automated software notation program or a sequencer.) Does it sound awful? Why? Or maybe it sounds different—but, hey, after a few repetitions you begin to get used to it, even like it.

This strategy enables you to dream up progressions you'd be unable to play—certainly, ones you're unlikely to create via casual jamming. It's possible to notate progressions that are essentially clichés, or sequences so contrived and complex as to be nearly unplayable or unlistenable. Some will work, some won't. Progressions developed notation-first may sound too busy or "chord-y." Sometimes a progression that sounds unworkable on its own will magically work when you find a *melodic* line that ties it together and makes it make sense. Learning to distinguish the unfamiliar and initially uncomfortable from the truly unmusical is an ongoing journey.

Overly complex progressions are a natural part of the learning curve with this technique. Be sure to listen back to your progressions and assess them for musical coherence. Expect to "thin out" your first notated versions as you play and tweak. Write yourself into a corner, then listen and play your way out of it. While you may initially "overwrite" using this technique, you eventually learn to use space and repetition more confidently, so your progressions use compositional time, duration, and harmonic rhythm—stillness as well as motion.

Cultivating Your Harmonic Mind's Ear

Recording technology and notation are powerful and complementary tools for developing harmonic skills. At the same time, you also want to cultivate your "mind's ear" skills for working creatively with harmonic material—your capacity for silent *auditory* experience of chords, away from an instrument or any physical realization of the sound. This work will gradually liberate your ability to design chord progressions from your instrumental limitations (or facilities!).

In theory, you can learn to hear individual chords in your mind's ear. But it is very difficult to hear unusual voicings this way, unless you're an instrumentalist who can conjure tactile, mnemonic images of your hands on your instrument to reinforce the sound. It's actually easier to hear *progressions*, because you're focusing not only on the imagined sound of the individual chords but on the sense and flow of the progression itself.

As you practice letting chord progressions resonate and "play through" in your mind, you'll start getting a feeling for the story the chords are telling. As you mentally track root tones, then bass lines, then inner lines that suggest qualitative shifts of major and minor chords, you'll trigger associated bodily movement and gesture, emotional associations, memory, and imagery. As you develop these skills, you'll also be less constrained by your physical chops as a player. You'll be increasingly able to imagine progressions that might be hard for you to play, and less likely to accept compositionally weak progressions just because they're easy to play.

CHORD PROGRESSIONS

We'll now look at ways to expand our vocabulary for working with the *sense* or meaning aspects of chords and chord progressions. Our goal is twofold: to expand our strategies for writing interesting and varied progressions, and to develop our sense for the emotional and narrative aspects of those progressions. You can use all the sound-based strategies discussed previously: working at, or away from, your instrument; and using recording technology, notation, and harmonic ear training to expand your abilities to hear, remember, and revise chord sequences and progressions.

Simple Chords

Writing "interesting" chord progressions is not synonymous with employing sophisticated harmonic vocabulary—lots of cool chords and chord changes. You'll need such vocabulary for certain genres, like bossa nova or art rock. But many genres are built on simple harmonic qualities and cyclic progressions: from country music, to early Motown, to old-school rock, to much contemporary pop writing. The chords in these songs can still make distinctive statements that support the meaning and emotion of the song. To write convincingly and authoritatively in these genres requires appreciation for the power of simple chordal structures and progressions.

Besides being better able to write to particular genre conventions and restrictions, there are good learning reasons to develop your skills for creating interest in progressions using relatively simple chords. Visual artists do "color studies" to wrestle with their materials in the purest form possible. Working initially with simple palettes of chords, we can more easily grasp the complexity beneath even apparently simple progressions. At Berklee, in part due to the college's jazz legacy, student writers with a lot of jazz theory training sometimes turn in songs where every chord is at least a seventh chord, and often more complex. These writers often lack a songwriter's sense for the *emotional* significance of even the basic diatonic "country" chords, much less their upper-structure citified cousins.

Another reason to focus at first on simpler chord structures, especially humble triadic voicings, is to more clearly hear relationships between chords and vocal melody. Compare the two harmonic settings in figure 6.3. In the first setting, doubling the melody note in the chord voicing on the FMaj7 and D–7(13) obscures the tension or "rub" of vocal melody against harmony. The second setting spotlights and clarifies melodic notes as non-chord tones against the simpler triads. This is not just an arrangement issue. You will make different melodic choices in writing based on the chord voicings you use.

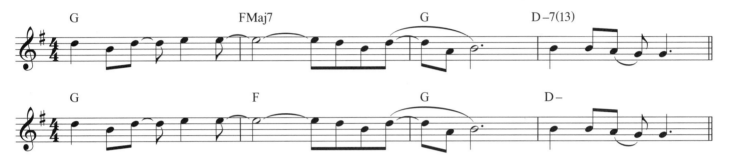

FIG. 6.3. Complex vs. Simple Chord Structures Against Vocal Melody

Using a simple *palette* of chords does not mean using only stock progressions. Even restricted to the "three chords and the truth" I, IV, and V chords, thousands of distinct progressions can be written. Only a few have been explored in the song repertoire as a whole, much less your individual writing. Each progression has a different story to tell. Embrace the power of simple chords—and occasionally, even the simplicity of power chords!

Chord Roots as Scale Degrees

In any given key, each chord takes on meaning based on where its root sits relative to the tonal center and scale. The *sound* of an F chord depends on its being an F. But an F *chord* in the *key* of F functions as a tonic chord; in the key of C, as a IV chord. While chord quality also matters, our ears seek out the *root* of the chord and assign it meaning.

While there are twelve available pitches in the equal-temperament system, the seven diatonic chords—with roots on one of the seven scale degrees for a given key—have special significance. In particular, the six "primary-color" diatonic chords (the three major triads and three minor triads), taken together, form an essential "chord palette" for songwriting. Consider this set of chords like a cast of characters, each with their own personality, affinities, disputes with other characters, and part to play in the tale.

EXERCISE 6.2. SIX CHORDS IN SEARCH OF A COMPOSER

Write a progression using all and only the major and minor triads of the diatonic scale (I, IV, and V major; II–, III–, and VI–). For this exercise, avoid the diminished triad (built on the seventh degree of the major scale). In practice, this chord often feels like a V7 (minus the root) rather than a distinct chord built on a different root.

It may seem dead simple to write a progression using just these six different chords. Yet it's remarkable how often student writers come back with a progression where they've "forgotten" to use the III– or II–. In addition, as you try to create variety in the progression, the highly constrained set of materials forces you to be more deliberate in your placement of chords. Even in the short six-chord progression example shown in figure 6.4, there are some less expected moves between chords, such as the direct move from III– to V.

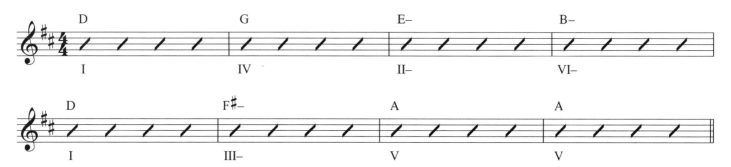

FIG. 6.4. A Progression Using the Six Primary Diatonic Triads

Exercises like this six-chord challenge, involving simple diatonic progressions written without lyrics or melody, with various constraints on choices of chords, can heighten your awareness of the effects of each chord relative to the tonal center, and of the moves *between* chords. It also encourages experimentation with less stock chord transitions and sequences.

Intervallic Motion in Chord Progressions

A chord in a sequence or progression takes on additional meaning by its placement within the flow of the chords. This flow establishes its own "melodic" line, independent of the vocal melody. As individual chords are complex vertical structures, various melodic threads can be heard: the root movement of chords, lines formed by bass lines or inversions, inner guide-tones, etc. We experience a given chord's root and quality relative to the overall key, but also relative to the roots of preceding and following chords. Here, it's necessary to review some aspects of harmony, always keeping in mind our purpose as songwriters: to develop our sense for connections of these chord movements to imagery, emotion, and story.

For example, a V chord in any key, anywhere in a progression, has its "scale degree" meaning, in terms of its dominant functional role. But heard in the two sequences I IV V vs. I II– V, the chord takes on different meaning because of the different scale degrees from which it is approached (IV vs. II–) and the intervals of those approaches (a second vs. a fourth). Because we listen via shifting windows of expectation and short-term memory, a chord's meaning in the context of a progression is also modified by the chord that *follows* it, and the interval by which we depart from it to that successor, e.g., I V VI– vs. I V IV.

Directional Effects of Chord Root Movement

The *interval of movement* from chord to chord also has specific meaning and effect, related to but not identical to the meaning of that interval as a scale degree. As songwriters, we need to understand these intuitions, because they affect our emotional responses to chord movements, along with imagery and narrative associations.

As a simple, consistent way to name and think about chord root intervallic motion, it's convenient to express these movements in terms of the "shortest path" between tones: i.e., movement by a second, third, or fourth, up or down respectively. Rather than talk about movement by wider intervals (fifth, sixth, or seventh), we "reflect" such movements back within the octave. Thus, we'd call root motion from D to A movement *down* a fourth, motion from D to G movement *up* a fourth.

Returning to our cast of diatonic chordal characters, we can characterize chord root motion, in common with vocal melody, by *direction* (up and down) and interval size or distance between the tones (in scale degrees). There is, however, a fundamental difference in our experience of vocal melody vs. the implied melodic movement of chords. In vocal melody, we hear contours as shapes in *pitch* space. In chord root motion, we hear contours in *harmonic* space, where intervals are mapped or reflected back to a scale degree relative to a tonal center, within the compass of a single octave.

Thus, there is potential ambiguity in how directionally we hear diatonic motion of chord roots. This distinction affects our experience of individual intervals, as well as contours created by successions of chord root tones. This is particularly true of root tone motion, especially since in some cases this motion is *implied* rather than directly stated in voicings of chords. The effect is less straightforward with the more clearly melodic contours of bass lines, inner guide-tone lines, and other voice leading effects.

The sense of directionality varies with the size of the interval of motion. For example, in theory we could hear root motion of D to E as movement *upward* by a major second, or *downward* by a minor seventh. But root motion by the relatively small interval of a second, up or down, is felt fairly melodically; here, harmonic and melodic motion come closest to coinciding. In this sense, D to E would be felt primarily as an *upward* motion (somewhat independently of how the chords might be voiced). Root motions by a diatonic third, such as D to F♯ or D to B, are larger intervals, but still felt largely melodically and directionally. (Curiously, though, they are felt as less strong harmonic changes, for reasons discussed on the next page).

Movement by fourths (or fifths) is directionally the most ambiguous type of diatonic root motion. In vocal melody, we clearly hear the difference between a leap *up* a fourth vs. *down* a fifth. These moves take us to different pitches, and create strongly contrasting pitch contours. Movement from D to G in chord roots, however, is directionally ambiguous: you arrive at the same harmonic tone. Thus, in chord root motions by a fourth, a spatial or directional sense of "up" or "down" motion becomes less potent than a different sense of movement.

These qualities of root tone movement can be better understood by considering the movements of constituent tones in the respective chords. Perceived *continuity* in a chord move depends on the "fate" of common tones shared between chords.

In movement by a diatonic second (up or down), there are no common tones between adjacent triads. Every voice moves in the same direction (subject to chord voicing and voice leading). This creates a strong sense of change and little continuity. These moves are thus the most "melodic" or scalar of chord transitions, and create the strongest *directional* sense, with corresponding emotional or descriptive associations of rising and falling.

This principle can be heard not only in direct chord movement but also in modulations. In old-school country music, a standard tool of the trade was to modulate the last chorus of a song upward, often by the interval of a major second. This created an audible "lift" in the music, along with the sonic effect of brightening tonal quality and raising the vocalist's range to add drama and tension. When this technique was inverted, as in the down-spiralling modulations of Johnny Cash's classic "I Walk the Line," the effect was surprising and equally strong.

In diatonic moves of a third, *two* common tones create strong continuity. This gives these movements a softened quality. I call such moves *color* moves; they suggest a shift of colored light on a scene rather than a change of scene. These moves make less strong harmonic statements than moves by fourths, and less directional statements than moves by seconds. In some situations, they may be heard more as changes of inversion or voicing than full harmonic changes. Such chord moves must therefore be used carefully, or they can "cloud" the narrative flow of the chord progression. However, precisely because they have intermediate strength as moves in harmonic rhythm, they can be great resources, especially used in unexpected patterns (e.g., VI– moving *up* to I).

Root movement by fourths and fifths share one common tone: the 1 of the I becoming the 5 of the IV, or the 5 of the I becoming the 1 of the V, respectively. Although we will *name* these root motions, for convenience, as movement by fourths (up or down respectively), the intuitive effect is *not* really up-and-down motion. Instead, we will use the terms *rising* and *falling*—but more in an emotional, narrative, and metaphorical than a directional sense.

Rising and Falling Moves

This way of understanding the "meaning" or affective qualities of different kinds of root motion sheds light on the affective power of simple chord progressions, especially movement among basic diatonic triads. Consider again the ubiquitous set I IV V. This set of chord roots combines the highly directional interval of the major second with two "hinge" moves of a fourth.

There are two paths of movement among these chords, that have very different emotional qualities. To distinguish these patterns of motion and their effects, it's helpful to picture the I, IV, and V chords arranged in a circular fashion:

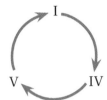
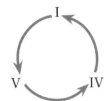

"Rising" Harmonic Motion   "Falling" Harmonic Motion

FIG. 6.5. Rising and Falling Harmonic Motion

Rising Harmonic Motion

One way to move through these chords can be depicted as *clockwise* motion around this circle: I to IV to V to I. This corresponds to the standard harmonic progression: from *tonic* (I) to *subdominant* (IV) to *dominant* (V), and returning back to the I. An implied metaphor and narrative is built into this progression, familiar to us through our associations of tonal music: we start from a clearly established tonic, "journey out" to the subdominant (IV), achieve suspense with the IV "rising up" to the dominant (V), and at last, resolve by "coming home to" the tonic.[16]

The experiential quality of these movements could be described as an overall *rising* gesture, in terms of emotion or energy. There are voice leading explanations for these effects.

- A transition between chords feels like more of a *movement* (a change) when the *root* of the chord we move to is *not* contained in the chord we move from, but "revealed" as the chord changes. We get this effect when moving *up* a fourth—I to IV, or V to I—the moves of the "rising" cycle above. This same effect can be heard in other diatonic moves up a fourth: e.g., II– to V, III– to VI, VI– to II–. (These moves are also the most likely to be intensified by shifting diatonic chords to secondary dominants: e.g., II7 or V7/V to V, etc.)

---

16. Some aspects of this discussion introduce different terminology than standard presentations on harmony. To compare this treatment of harmonic motion with the approach used in Berklee's jazz harmony curriculum, I recommend *The Berklee Book of Jazz Harmony*, by Joe Mulholland and Tom Hojnacki (Berklee Press, 2013).

- With V to I, we hear a particularly strong resolution back to the tonic. The third of the V chord, the seventh degree or leading tone of the scale, resolves upward by a half-step to the tonic. This is the classic leading-tone resolution of tonal harmony.

- As discussed earlier, we hear root movement by seconds as more "melodic" in implication. Thus the upward direction of the major second, IV to V, "lifts" us and builds energy. This effect is arguably based more strictly on root tone motion alone.

Falling Harmonic Motion

We can also move between these chords in the *other* direction, depicted here as counterclockwise motion around the circle: I to V to IV to I. These root movements have a different energetic quality. In standard music theory, the cadence from IV to I is sometimes referred to as a *plagal* cadence. Moving from I *straight to* V (without passing through IV) is a similar root motion (down a fourth). While a different effect with respect to the tonal center, it shares something of the quality of the plagal cadence. To convey the complementary quality to the "rising" set, we'll call these "falling" moves.

Rising movement is typical of the harmony predominant throughout the Great American Songbook-era repertoire. It is intensified by use of secondary dominants, and tonal modulation. But the "falling" type of chordal root movement is also ubiquitous in many styles and idioms, often associated in particular with genres such as blues, rock, and gospel, as well as bluegrass, Celtic, and Southern roots styles. There's even a complement to the old-school "circle of fifths" pattern in rising motion—the "circle of fourths" progression—made famous in '60s era rock by Hendrix's "Hey Joe" and various songs of the Beatles, including "Lucy in the Sky with Diamonds."

Rising and Falling By Seconds and Thirds

We can extend this rising/falling polarity to chord moves of seconds and thirds. Because of melodic implications of root movement by a second, the move V to IV has a downward or "falling" effect, with corresponding spatial and gestural associations.

The classic twelve-bar blues progression, in a simplified version, is actually an interesting hybrid of the two types of movement:

I7	I7	I7	I7
IV7	IV7	I7	I7
V7	IV7	I	I (V7)

FIG. 6.6. Rising and Falling Harmonic Motion in Classic Twelve-Bar Blues

Here, the first of the three phrases establishes the tonal center (typically voiced with a seventh chord, for a Mixolydian or blues rather than a straight major-key feel). The *initial* chords of each phrase (heard in almost an acrostic way) outline a "rising" progression: I to IV to V. But the movements *within* each four-bar phrase are all "falling" transitions: IV to I, then V to IV to I. Even the optional (parenthesized) turnaround in the last phrase adds an additional I to V "falling" move, before a quick "rising" move back to I and the cyclical repetition of the form.

The circle depiction is a reminder that movement in terms of these cycles need not start or stop at the I chord. The direction of motion carries a similar rising effect moving from V through I to IV, or a falling effect from IV to I to V. This is why I have not defined these moves in terms of standard "cadences" or ways of ending phrases. By beginning and ending phrases on chords other than I, a variety of effects can be created. These may at times weaken or leave ambiguous the apparent tonal center, leading the way to more fully modal progressions. We'll revisit these possibilities at the end of the next chapter, "Melody/Harmony Connections."

The affective qualities of different directions of root movement by thirds is more subtle to discern. In movement *downward* by a third, e.g., I to VI–, the new chord's root (the sixth degree) is *not* contained in the chord, and thus creates a stronger impression of a harmonic change. As a result, although root motion might be considered *down* a third in this case, the overall affective quality binds more closely with the "rising" moves of upward fourth and second. Sequences built around movements of upward fourths can always be punctuated by moves of downward thirds, as shown in the boxed transitions in figure 6.7:

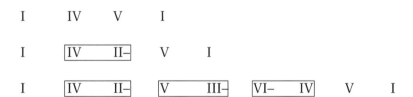

FIG. 6.7. Rising Progressions (with Downward Diatonic Thirds)

Although roots move in both directions in absolute terms, there *is* an overall "rising" effect in each of the above progressions.

By contrast, in movement *upward* by a third, e.g., I to III–, the new root is contained in the departed chord (the third of the chord, carrying the quality of the chord). Thus, perhaps somewhat counterintuitively, movement *upward* by a third has the more unexpected, "falling" quality. Thus, these movements can punctuate sequences built out of other falling movements. In figure 6.8, we see a few example sequences built out of all "falling" transitions, including some upward thirds (again, shown in the boxed transitions):

I	V	IV	I				
I	V	IV	VI–	III–	II–	VI–	V
VI–	I	V	IV	III–	V	II–	VI–

FIG. 6.8. Falling Progressions (with Upward Diatonic Thirds)

Functional Considerations

The movement qualities described previously are not substitutes for functional harmonic roles, but rather describe some additional qualitative effects of simple diatonic progressions. These effects are modified by functional roles of the chords with respect to key/tonal center and scale degree position. The progression I IV V can be described as a "rising" intervallic sequence "up a fourth, up a major second." The progression II– V VI– follows the same intervallic pattern, but with different chords relative to the tonal center. Both I to VI– and III– to I are moves downward by a diatonic third, an overall "rising" effect. However, each could take on a more "coloristic" or prolonging harmonic effect, or a more functional effect, depending on context.

To summarize: We can hear any chord progression in dual respects: as a sequence of chords with roots on particular scale degrees, and as a sequence of chord "moves" or *transitions*. Ascending fourths, ascending seconds and, to a more limited extent, descending thirds have a *rising* quality or affect; descending fourths, descending seconds, and (again, conditionally) ascending thirds, a *falling* quality.

EXERCISE 6.3. ANALYZE A PROGRESSION BY ROOT MOTION

A powerful way to put these concepts into action is to analyze a given diatonic progression in terms of both the specific chords used, and root movement in rising and falling directions respectively. Most progressions mix these types of moves. Note where reversals or "flips" of direction occur; reflect on how these affect the meaning and emotion inherent in the progression. (This is a powerful preparatory technique when *framing* from a chord progression to narrative or thematic content, or *setting* from chords to lyrics by sense.)

We'll illustrate with the example in figure 6.9. For consistency and conciseness, we label moves according to the diatonic interval involved: e.g., D2 means downward movement by a (diatonic) second; U4 means upward movement by a fourth. (This makes sense: who could imagine U2 standing for anything but rising energy?) As a second-order visual indication below the interval markings, diagonal arrows (↗↘) indicate rising or falling effect, respectively. We can thus see spotlight points where the rising/falling quality of root movement shifts. Implied root movement at transitions between phrases, or at the end of the section assuming a cycle back to the start, are indicated with parenthesized courtesy chords and step indications.

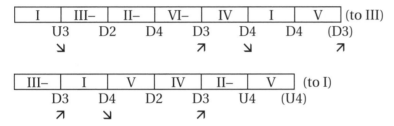

FIG. 6.9. Sectional Progression Labelled with Rising/Falling Root Motion

Here, the progression was written with the intent of favoring falling movement; yet, the VI– to IV transition, a rising move, naturally intruded. Viewing the section as a whole, a symmetry emerges: the first line primarily falling, but with a rising moment midway through the line; the second line beginning with a rising move, falling back to falling, ending with rising moves. If the section is cyclical, the V to I transition is a final rising move to start the journey again. By listening for such hidden "narratives" in chord progressions, we can work from harmony to other facets, or add harmony to other material in less arbitrary, more prosodically sound ways.

Working with Root Tone Contours

Music breathes and flows, not by constantly maintaining strength, but through ebbs and flows of energy. Varying rising vs. falling movement between chords can create dynamics and interest in even apparently simple progressions.

These terms are only intended to be suggestive. This polarity could also be characterized as *active* vs. *receptive* energy. I have at times described the V to I cadence as returning in pride or triumph, IV to I as returning in humility or surrender. However you experience or name these complementary patterns of root movement, focus in your songwriting on their distinct qualities. As you play through progressions moving in these varied directions, you should gradually get a sense for the polarity or energetic contrast in their effects, and be able to notice when the directions of chord movements change. You should also cultivate associative resonance of these aspects with other facets, especially lyrics. Listen, and find your own imagery, associations, and spatial or gestural sense. What's important is that the chord *moves* begin to take on narrative qualities for your writing.

What is critical, for our purposes as songwriters, is that we have access to all these types of motion in our progressions. It seems simple to write a simple progression using just the six basic diatonic major and minor triads—yet we can miss some. It's easy for us as writers to fall into habitual families of progressions, limited in key respects. Similarly, we can have blind spots when it comes to movements between chords along various paths. Each transition carries distinctive emotional and narrative connotations. When we expand our repertoire, "chord progression first" writing can get us to a much wider range of thematic material, and expand our options when setting *from* other facets to chords and progressions.

EXERCISE 6.4. WRITE A PROGRESSION USING SIX INTERVALS OF ROOT MOTION

This exercise is a "dual" to exercise 6.2, where we wrote a progression using all and only the six (major and minor triad) diatonic chords. In this variation, your challenge is to write a sectional progression using all and only the six *diatonic intervallic moves:* up a second, up a third, up a fourth; down a second, down a third, down a fourth. As before, the result should make musical sense! Figure 6.10 shows an example of a repeating sectional progression.

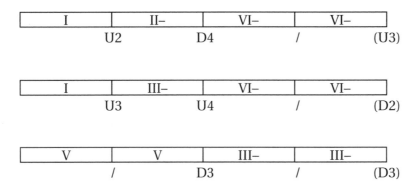

FIG. 6.10. Diatonic Progression Using All Root Movements

As an extra challenge, try to avoid using the same intervallic move twice in succession, except across phrase boundaries. In the example, two such repetitions occur: one across a phrase boundary, one at the repeat of the entire section (assuming it will be performed cyclically). In particular, two or more consecutive moves of a second in the same direction start creating an overly linear feel—less of a true progression, more an outline of the scale in the root tones. Two or more moves of a third outline an arpeggiated chord in root movement (though not necessarily one of the chords played). This can also work against the decisiveness and vigor of the progression.

HARMONIC RHYTHM

The functions that chords provide in the song have dual aspects, overlapping but not identical to rhythmic accompaniment. Along with nonharmonic instruments (e.g., drums and other percussion), harmonic instruments play their part in expressing *accompaniment rhythms*—through the strum of the guitar, the vamping on the piano. Interlaced within this accompaniment, however, are more compositionally essential rhythmic patterns expressed by *harmonic movements* of the chords. We'll refer to the rhythmic patterns created by these movements as the *harmonic rhythm* of the progression in the song. Harmonic rhythm is not defined by where chords *sound*—a function of chords as accompaniment—but rather, the rhythm of *where chords change*.

Harmonic rhythm plays a complex role as a core compositional element of the song. Chords help to outline overall phrase and sectional structure for the listener's ear. Chord movements can coincide with key spots in vocal melody and act as a spotlighting technique. Chords can also move when vocal melody does *not* move. At the same time, the movement of the chords makes a separate rhythmic statement—a rhythmic line moving slower than vocal and melodic rhythm, but in constant interaction with it.

This sense of harmonic rhythm may appear analogous to the modified concept of melodic rhythm presented in the "Melody" chapter—rhythmic patterns of *changing* pitches in the melodic contour. However, there's an important distinction. To understand the unique qualities of harmonic rhythm, we must consider the role of chords in the texture of the overall song, and in connection to the other facets.

Lyrics and melody are intimately connected in the vocal line. Since singers must breathe, vocal melody breathes, naturally breaking into phrases where the singer takes a breath, or where a thought concludes and a new thought begins. In contrast, chords need not "breathe"—or at least need not pause with the vocalist's breaths. They may roll forward in an uninterrupted stream, a continuing backdrop behind vocal phrases. Sometimes, we'll move chords most busily during pauses in the vocal melody—a countermovement principle intrinsic to the nature of accompaniment. Chords move in phrases of their own, which don't interlock directly with vocal phrases. Regardless of whether the chords "pause for breath" between phrases, the underlying harmonic motion provides a continuing orientation in time, and to the key and tonal center of the song. Even when chords are not sounding, during an a cappella section or a moment of complete silence, we can still perceive this implied harmony. This is what gives harmonic rhythm its unique quality. Events in harmonic rhythm are perceived shifts in what's experienced as an unbroken "thread" of harmonic texture.

Harmonic rhythm shapes the meaning of chords and chord progressions in varied ways. A chord receives more emphasis by being placed on metrically stronger beats and phrase positions, and by longer duration. This harmonic rhythm creates its own patterns, interwoven with the specific chords in the progression. Sometimes, it's more important *when* we change a chord than *what chord we change to.*

Figure 6.11 shows an example progression, written in three notations. Roman numeral notation is shown to the left. A "harmonic rhythm map" is shown in the center. This is a useful informal notation for mapping a progression's harmonic rhythm as a visual pattern: an "X" signifies a change of chord, a "\" indicates a continuation of a chord. Shown to the right is a variant of Nashville notation blending functional harmonic notation with some rhythmic indications such as the continuation marks of the harmonic rhythm map.

Roman Numerals				Harmonic Rhythm					Nashville			
I	II–	VI–	VI–	X	X	X	\		1	2–	6–	\
IV	I	V	V	X	X	X	\		4	1	5	\
IV	V	III–	III–	X	X	X	\		4	5	3–	\
IV	IV	V	I	I	X	\	X	X	\	4	\	5	1	\
IV	V	IV	IV	X	X	X	\		4	5	4	\
IV	V	IV	IV	\	X	X	\		4	5	4	\

FIG. 6.11. Analyzing a Progression in Terms of Harmonic Rhythm

Though each line of this progression has distinct sequences of specific chords, the harmonic rhythm repeats for the first three lines. This unifies the section, despite the through-composed arc of these phrases. As with intervallic contour, we must pay close attention to chords that start phrases or sections, or at repetitions. These junctures may either continue or change preceding chords. Transitions across structural boundaries are less prominent than midphrase transitions. As a result, apparently identical chord sequences may also have different harmonic rhythm effects, as with the last two lines.

Since different sequences can share harmonic rhythm profiles, while identical sequences can take on *different* harmonic rhythm profiles (depending on context), the harmonic rhythm aspect can fully "counterpoint" against the progression's functional harmonic meaning.

You can extend harmonic rhythm notation to indicate anticipations or "pushes" of particular chords. These rhythmic effects represent a middle ground between harmonic and accompaniment rhythm. Some pushes are structurally and compositionally essential; in other situations, they represent arrangement or performance aspects. (Nashville notation "pushes," discussed in the sidebar on page 134, show such additional harmonic rhythm aspects with particular visual clarity. These can be imported into harmonic rhythm maps.)

The complex vertical structures of harmony create grey areas in how definitive a change we feel in a given harmonic transition. Changes of inversion or bass line, or chord quality (major or minor, suspensions or upper-structure tones) will shade perceived harmonic rhythm in subtle ways. Building on our earlier discussion of qualities of root tone intervallic motion, movements of a diatonic third can even be heard as softer "color" moves in harmonic rhythm, as compared to the more definitive movements of seconds or fourths.

Still, even a simplified picture of harmonic rhythm reveals patterns that strongly affect the meaning and emotional impact of a chord progression. Working intentionally with harmonic rhythm allows us to vary timings of chord placements in flexible ways, adding meaning and interest to the chords' rhythmic statements in relation to other aspects of the progression, and to other facets.

CYCLIC VS. NARRATIVE PROGRESSIONS

Writing fresh, innovative chord progressions requires more than jamming over familiar chord riffs and cycles. It involves thinking of *progressions* as musical ideas, with their own inbuilt interest. This enables us to write distinctive progressions that avoid cliché patterns. But the distinctiveness and evocativeness of a progression is not a direct function of its structural complexity. In this section we look at chord progressions in terms of their relative degree of internal repetition and variation, distinguishing between cyclic and narrative types of progressions.

Cyclic Progressions

Cyclic progressions are ubiquitous in contemporary music—from mainstream pop, hip-hop, and neo-soul to the growls of indie rock and the plaintive strains of acoustic singer-songwriters. One reason to pay close attention to the qualities of chords and chord transitions, as discussed earlier in this chapter, is to understand how different cyclic progressions can create distinctive emotional qualities. One ubiquitous cycle, VI– IV I V, can be heard in countless contemporary songs. (Dubbed by some the "sensitive singer-songwriter progression," it might be considered the modern successor to the classic "Heart and Soul" progression: I VI– IV V.) Some of the staying power of this progression, which might be said to poignantly evoke the shifting emotional landscape of contemporary angst-ridden youth, can be understood through the alternation of rising and falling transitions in the sequence.

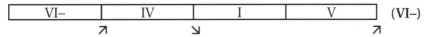

FIG. 6.12. A Common Cyclic Progression

Some cyclic progressions effectively serve the thematic needs of the song. But writing only in cyclic forms is sometimes symptomatic of a process of developing progressions only by jamming and improvisation, and can be very limiting in scope. One weakness in cyclic progressions lies in how cycles create and support sectional form. When you simply repeat a four-bar chord cycle four times for your verse, the chords per se contribute little to outlining or reinforcing sectional form, or transitions between sections. You're forced to fall back on other elements, such as dramatic leaps in vocal range between verses or production effects, to create interest and sectional contrast. Making even one small alteration in the verse—for example, one chord in the last repetition— can shift listeners' perceptions: from a four-chord cycle repeated four times, to a sixteen-bar "statement" with closure or a build of energy toward a new section. (See exercise 6.5.)

Narrative Progressions

Another way to move beyond stock and cliché progressions is by writing longer, through-composed sequences of chords that create and outline sectional form. I call these *narrative* progressions, because the flow of the chords and their transitions often evoke the sense of a story or journey. When writing a narrative progression, whether working from the progression to other facets such as melody or lyric, or writing the progression in response to these elements, I focus on the story the chords are telling.

By "narrative," I don't mean a literal story or even a single emotional interpretation. Rather, I mean a "narrative-seeking" progression—one that sparks associative thinking for the writer, naturally leading to melodic, lyric, and thematic ideas. The "journey" is also not confined to standard progressions. Using the full palette of diatonic chords and transitions, and employing shifts in harmonic rhythm and pace, are key tools for creating interest in these progressions.

I suspect I absorbed this approach from chord-driven styles like bluegrass, and from my experience as a guitar accompanist for Celtic music. But narrative progressions can be used in any style or genre. Consider the harmonic structure of Jimi Hendrix's immortal "Little Wing." Besides Jimi's timeless guitar voicings and solo, and evocative lyrics, the chord progression itself carries inherent emotional meaning. Though it's a single sectional chord progression, repeated for the opening instrumental, two verses, and a closing instrumental, it presents more as a narrative than a cyclic progression. Or consider the music of the Beatles. Each song has the freshness of a new experiment, often in the chord structure—something they (and the world at large) had not tried or heard before. Pop writing in the mid '70s was another golden era for narrative progressions.

A narrative progression has several essential qualities:

- It's more than a short cycle of chords repeated for the duration of a section. It moves in the direction of being "through-composed," with different chords or transitions between chords used over the course of the progression.

- Though not repeating, the progression must still make musical sense to the listener, both in its moment-to-moment flow and as a whole. Particular chords used (relative to key and tonal center), and moves between these chords, create meaning and emotion, separate from whatever melody and lyrics may be put to the chords in the final song.

- This "through-composed" quality and continuity combine to create the sense of a story or a journey that extends through the duration of the progression. If the progression covers a verse, there's a distinctive beginning, middle, and end to the verse. As a result, a narrative progression creates structural spotlights in a section or overall song. A narrative progression can also cover an entire song form of many sections, but in this case is still more than just a sequence of simple chord cycles outlining the main song sections.

Both cyclic and narrative progressions work because of a sense of "flow" from chord to chord. A cyclic progression creates a tight loop with that sense of flow; a narrative progression creates more of a sectional "arc" with a clear beginning, middle, and end. Narrative progressions can incorporate cliché sequences, but generally set them in a context that makes them sound fresh. While there are genres built on short chord cycles, "stock" narrative progressions are rarer. Almost by definition, such progressions have some unique aspect that is likely to become associated with a particular song. Reusing the progression will therefore sound more derivative of that original song. Though chord progressions are not protectible by copyright, any songwriter who reused the main progression of "Little Wing" without giving due credit to the work as a tribute or adaptation would likely call down the wrath of legions of Jimi's fans.

MOTIVIC PROGRESSIONS

Cyclic vs. narrative chord progressions are best thought of as end points on a continuum. In the middle range are progressions involving a fair amount of repetition (like cyclic progressions), but also varying the progression to create a clear sense of a journey throughout the section (like narrative progressions). The repetitions and variations in short sub-sequences of chords form question-answer patterns; hence, I call these *motivic progressions*. You can understand a given chord progression motivically by breaking the progression as a whole into repeating and varying sub-sequences. These chordal "motives" are similar to motives in melody, but unfold at a slower pace within the song. A workable rule of thumb is to treat the chords accompanying each lyric phrase as a unit.

Also, unlike vocal melody, which is naturally punctuated into lyric phrases, the stream of chords in a progression may flow steadily across phrase boundaries. Thus it can be more arbitrary to "parse" a chord progression into motivic units.

Figure 6.13 shows some short examples of these three kinds of progressions.

Cyclic Progression				Motivic Progression				Narrative Progression			
VI–	IV	I	V	VI–	IV	I	V	VI–	IV	I	I
VI–	IV	I	V	VI–	IV	I	I	V	II–	VI–	VI–
VI–	IV	I	V	VI–	IV	I	V	IV	I	V	V
VI–	IV	I	V	VI–	IV	V	V	II–	IV	I	V

FIG. 6.13. Example of Cyclic, Motivic, and Narrative Progressions

- *Cyclic progression.* Repeats or cycles a chord sequence multiple times to create the section. Often the sequence is a chord cliché, but novel sequences can be used in a cyclic fashion.

- *Motivic progression.* In the example, the second line contrasts with the first by holding the third chord (I) for two bars, slowing the harmonic rhythm. The fourth line makes a similar change in harmonic rhythm, this time with the V. This chord has additional "motivic" meanings: as a "question-answer" to the I chord in the second line; or as an accelerating metric displacement forward of the V chord in the preceding third line.

- *Narrative progression.* The third example begins by moving through the same chords as the cyclic version, but with different phrasing and harmonic rhythm (X X X \). The second line uses different chords from the first, but repeats its harmonic rhythm. The third line maintains the same harmonic rhythm, repeating individual chords already heard as well as one transition (IV to I), but displaced metrically forward. The fourth line accelerates or makes more dense the harmonic rhythm, with a change of chord in the last bar (X X X X). Unlike the motivic version, each line in this progression is different. Yet there's enough connection across the different phrases to create a narrative "thread" or through-line.

When I first arrived at Berklee, as a roots-oriented songwriter and Celtic accompanist, I was not a fan of cyclic chord progressions. I felt they were inherently lazy, the sign of lack of harmonic thinking. I have genuinely come to an appreciation of the possibilities for creating meaningful, evocative progressions from anywhere along this continuum. There are also risks and pitfalls with each style of progression—if thrown together in a haphazard way. Cyclic progressions can tell too little of a story. Narrative progressions can wander and meander, telling too much of a story, or too many stories. Motivic progressions, if crowded with too many audible echos and resonances, can bring the progression too much to the foreground, overpowering lyric content or melodic flow.

Whether writing cyclic, narrative, or motivic progressions, in writing from a chord progression as a starting point, the *progression* is the first object of your creative attention. You're trying to work with something fresh and original in the progression—an idea to spur the rest of the song. But even uniqueness and innovativeness is not always required, especially in genres built around canonic progressions. What is important is matching the meaning and emotion of the progression to the overall song.

EXERCISE 6.5. UNWINDING A CHORD CYCLE TO A NARRATIVE PROGRESSION

Begin with a four-chord cycle repeated four times to form a song section. Make a series of one-chord-at-a-time revisions to the cycle, seeing how these changes gradually create more of a motivic, then a through-composed feel for the section. End with a "narrative" version where no line is literally repeated. Test that the section makes narrative sense by seeing whether you can play through it from memory, or even hear the progression "in your mind's ear." Use functional notation (Roman numerals or Nashville notation as you prefer), and notate as well the root intervallic contour, the rising/falling root pattern, and the harmonic rhythm of the progression. You can use these auxiliary notations to help guide your incremental revisions, or to assess and possibly polish the final result. In figure 6.14, I've applied this cycle-to-narrative revision strategy, starting from the "sensitive-songwriter" VI– IV I V cliché discussed earlier.

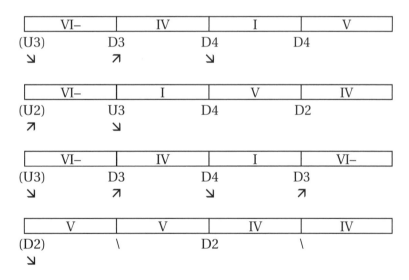

FIG. 6.14. Adding Some Sense to the Sensitive Singer-Songwriter Progression

Note the new motivic interest in the progression: With the variations introduced, the remaining repetition of lines 1 and 3 now form a more distinct *abac* phrase pattern. The chord motive I V is repeated but metrically displaced forward across lines 1 and 2. The chord motive V IV in line 2 recurs, decelerated by rhythmic augmentation, as line 4. Study the progression, seeing what motivic devices you can identify in patterns of chords, chord moves, harmonic rhythm, and phrase structure. Compose your own "unwinding" of the Sensitive Singer-Songwriter Progression. Then start with your own simple four-chord cycle, unwind it into a narrative progression—and make it into a song.

We've explored a few interrelated yet independent ways of creating meaning and emotion in chord progressions: harmonic functions of chords relative to tonal center, key, and mode; intervallic root motion; harmonic rhythm; cyclic, narrative, and motivic progressions. By working with each of these aspects of chord progressions, both in isolation and in interaction, we can create more evocative progressions that are truly "progressive" in a more fundamental sense—possessing that elusive quality Oliver Wendell Holmes Sr. called "the simplicity on the other side of complexity."

CHAPTER 7

Melody/Harmony Connections

In this section, we outline a series of melody/harmony strategies, in order of increasing independence of melodic and harmonic elements. Rather than outline separate process directions of setting *from* melody *to* harmony or vice versa, we'll describe a series of melody/harmony strategies in terms of *textures* that combine melodic and harmonic material in varying ways. Where appropriate, we may describe complementary textures that invert a given relationship of melody and harmony. While there is no intended aesthetic preference in the order in which these strategies are presented, there is an implied progression in terms of skill levels. Each texture has distinct emotional connotations and spotlighting effects, bringing various facets to the foreground or background.

Used appropriately, each of these textural effects can serve the needs of the song. Some textures may be useful in earlier stages of writing, and then may be transformed or developed as the song progresses. But there's always a risk of any texture devolving into a "lazy" strategy. We may fall back on certain textures more by habit than by design, and wind up with mismatches between the texture employed and our desired effect. If you're thinking harmony as you write melody, you'll tend to fall back on melodic habits requiring less thought, and vice versa.

Imagine the songwriting facets as boundaries inscribing a creative *space* of possibilities. We want to be able to create material anywhere in this space. We're not just looking for a life raft to take us from facet to facet; we want to swim in the whole ocean. That means being able to write different kinds of melodies—melodies locked tightly to harmony, melodies that float independently of harmony, and melodies that fall anywhere along this spectrum of possible melody/harmony textures. Rather than thinking in terms of a single creative operation—"setting from melody to harmony"—think of transforming a melody along the melody/harmony continuum. We want similar freedom in our chord progressions, whether we write these in response to melodies or as a springboard for melodies to come.

INDEPENDENCE OF MELODY AND HARMONY

In theory, you can start from a song seed in any facet (rhythm, lyric, melody, or harmony) and set it to material in any facet. But as Einstein is reputed to have said, "In theory, theory and practice are the same. In practice, they are not." A repertoire of different strategies helps if applying them gets you to different results. But if the seeds we start with are not actually separable but composites, the promised fruitfulness of this process flexibility is a bit of a fiction. Nowhere is this more of an issue than in relationships between melodies and chord progressions.

Achieving true independence of melody and harmony is not so easy, even when apparently working with each element in isolation. To put this to the test, try to invent a song melody singing a cappella (without playing chords behind it). You'll likely still hear an *implied* harmony—your melody generated with associations to imagined chords. Try to write *multiple* chordal settings for the melody. As you put different sets of chords to melody, the expected "already heard" chords will sound right; significantly different choices may sound "funny."

This close linkage of melodic and harmonic materials is in part a consequence of our spending our lives listening to harmonically saturated music. Conventional training in music theory can even work *against* you, making it more difficult to hear or create melodies without a harmonic context. Most Western-trained musicians and listeners are acculturated to harmony, by osmosis if not by formal training. Thus, they tend to hear a kind of silent chordal accompaniment when listening to even a solo melody.

Working the other way, *from* chords to melody, presents different problems of independence. We can more easily write chord progressions without singing melodies over them. We may hear filler melodies as we write the chords, but it's not too hard to hold these in abeyance and revise them later. The challenge here is, I believe, twofold: to find melodies that move sufficiently independently against chord progressions, and to find progressions not confined only to the logic of standard tonal harmony. Again, the influence of our harmonic training and expectations can be surprisingly stubborn. I often challenge student writers to create unusual chord progressions, and then to write melodies to those progressions. A writer may create a distinctive progression, one genuinely new for them. Yet, melodies they write to those progressions frequently sound as if they were written, not to the more innovative progression, but instead to an intuitively heard cliché progression that follows more expected harmonic paths and phrasing.

Musicians with better-developed chops on a harmonic instrument like piano or guitar can generally devise more complex progressions, and even hear them away from their instrument. But that doesn't translate directly to the skill of writing melodies over those chords that move in a more independent way. To develop this kind of bilateral independence between melody and harmony, we need to both learn and possibly *unlearn* some things.

If we start only from melodies where chords are already embedded or implied, or can only hear melodies to chord progressions that are "locked" to those progressions, then writing in "different directions" won't yield fundamentally different kinds of songs. To expand the range, scope, innovativeness, and integrity of our songwriting, we want to find our way to new kinds of melodies, chord progressions, and combinations thereof. This is where the proverbial melodic rubber meets the chordal road.

MELODY/HARMONY COUNTERPOINT

We'll organize our survey of the repertoire of melody/harmony textures by analogy to principles of counterpoint, adapted to our songwriting context. We'll further broaden this analogy to counterpoint in our next chapter on structure, adapting the principles to contrasting (i.e., "contrapuntal") structures and motivic patterns in different facets.

Music theorists first articulated melodic principles in the context of *counterpoint*—interwoven *multiple* melodic lines. Some songwriting forms and genres, such as choral writing or a cappella group arrangements, are intimately tied to multi-voice textures. Our restricted scope of songwriting, here, involves a single vocal melodic line sung to chordal accompaniment. Still, we can adapt some concepts from traditional counterpoint for this more specific songwriting context.

A primary goal of counterpoint is independent motion between voices (though similar and even parallel motion are constituent textures). Similarly, we can recognize a "contrapuntal" relationship between a song's melody and harmony. Treating the harmonic accompaniment in a song as a "voice" depends on hearing the various implicit "melodic" lines in the chord progression, as discussed in the "Harmony" chapter. Any of these "line" aspects of chord progressions can be heard as countermelodies against the vocal melody, analogous to the multiple peer melodies of choral textures. The analogy is only approximate, however. We respond differently as listeners to vocal melody and to melodies in chord progressions, especially melodies formed by sequences of root tones.

As in traditional counterpoint, we want an overall flexibility of independent motion between these voices, though that may involve passages of similar or parallel motion. We also want process flexibility—the ability to work (set) from either chords or vocal melody as the "given" (i.e., "cantus firmus") material to which we respond.

Species Counterpoint in Melody/Harmony

Traditional counterpoint[16] developed the notion of various *species* of contrapuntal motion, in part as a pedagogical sequencing into textures of increasing compositional challenge. In first-species counterpoint, notes of respective voices move 1-to-1, at the same melodic pace. Further species change this relationship, so voices move 1 note against 2, 1 against 3, etc. Lastly, "florid" counterpoint allows more freedom of pace across and among voices.

There are characteristic pace relationships between the implied "melodies of the chords" and vocal melody in a song. Typically, movement of chords (and thus of their implied melodic lines) is slower than the changing pitches of vocal melody. Thus the basic melody/harmony connection in songwriting generally feels like counterpoint of species 2 or 3, in contrast to the shifting rhythmic and pace relationships between lyric rhythm and melodic contour (discussed in the "Melody" chapter).

The proportions and pace are not strict. Given overall differences in pace for both melodic and harmonic motion, there's great freedom in ways these two threads can move. A chord may be held while the melody moves, or chords can move when the melody is still—e.g., behind a long sustained note (or repeated pitches) of the vocal melody, or around phrases. Figure 7.1 shows a simple example section exploiting this variability in the pace of melodic and harmonic movement.

FIG. 7.1. Varying Melodic/Lyric and Harmonic Pace

This sense for the relative pace of motion in vocal melody and chords respectively has practical implications. First, we need to pay close attention to moments where vocal melody sounds against *changes* in the chord progression. Chord changes are rhythmic spotlight positions, heightening effects such as chord tone vs. non-chord tone relations between melody and the "chord of the moment." Second, it's at the slower pace of the "melody of the chords" that rhythmic patterns of the chord progression itself— the harmonic rhythm—are articulated. These patterns are hard to hear, not just because they move slower than rhythmic patterns in vocal melody; they're also only heard superimposed on (or heard beneath) the melody, unless you work with the harmony *in isolation.* Chords-first writing helps you to hear this harmonic rhythm more clearly,

16. Traditional counterpoint studies were canonized by Joseph Fuchs' classic *Gradus Ad Parnassum* (1725).

and eventually to compose and execute more elusive rhythmic patterns. This enables you to experiment more boldly with effects such as rhythmic shifts in the chord progression: varying durations on chords, using anticipations and moves on weak metric beats, etc.

Contrapuntal Motion in Melody/Harmony

Another key concept in counterpoint involves different kinds of motion between voices:

- In *similar* motion, voices move in the same direction (higher or lower in pitch). *Parallel* motion is similar motion by the same interval (in diatonic scale degrees; that is, one voice might move a minor third while one moves a major third, etc.).
- In *oblique* motion, one voice stays still as the other moves.
- In *contrary motion*, voices move in different directions.

Contrary motion is given a certain esteem in contrapuntal thinking: in part because it requires the most skill and preparation to conceive and perform, and in part because of its effect on the ear, creating a simultaneous pull of focus to both voices. However, practical contrapuntal textures mix all these types of motion in any extended passage, balancing independence of separate voices with harmonic agreement in their juxtaposition.

MELODY/HARMONY CONTRAPUNTAL TEXTURES

These different types of contrapuntal motion have counterparts in the varied textural strategies for melody/harmony connections in songwriting we'll explore in the following sections.

Pedal-Point Melodies

The term "pedal" or "pedal point" is usually applied to a note in a lower bass line of the harmony, repeatedly sounded under a melodic passage. The harmony is usually active during such passages. In a songwriting context, however, simply holding one chord, or even a drone or partial chord, for a passage or a section can be viewed as an extension of this kind of texture.

We can also consider a complementary texture, where the vocal melody maintains a held tone against changing chords—in effect, a "pedal point melody." This texture echoes the contrapuntal idea of *oblique motion*, where one voice is still as another moves. The quiescent melodic line spotlights or moves to the foreground the root or bass line motion of the chords, which in turn recolor the harmonic interpretations of the held melody note. Using a chanting tone melodic contour is also a good strategy for focusing attention on lyric content. Rhythmic effects are often used in pedal-point melody for additional interest.

Great songwriters and composers in all styles and genres have used this texture to compelling effect: from Antonio Carlos Jobim's classic "One Note Samba" to the opening phrases of Donovan's "Catch the Wind." It's a sound now iconic in the music of contemporary acoustic singer-songwriters. A simple example is shown below. Chord roots are indicated in the bottom staff. The "pedal-point" melody creates pleasing effects, as the held C note shifts between chord tone and non-chord tone roles against the chord of the moment: 5 of the F, 6 of the E♭, 3 of the A♭, 2 of the B♭. A bit more interest comes through varying the rhythmic pattern across the four bars.

FIG. 7.2. Pedal-Point Melody. Relatively dependent on chord progression.

A pedal-point melody can hold notes on different scale degrees relative to underlying chords, forming varying chord tone and non-chord relations. Here's another example over the same chords, with the held note forming successively a 2, 3, major 7, and 6 (resolving to a 5) against the underlying chords:

FIG. 7.3. Non-Chord Tone Melodic Pedal Point

The biggest risk in pedal-point textures (of either variety) is when they're used as an improvisational "cheat," rather than a compositional choice, to achieve a specific emotional or narrative effect. But used with intent, they offer a powerful technique for spotlighting, and especially for sectional contrast.

Ostinato Melodies

An extension of the pedal-point melody strategy sets up a repeating melodic figure or ostinato against a sequence of changing chords. As with a single-note pedal, the repeating melodic figure is recolored by the shifting interpretation against the changing chords. This recoloring is more effective when the melodic figure isn't too closely tied to a single chordal area (as with a scalar passage or arpeggiated chord).

Often, repeated rhythms help reinforce the ostinato pattern, as in figure 7.4. Here the E note in the repeated ostinato figure takes on shifting non-chord tone roles over each chord, until it resolves as the third of the C chord.

FIG. 7.4. Melodic Ostinato over Changing Chords

This strategy extends a sense of oblique motion to the border between melody per se and phrase structure—not the melodic note, but the melodic figure or *motive* remains fixed as the chords move. The example shows a typical template: the melodic motive is varied (by truncation) at the end of the phrase, setting an *aaab* melodic structure against the through-written chordal line.

A melody that shifts in range and/or contour against a cyclic chord progression within a section inverts this texture. As repetition or cycles are brought to the foreground in either melody or harmony, a secondary "pace" is created at the motivic level. This pace interacts with other rhythmic aspects of the song.

Parallel Textures

The contrapuntal device of *similar* or even *parallel* motion is reflected when vocal melody follows a melodic aspect of the chord progression. The paralleling can track various melodic threads in the harmony. Also, as with pedal-point melody, the vocal melody can "track" the chord melody at varying intervals, such as at the third or fifth, or with non-chord tones. The most audible, and potentially problematic, case is when vocal melody sounds or doubles chord roots. Figure 7.5 shows two largely parallel-motion melodic settings for a chord progression: one doubling chord roots, the other hovering around the 3rd of the chords.

FIG. 7.5. Melody Moving in Parallel to Chord Root Tones

As the second example above shows, this type of similar or parallel motion might be disguised by activity in the melody, yet still contribute a weakness to the overall texture. The vocal melody can be very active in relation to chord movement, yet still be moving in a harmonically parallel way. This is a case where vocal prowess in particular needs to be applied with caution. Vocalist-writers will easily add flourishes around a melody that still essentially parallels the harmony. This may yield a compelling vocal performance, but a less interesting melody and song.

Discerning the underlying relationship requires distinguishing *anchor tones* and *ornamental tones* in the vocal melody. Anchor tones are notes spotlighted by falling on main metric stressed beats, or on beats where chords change (even if metrically weak). Ornamental tones can embroider around anchor tones, but the relations of anchor tones to the underlying chords knit the bones of the song. In general, less stable tones or non-chord tones suggest more independence between melody and harmony. But this can be deceptive. A parallel voice-leading texture can be created even with (usually mild) non-chord tone intervals, if they're maintained between melody and chord roots for an extended passage.

A good technique to evaluate if your melody is moving against the chords in too parallel a fashion is to annotate the scale degree (whether chord tone or non-chord tone) formed by each melody note falling on important metric positions where the chords change. If you discover a long series of melody notes chiming in unisons or thirds with the progression's roots, you may have a problem on the "parallel bars."

Effects and Uses of Parallel Motion

Similar or parallel motion in any materials *intensifies* motion or thickens texture. It's a strong effect, best used when you intend to reinforce that movement. For example, you can use parallel motion to create a distinct, strong texture in one song section; then shift texture in another section, supporting cohesion within and contrast between the sections.

Risks with Parallel Motion

Where pedal-point melody tends to keep melodies in a very confined range, paralleling root motion with vocal melody tends to introduce larger leaps in the melodic range. In writing the melody, you can transpose these intervals in various ways (just as bass players make register and octave choices, even in a largely chord root-oriented style, that dramatically affect the shape of the bass line). Still, what works well as a chord sequence, or a "melody of chord root tones," may not translate well into vocal melody (and vice versa). A complementary problem can arise with chord progressions written in too "melodic" a way. Overuse of step intervals in root motion, and particularly sequences of scalar motion in chord roots (e.g., IV III– II– I) can be a sign of thinking too "melodically" with your chords.

Also, as with pedal-point or ostinato textures, similar or parallel motion between melody and harmony can be a bit of a "cheat" in the writing process. If you play your instrument and compose and sing your melody at the same time, you're likely to slip into parallel phrasing simply because it's hard to improvise two independent ideas at the same time, like rubbing your harmonic tummy while patting your melodic head. The results may not suit the expressive needs of the song. If a progression is not intrinsically interesting, seconding it in vocal melody won't necessarily improve it. (It's a bit like those jingoistic tourists in a foreign country, who think shouting in English rather than speaking in English will somehow make their meaning clearer.)

Similar rather than parallel motion, parallel motion maintained at non-chord tone intervals to chord roots, parallel motion following interior guide-tone lines rather than root tones, and parallel motion to root tones in the presence of a strong bass-line idea in the accompaniment, are all ways to mitigate the overdramatizing effects of parallel melody/harmony texture. Or—as with any textural strategy—when all else fails, rewrite.

Lazy Melodic Lines against Chords

Another texture, prevalent when setting *to* melody *from* a chord progression, creates a vocal melodic line moving in a "lazy" or "least motion" kind of way, with a preference for repeated notes, small intervals or step-wise motion, and frequent changes of direction. In a nutshell, to create a lazy line:

- Pick a starting note against your first chord—usually (but not always) a chord tone.

- Move *only when you have to* (the "lazy" part of the strategy) in response to changing chords. At each new chord, stay on the same tone or make a *small intervallic* move—usually to a chord tone relative to the new chord.

- Move directionally in ways that maximize balance, so the melody tends to circle around the initial tone, extending the overall range as little as possible.

Held notes will feel like a pedal-point texture; moving notes may parallel root motion of chords, especially chord moves by seconds or thirds. But the lazy pull toward minimal melodic movement fights against the tendency to parallel chord roots when the roots move by intervals of a fourth (or fifth). If melodic contour stays with common or close tones, the relation of melody note to chord root changes, as in the following small example over a cliché chord sequence (I IV I V) cycled twice, where the relation shifts from 3 to root to 3 to 5.

FIG. 7.6. Melody Dependent on a Harmonic Progression

Though my term "lazy" may sound vaguely judgmental, this is actually a time-honored strategy useful in many situations. Since smaller intervals are generally easier to sing than larger leaps, they yield more singable melodies with better continuity. Directional changes circling around the starting tone keep the overall melodic range confined. Thus, it's a natural strategy for singer/ writers who are not very confident about their range. It also approximates the techniques harmony singers use to find harmony parts by ear: find your "tonal zone," then move lazily. (For harmony singing, also avoid doubling notes of neighboring voices.)

But melodies you find this way are not always interesting in contour or shape, or vocally challenging and dramatic in range or intervallic variety. They can tend to "drift" or "undulate." Mostly, these problems arise when the melodic idea is not just responsive to but *too dependent on* the chord progression. There's nothing wrong with using lazy melody; just don't be lazy about it!

Using only chord tones is not fundamental to this texture, but it's often a characteristic of the style applied in a less intentional way. As with the strategies seen earlier, it's also possible to rely too much on easy non-chord tone relations (singer-songwriters seem to love 2s and 9s these days), providing a kind of surface tension but not real interest or melody–harmony independence.

By nature, this melodic texture, being both "chord-led" and "lazy" (minimizing melodic activity), spotlights the chords. Applied to stock or cliché chord sequences, as in figure 7.6, this can lead to a bland overall texture. Providing some rhythmic interest then becomes almost essential, such as the anticipations and slight variations shown.

On the other hand, this effect of bringing chords to the foreground can be useful when the chord progression *does* hold intrinsic interest, especially with edgy or surprising chord moves. In these circumstances, lazy melodic lines can serve as voice-leading "glue," smoothing over otherwise disorienting harmonic changes.

EXERCISE 7.1. LAZY MELODY OVER CRAZY CHORDS[17]

Write an 8- to 12-chord progression, choosing freely and somewhat randomly among a mixed palette of major, minor, diminished, and augmented triads, *not* diatonic to a single key or mode. For the purposes of this exercise, the effect of the progression on its own should be as random and disorienting as possible. Get as wacky as you like!

Now write a "lazy" melody to the progression. Exploit common tones where they occur in chord transitions, or move lazily to the nearest chord tone in the next chord. You can use only chord tones for each chord of the moment, or let lazy voice leading suggest non-chord tone relations by holding chord tones against the next change or anticipating chords. Start in turn with each note of the first chord, and move lazily ("drift") up or down, or let the melody undulate

---

17. This is an adaptation of the "48 x 48" exercise from Mick Goodrick's *The Advancing Guitarist* (Hal Leonard Corp., 1987). In that book, the context is melodic improvisation on guitar, but it's a great exercise for songwriters as well.

around the starting note. This yields a variety of distinct melodic "strands" to explore. Compare the effect of the progression on its own and with each of these "smoothing" melodies. Since the chords are not (intentionally) related by key or functional progression, you can also reverse (i.e., retrograde) such a progression and melody, and/or rotate it to start on a different chord. Music for haunted calliopes and zombie movies…. Loads of fun!

Chord-Driven Melodies

Another common melody–harmony texture could be characterized as "chord-driven melody." These melodies move more freely and energetically than lazy voice leading. Since the technique is freer with overall range and intervallic motion, it can yield more vocally engaging and dramatic melodies. (After all, unless we're singing "Up a Lazy River," we don't want our vocalists to sound lazy!)

Like lazy voice-led melody, though, these more active chord-led melodies are also locked to a preconceived chordal substrate that's directly audible in the melody, often to less than satisfying effect. Play such a melody without chordal accompaniment, and you'll still hear harmony strongly implied. Some telltales of chord-driven melody are a preponderance of scalar steps or skips forming arpeggiated chords, and anchor tones that are mostly chord tones. You can't write a melody that completely avoids these kinds of figures, but they dominate the texture in chord-driven melodic lines. There's also a tendency towards a busy, florid, or notey pace relationship between melody and harmony, with steady propulsive rhythms in both facets.

Like lazy melody, chord-driven melody tends to arise when chords are written first and you set melody *to* those chords. The busy melody can be an attempt to create interest over a relatively dull progression or a reaction to a progression with lots of its own twists and turns. In the latter case—with busy, complex chords—the melody is often tied to the chords simply because compositionally, we're struggling to keep up with them. In this sense, chord-driven melody is less like part-singing in a choral setting, and more similar to melodic instrumental soloing over chord changes. The danger is that such melodies, through being locked too closely to the chords, can lack melodic narrative or flow.

Figure 7.7 is a chord-driven melody of this kind, written over a busier chord progression than our earlier examples:

FIG. 7.7. Freely-Moving Melody Locked to a Chord Progression

This melody has reasonable range and intervallic motion for vocal melody, and displays some motivic interest—such as the ascending passage in bar 1 echoed, with a rhythmic variation, in bar 2. But it feels and sounds "chordy," a bit busy and instrumental. Many of the scalar passages are passing-tone elaborations of chord arpeggio "skeletons" woven throughout the melody. The few stressed non-chord tones, e.g., the appoggiaturas in the middle of bars 2 and 3, resolve quickly to chord tones. That gives the melody the feel of being mostly "tugged along" by the chords, sometimes pulling, but without its own thread or line. To a jazz musician, it might sound like an amateurish solo.

Even when writing melody first in process, we can wind up writing chord-driven melodies, because we're instinctively hearing chord progressions in our mind's ear. Since these chords are almost subliminal, they're more likely to be "stock" or cliché rather than progressions with intrinsic interest. Now, we have the effect of bad melodic soloing, but at least over banal chord changes—woo-hoo! Chord-driven melodies are typical of writers with more of an instrumental background, and they can tend to move in the direction of instrumental melodies. In the roots music world, many recently composed fiddle tunes sound like this—often a sign of thinking chord progression first, then filling in melody over chords. (As a fiddle tune composer or "tunesmith" as well as songwriter, I can say these are generally not my favorite new fiddle tunes.) Improvising soloists who know a progression well can anticipate the chords enough to make the melody sound like it's at least pulling rather than being pulled by the chords, but the horse is still hitched to the wagon.

Two complementary strategies can help you move beyond limitations of harmony-led melodic textures:

- When working *from* chords *to* melody, make ample use of non-chord tones, especially on metrically strong positions. Don't use these simply to be *contrary* to the harmony. Find melodic lines that make their own sense as contours and narratives. Let these lines cross against and "fight" chords with momentary tensions, and don't shy away from them.

- Conversely, to move beyond writing only to preconceived chord progressions when working melody first, practice writing melodies over a *tonic drone*. The drone can be arhythmic or pulsed, a single note or octave or thickened by a 1–5 voicing, or even a single-chord rhythmic riff (though denser chord structures will influence your melody). Focus on the varied effects of stability/instability and tone tendencies in melody alone, relative to the tonal center and key/mode. This practice will gradually increase your ability to write melodies that move more independently, even in the presence of a chord progression. To paraphrase a jazz musicians' dictum: Play (or in this case, write melody to) the key, not the chord. Your goal can be a melody that stands alone in the final texture of the song, *without* chordal accompaniment: either melodies over a drone texture or true a cappella songs. Or use this as a process tool for early melodic sketches, adding chords later.

Independent Tonal Melody

In his seminal book *Melody in Songwriting* (Berklee Press, 2000), Jack Perricone introduced the notion of *independent melody* in the context of songwriting: as a melody sufficiently well formed to be interesting, engaging, and memorable without harmonic accompaniment. Contrast a piece like "One Note Samba" (mentioned earlier in the context of "pedal-point" melodies) with "Over the Rainbow." In the former, melodic interest is created through interaction with the harmony. The latter tune stands on its own, with intrinsic melodic interest. Unlike a chord-driven melody, its contour with its varied leaps and scalar passages is memorable, expressive to sing. This expressive contour is inherently *evocative*—seeming to contain or echo the narrative theme, imagery, and character of the song. Thus, this melody is independent in the sense of "distinct and memorable." It doesn't require the presence of chords to be effective, and could even be sung beautifully a cappella. Note it's not a superior piece of *music* to "One Note Samba"; it's a different *type* of tune. "One Note Samba" uses its chanting-tone melody just as artfully.

Figure 7.8 is a melody in an "Over the Rainbow" vein—though not nearly as good. (Like its immortal precursor, it has an octave leap—but at the end of the section, and down instead of up!) It was written *without* an explicit, predetermined chord progression in mind.

FIG. 7.8. Stand-Alone Tonal Melody. Good melodic continuity.

This melody moves relatively freely in range and intervallic variety, showing both continuity and unity. It covers a good range for vocal melody: an octave plus diminished fifth, from the leading tone below the tonic to a fourth above the octave. It mixes steps, skips, and leaps, avoiding extended passages that are purely scalar or arpeggiated. The phrases cadence on structural tones that take on meaning and create contrast in terms of stable vs. unstable relation to the tonal center (F). The melody uses several motivic devices, including repetition, sequence, and extension. It has an arc, a narrative; it stands on its own and tells a story.

Partly as a result of these attributes, one could harmonize this melody in various ways. Two possibilities are shown in figure 7.9.

FIG. 7.9. Alternate Harmonizations of a Stand-Alone Tonal Melody

As these alternate harmonizations demonstrate, different harmonic settings can shift chord tone/non-chord tone relationships of given notes, e.g., the C(add9) chord against the D note in the last line of version 2. We can range from what a more restrained jazz "comper" might do, towards more extensive reharmonization—even shifting tonic, subdominant, or dominant harmonic functions on key notes (as in the fifth measures of the respective versions). Because of this freedom, progressions can follow their own voice-leading or bass-line logic, as in the line cliché in the second line of version 1, or the more unexpected linear bass line in the second line of version 2.

This harmonic flexibility can be used in developing or revising the song, or structurally—varying harmonizations of different repetitions of the same melodic figure or phrase within or across sections of the song. What's remarkable is that harmonic progressions of such distinctive design can be created "after the fact," set to melodies initially composed largely by reference to a tonal center and motivic principles. However, a key to this flexibility is that both melodies and harmony are, in the end, firmly rooted in the feel of major/minor tonality. This is evident from certain aspects of the example melody. The key is unambiguously suggested, by clues such as the leading-tone interval resolving back to the tonic, and the presence of tritone intervals (such as the E and B♭ in measure 6). Even the melody's motivic construction is typical of techniques used for tonal melody. By relying heavily on *sequence* (both consecutively and at matched points in phrases) at the interval of the second, the melody combines figural integrity with the effects of recoloring chord tone/non-chord tone relations of constituent notes to the tonal center.

I believe these techniques lie at the heart of the elegance and sophistication of the Great American Songbook and related styles. While these vocal melodies characteristically moved in ways very different than vocal lines developed for early polyphonic music, it could be argued that the melody/harmony relationships of this classic era of song repertoire express deep contrapuntal principles. Certainly, they represent an apotheosis of the progressive set of techniques explored so far in this chapter, for achieving independence of vocal melody with underlying harmony. These techniques allow creation of melodies with intrinsic interest in melodic contour, well suited to expressive styles that emphasize range and other aspects of vocal performance. The generations of interpreters, arrangers, and improvisers that have used this repertoire as a foundation have built their art on these inner principles of construction in the songs themselves.

For contemporary songwriters, these techniques also extend process flexibility, allowing us to work either melody first or chords first while still achieving a measure of independence in the resulting texture. A critical question remains. Can these techniques be applied and extended—or can comparable techniques be found—in other melodic and harmonic traditions?

MODAL MELODY/HARMONY

Much of the world's melodic music, and much contemporary popular music as well, is not driven primarily by functional harmonic progressions. I'd include in this category a vast territory of modal and pentatonic melody that can be found in music of many cultures and eras. (I won't address purely *atonal* melody here; this would take us into domains of experimental composition beyond our scope.) One characteristic of such melodies is that they hold intrinsic interest without chords. Many such melodies were composed by musicians with no training in formal harmony, and in communities and styles where harmonic accompaniment was not part of traditional ensembles. This independence from a harmonic substrate can extend to ambiguity of where the tonal center is felt to be. For certain pentatonic melodies, even hearing them in the context of a full diatonic modal scale allows for alternate interpretations.

Such traditional melodies are beautiful and memorable in their own right, and in some traditions (such as Irish *séan-nos* or "old-style" unaccompanied ballads) are performed even today with no harmonic accompaniment. However, as traditional music styles have made the transition to contemporary audiences, one aspect of this evolution has been adventurous exploration of diverse approaches to harmonic accompaniment—for music originally conceived and performed in primarily melodic contexts. Accompaniment generally makes such music more accessible to modern harmonically acclimatized ears. Yet, the modal structure of the music allows for intriguingly open possibilities for harmonic interpretation, since many of the tunes were not originally constructed around preconceived harmonies. Contemporary traditional musicians explore these alternative harmonic possibilities in innovative arrangements and adaptations.

Expanding the Songbook

Even when working melody first, the Great American Songbook writers composed from an intuitive grounding in the language of tonal harmony. Like natural language, we absorb this vocabulary and "grammar" through acculturation and continual exposure to music in that harmonic style. Similarly, to learn to compose modal or pentatonic melodies, you need to gain some familiarity with the repertoire, idioms, and traditions where such melodic forms are native. It's helpful to learn various modal and pentatonic scales, and to set out bravely to write in them. But to write convincingly in these styles, and more importantly, to make such resources part of your vocabulary as a writer, there's no substitute for full immersion in the real stuff. I developed much of my own musical style through years of listening to diverse folk and world music repertoire, particularly Irish and American old-time ballads and fiddle tunes rooted in modal and pentatonic melodies.

To expand your work in the full 360° songwriting sense, I warmly recommend that you check out "the music of the rest of the planet." But though I love these traditions, and hope you'll find new (and old) music you'll fall in love with as well, I also believe these resources can be applied broadly across genres and styles. Through my continuing education in contemporary music by my Berklee students (that is, teachers), I'm struck by the strongly modal and pentatonic aspects of melodies across a wide variety of current music—from neo-soul to topline pop writing (not to mention the resurgence of interest in roots music styles).

Counterpoint in Modal Melody/Harmony

Just as they're conceived independently of chords, modal and pentatonic melodies also exhibit intriguing freedom in rhythm and phrasing. This rhythmic freedom stems in part from an intimate connection of song melodies to lyrics, although melodies and lyrics also intermix and recombine over time. Irregular time signatures and phrase lengths might exactly match the lyrics' ebb and flow, or might sometimes mischievously fight the lyric with archaic mis-settings, breaking "conversational prosody" rules right and left.

Because many earlier traditional melodies were not composed based on a harmonic substrate, they depend for their musical interest and integrity, not just on a richer variety of tonalities to modern ears, but also on a remarkable dense web of *motivic* relationships within the music. This dense motivic approach can be applied to working chords first, with chords drawn from modal scales. In principle, this polarity between tonal and modal resources could be explored in a full 360° songwriting sense, working from directions of both melody and harmony. The resulting musical possibilities hold the promise of achieving a different kind of independence.

To bring these various musical worlds together, into a comprehensive "global school" of songwriting, is work for another day. (I admit it—there's my "hole for a sequel, big enough to drive a truck through.") But as a suggestive example, I offer, in figure 7.10, a melody composed without a preconceived single harmonic interpretation. The melody is mostly pentatonic, shifting to a modal feel at the end of the phrase. Yet, it is not strongly marked as being in any particular folk or ethnic style.

FIG. 7.10. Pentatonic/Modal Melody

This melody was neither generated in response to chords nor locked to an implicit set of chords. Though quite different in character from the tonal melody example in figure 7.8, like that melody it has characteristics well-suited to *vocal* melody. The melodic contour is shaped by a unique peak or high point (the G in measure 1), and valley or low point (the D in measure 5). It uses varied interval sizes and directional changes. The only arpeggiated chords occur across measure and implied subphrase boundaries (F D A across measures 2 and 3, and A F D across measures 4 and 5). Though using a range of rhythmic durations, the melody does not depend for interest solely on repeating rhythmic figures; it's no more rhythmically than harmonically driven.

Rather, the sense and narrative of the melody derives largely from its *motivic* construction. The melodic contour elaborates an initial figural idea (D G F D) with a variety of motivic devices. Again, as with the tonal melody of figure 7.8, it uses sequence—but at the distance of a fourth. The result is a weakening of the sense of tonal center, with melodic contour taking more prominence. It also employs other devices such as isomelody (same melodic contour, varying rhythmic pattern), displacement (C A G A in measures 4 and across measures 6 and 7), and truncation.

As we sketch various harmonizations of this melody, differing chord choices change the chord tone vs. non-chord tone roles of various notes. Not only individual chords, but the overall apparent tonal center and mode (and therefore the palette of available diatonic chords) can shift. We might select from alternatives sketched during composition, or structure several alternatives directly into contrasting harmonizations of repeated melodic phrases.

Figure 7.11 shows four different "melody-led" harmonizations for the melody of figure 7.10. Harmonizations (a) and (b) interpret the melody in the tonal centers and modes of D Dorian and G Dorian respectively, made possible by the pentatonic figure and use of sequence. Harmonization (c) uses surprising juxtapositions of chords against the melodic line, as root motion in the progression takes on its own "melodic" and motivic aspect against the vocal melody. Harmonization (d) shows how the melody can preserve narrative flow, set against a suspended chordal drone.

FIG. 7.11. Harmonizations of Melody from Figure 7.10

Modal Palettes and Mosaics

While these various harmonic settings reveal something of the flexibility of the source melody, they are not necessarily distinct, in sound or process of generation, from tonal harmonizations showed earlier. If you build modal progressions seeking only the same kinds of "narrative progressions" we associate with tonal harmony, the resources can appear limited, and even confining. However, there is a different approach that can produce strikingly different textures. If, in an independent tonal melody, we melodize the key, not the chord, perhaps "independent modal harmony" involves harmonizing the mode, not the tune.

Where the link between independent tonal melody and harmony depends on a shared tonal framework, the link between modal/pentatonic melody and harmony can be thought of as a kind of "canvas"—painted or colored by chords drawn from various "palettes," each defined by a given mode. Since melodic phrases can move between modes or, with pentatonic materials, allow for alternate modal interpretations, sometimes multiple palettes are available.

You can draw chord sequences from these palettes that create their effect more strongly by motivic principles—a kind of chord "mosaic" as it were. Such mosaics may involve rapid changes of chords compared to more conventional progressions, though the chords themselves are largely diatonic to a mode (at least in any adjacent passage). In contrapuntal terms, the chord sequence "thread" is brought to more prominence relative to the melody than in typical melody/harmony textures. (In a songwriting context, of course, these denser contrapuntal melody/harmony textures need to be reconciled with an appropriate focus on the lyric.)

In figure 7.12 we show some additional harmonizations for the melody of figure 7.10, in this "mosaic" textural style. For ease of comparison, I've kept harmonic pace consistent across the versions. From a process perspective, these chord mosaics can be generated in a more independent fashion, following their own design rules and implicit "root tone melody" relationships. Thus they may interact with the vocal melody in complex and surprising ways. Unusual non-chord tone relationships can be smoothed by the linear context of the moving chords, while even chord tone matches can be surprising in context. Shifts to alternate chordal palettes can "presage" or "echo" characteristic tones in melody (or vice versa). Note the use of motivic devices such as retrograde, sequence in root tone motion, and even rotational displacement—used not only within a given "mosaic" progression, but across the alternatives as well.

FIG. 7.12. Alternate Mosaic Harmonizations of Melody from Figure 7.10

Whether setting chords to melody or melody to chords, the contours of modal and pentatonic melodies seem to lend themselves to the slowly unfolding "melodies" of these flexible harmonic settings—moving in simple cycles, narrative progressions, or the chord "mosaics" discussed above. Achieving this independence in its fullest sense depends on understanding the contour principles discussed in the "Melody" chapter, the qualities of root tone motions discussed in the "Harmony" chapter, and the progression of contrapuntal strategies laid out in this chapter. I believe this is new territory to explore, potentially comparable in expressiveness to melody/harmony relationships in the tonal vocabulary of the Great American Songbook. Call it the Great Global Songbook—still to be written.

CHAPTER 8

Structure

In each facet we've toured—rhythm, lyrics, melody, harmony—we've engaged with structural aspects. Yet I've held off detailed discussion of structure as a whole until now. We tend to associate different kinds of structure with different facets: rhyme schemes for lyrics, phrase structures in melody, etc. But structure in songs is not the province of any one facet; rather, structural patterns are expressed in layered ways in multiple facets. Through structure, we *unfold* or "grow" seeds in *any facet* into matching question/answer phrases, up to an entire section. We also use structure in a top-down way, architecting songs from well-worked forms and using seed material to *fulfill* those structural plans.

STRUCTURE IN THE SONG

In this chapter, we'll touch on three aspects of structure in the context of the song:

1. *Phrase structure.* Melody, lyrics, and chords weave together in a *structural phrase*: a duration (e.g., a number of bars if the phrase is metrically regular, though it need not be) marking a unit of musical time. The boundaries of a structural phrase are generally conveyed to the listener's ear by some marking event in one or more facets—the first syllable of a line, the attack of a chord. But the overall structural phrase is not determined by the phrasing of material in any one facet. At times, it might only be expectations based on prior phrases, anticipated symmetry or regularity in structure, or genre conventions that tell the listener where to hear phrase boundaries.

   This allows us to counterpoint structure in any facet, not only against material in other facets, but against perceived boundaries of the phrase itself. This can be seen particularly clearly in lyric settings that shift the start of the lyric line in front of or behind the musical downbeat. The start of that next phrase *might* be cued with a chord change, but might be implied. As we'll see later in this chapter, a similar principle is active when chords change on weak metric beats. Harmonic expectations may be set against the expectations established for the phrase length.

2. *Motivic structure.* In each facet, material is structured into patterns of similarity, contrast, and heard transformations. We've alluded to this as *motivic* structure, and seen its importance for creating compelling and memorable melodies and chord progressions. As motivic structure involves a great deal of repetition, it's important to note that it appears strongly in the lyric facet as well. We tolerate and are moved by a remarkable amount of repetition in lyrics—repetition that would feel marked and mannered if heard in ordinary speech or even poetry. This is motivic structure "peeking out at us" through the lyrics.

3. *Song form.* Lastly, structure manifests at the broadest level as *song form.* Here, though more removed than phrase structure from close interactions with the facets, structure aligns directly with the world of content. Genres and styles are built on repertoires of song forms like verse/chorus, AABA songs in musical theater, blues stanzas, and the like. These song forms orient listeners and guide writers to genre, expected themes, and even emotional and lyrical tone.

Knowledge of a range of different song forms and their properties is essential to make effective decisions about song structure at all levels. It's beyond the scope of this book to catalog these forms and their attributes, however. You can benefit greatly by studying example songs as models, replicating their structures but using your own song material. In the rest of this chapter we'll explore phrase structure and motivic structure, across the multiple facets of the song.

Starting from Structure

Since structure touches all facets, which all touch each other, you might consider structure our Fifth Facet—the George Martin to our Fab Four. One key difference, though, is that structure rarely emerges directly from encounters with the sensory world of content. Rather, structure—at all levels—tends to emerge as we work with fragments of melody, chord progressions, or lyric lines. Thus, we've depicted structure at the center or hub of the Compass: directly touching the facets through creative operations of unfolding or fulfilling structure, but resonating with theme and content—the World—primarily through the facets.

Nonetheless, the songwriting process can begin from structure as a starting point. In project-based writing, structural requirements, constraints, and challenges may accompany requirements about topic or theme, genre, tempo and groove, etc. In writing for specific markets and formats, for theatrical situations, etc., structural requirements may be dominant factors constraining your compositional choices. If you learn to maneuver through them, and enjoy them, such constraints can lead to extremely efficient and productive writing; so many decisions have been made for you!

Our writing can also be sparked by structures discovered in example or model songs. Here, what inspires us about the structural expression is especially likely to be grounded in material of the facets: chords, lyrics, melody. We might want to try a particular rhyme scheme, or use a distinctive sectional form as a template for a new song. Together with listening and analysis, writing to examples as structural models is a great way to learn song form.

Whether writing from a model or example song as a learning exercise, or for the marketplace, it's good to avoid actual plagiarism! When imitating one structural aspect of a model song, *change* structural elements in other facets. The more dramatic these other changes, the more you'll learn about working with that particular structure. (A student once brought in a song directly using the intricate rhyme scheme of Dylan's "Tangled Up in Blue"—but I made sure she changed the chord progression, subject matter, phrase lengths, etc.).

Structural Challenges

Given workable ways of notating structure—such as rhyme schemes or *phrase maps*, like *aabaac*—you can also work directly with structural patterns themselves. This becomes both a tool for study and a basis for an advanced form of *challenge writing*: i.e., create unique patterns for which you know of no existing song, then try to write to them. Fair warning: you'll feel a bit nerdy if you try this! But even the possibility of this approach is a testament to the power of *notation* in creative work.

PHRASE STRUCTURE

The *temporal framework* discussed at the start of the "Rhythm" chapter begins with pulse, tempo, meter, and groove. As this temporal horizon widens to phrases, sections, and overall song form, subdivisions of time are gradually felt less rhythmically than *structurally*: through balance, expectations, symmetry, closure/lack of closure. The level of this structural experience of musical time that interacts most closely with the facets, for both writer and listener, is the *phrase structure* of the song.

We set a lyric line with a certain number of stresses, or unfold a melody over a certain number of beats, in the context of a common structural phrase. Though this phrase roughly coincides with a sung lyric line, we can shift that line in relation to the structural phrase: start the line before or after the downbeat of the phrase, run the line across the phrase, or leave space in the phrase after the vocal line comes to its breath.

EXERCISE 8.1. SHIFT A LYRIC LINE AGAINST THE PHRASE

Take a five-stress lyric line and speak it rhythmically, feeling it initially in the context of a two-measure structural phrase. Gradually shift the line backward in the phrase, feeling the phrase begin *before* the first lyric syllable. Continue this until you feel the length of the structural phrase itself shift. Practicing this without the support of chords or an accompanying track helps you internalize and strengthen your sense for the structural phrase as an independent element.

I find the informal notation below useful for this exercise. Numbers refer to beats in the measure; italicized numbers represent the starts of measures. You can place dots (•) at will in the lyric line to line up with beats, in spots where rhythmic placement of the syllable gets tricky to follow.

I am trying to	find my	way to	love			
1 2	3	4	*1*	2	3	4

	I am	trying to	find my	way	• to	love
1 2		3	4	*1*	2	3	4

By leaving certain numbers out (always including the "1"s to account for each measure), you can quickly map the felt phrase length of a lyric line, while leaving the precise placement of certain syllables open if that specific lyric rhythm is not yet decided:

	I am	trying to	find my	way	to	love
1	-	3	4	*1*	-	*1*	-	*1*

As you pull the lyric line backward, add in pauses as needed so that the line still feels well-set and expressive of the intended meaning. For the first few moves, you will be able to accommodate the shifting lyric line placement within the structural phrase as is. At a certain point, though, you'll feel the need to "add more time" to the phrase. At that point you are manipulating the structural phrase directly—"changing time."

Independence in Phrase Structure

Rhythmic aspects beyond the rhythmic phrase, such as accompaniment and groove, can blend into our sense of the phrase structure of the song. But an even stronger connection is felt with the chords. Structural phrases tend to be marked most definitively by chordal movement—a consequence of the "seamlessness" of the chord progression, which links harmonic flow with purely temporal flow. Because chords generally move more *slowly* than vocal melody, because chords *accompany* the song, and because the sense of the chords is seamless and ever-present, chords align closely to phrase structure and even sectional form. Most often, chord changes cue starts and ends of phrases for our ears. In fact, many songwriters can only conceive of and work actively with phrase structure through the chords; harmony and phrase duration are tightly locked together.

This creates a potential limitation. Listener expectations can mark phrases based on anticipated symmetries and regularity of phrasing, or on genre-specific forms (such as the archetypal ternary 12-bar blues pattern). If you're writing within these conventions, you can let the norms do the work of establishing the phrasing for you. But to write something innovative or irregular in phrasing, songwriters need the skill and flexibility to mark phrase structure with any combination of elements. This requires being able to feel, and shift, phrase structure *independently* of material in any facet—including the chord progression.

While struggling to articulate this concept, I stumbled on a compelling analogy in the domain of juggling. You learn juggling by building up: first juggling one ball or club, then two, then three. Recently, as I practiced juggling my one lone club, I was putting my whole body into it: bending my knees as I caught the club, giving a cute little lift with my torso as I tossed it again. My juggling teacher, Jen Agans, said: "Actually, jugglers need to keep their body still and let the movement happen *at the periphery*, with the clubs. If you mimic the movement of the club with your body, it will feel good, as long as you have just one club. But as soon as you're juggling three, that will work against you. Your body won't know which club to track with its extra movements."

Consider songwriting via the facets as a kind of juggling, where rhythm, lyric, melody, and chords can be "tossed" independently, creating cool cascades and fountains in their interacting patterns. You need something to "hold still" so that all these elements can shift freely in relation to each other. That something is the *phrase structure* of the song—the temporal landscape you retain in mind's ear while shifting lyrics, melodies, or chords.

Cultivating independence between chord progression and phrase structure directly affects our range of options for writing chord progressions. It allows us to work more flexibly with harmonic rhythm—for example, moving chords on unexpected, especially *weak* metric beats. This internal sense must be even stronger to use asymmetrical, unbalanced forms such as odd-beat or odd-bar phrases, or sections with unbalanced numbers of phrases. You also need this skill for compositional process, to *change durations* of phrases by intention in the course of developing or revising a song. A simple technique is to take a section written with regular, symmetrical phrasing and experiment with adding or removing durations to various combinations of lines. The following exercise involves weak-beat metric placement and, accordingly, odd time signatures.

EXERCISE 8.2. SHIFT A CHORD SEQUENCE AGAINST A STRUCTURAL PHRASE

Write a four-measure chord sequence[18] that includes some shifts on *weak* metric beats, e.g., beats 2 or 4 in 4/4 time. The following harmonic rhythm pattern is an example:

Place this sequence into varied phrase structures—without changing the sequence's harmonic rhythm internally, but only the duration at the end completing the structural phrase. The exercise is illustrated, for the rhythmic pattern above, in figure 8.1.

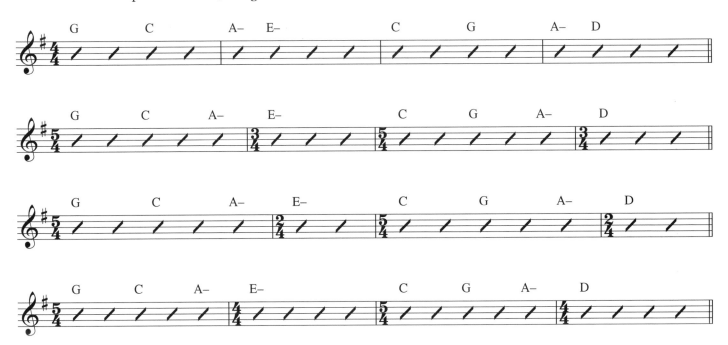

FIG 8.1 Shifting Weak-Beat Chord Movement and Phrase Structure

The first line sets the chords to the harmonic rhythm, with weak-beat movement in measures 2 and 4. The second line reinterprets the sequence with odd-beat time signatures, such that the weak-beat chord moves now are heard to take place on strong metric beats of new measures. This transformation does *not* change the overall length of the structural phrase, just requires you to hear it a different way. (For this very reason, though, it may perhaps be the more difficult of these transformations.) Lines three and four *shorten* and *lengthen* the overall structural phrase respectively, responding to the shifted chord.

A flexible sense for structural phrases is essential for working with a wider range of functional and modal chord progressions. Progressions take on harmonic and tonal meaning in relation to phrasing; once we can shift progressions relative to structural phrases, and vice versa, we can not only shift metric placement of individual chords, but "recolor" entire cycles or sequences in a rich variety of ways.

---

18. For clarity here I refer to a "sequence" rather than a "progression," meaning a smaller unit than an entire sectional progression, analogous to the single lyric line we worked with in exercise 8.1.

MOTIVIC STRUCTURE

Structural phrases divide up the stream of musical time. As we write songs, we fill these phrases with lyrics, melodies, and chords. These elements are also streams of a sort, which we in turn divide into units. These units are characterized not simply by duration, however, as with structural phrases, but by a succession of *motives:* distinctive figures that attract our attention and play a structural role in the song. Motives—the "atoms" of structure as it were—and motivic structure, embodied as patterns of repeating and transformed motives, can be expressed in material of each respective facet: in lyrics, melody, chords, or in rhythmic patterns of any of these elements. Even distinct changes in the length of structural phrases themselves can become a motivic element that interacts with motivic patterns in other facets.

In the writing process, we can create motivic structure in complementary ways: *bottom up*, via transformations or operations on individual motives, building (or *unfolding*) them into larger structural units; or *top down*, filling (or *fulfilling*) overall structural patterns with motivic material.

Motives vs. Song Seeds

Though motives, like song seeds, can be expressed in each facet, motives are not quite the same as song seeds. In process terms, seeds are fragments captured via discovery. Just as some song seeds may arrive as composites of multiple facets, a song seed might already contain several motives, or a motive bundled with an interesting transformation. In fact, the essence of the seed's interest may be the motivic transformation itself.

To skillfully develop a seed of this kind, you may need to break it into smaller, individual motives when composing gets under way. Not all seeds function as motives in the final song. A hook or title may have a key place in overall song form, yet not be intrinsic to motivic structure. And just as not all seeds are motives, not all motives begin as seeds that we catch or stumble upon. We can construct or *compose* motives.

Unfolding: Motives into Structure

We work with motives by repeating, contrasting, or transforming them in various ways. Though an individual motive may have a distinctive figural quality that attracts our attention, we often recognize motives because of their repetition and transformation in the song's structure. Indeed, those transformations often create the sense of that structure for the listener. The structure may also emerge incrementally as the writer *unfolds* the motive into larger phrases or sections.

We can create diverse patterns simply by repeating and interchanging contrasting motives in various ways, within various sectional structures. For example, patterns with two motives *a* and *b* could include *aaab*, *abab*, *abbb*, or *abbabb*. But motivic structure can go deeper than just successions of distinct motives. The perceived identity of *musical* motives (including *sound* aspects of lyrics) is a continuum: from exact repetition, to similarity with variation, to strong contrast. We often create different motives for a pattern by transforming a single motive. Thus, in an *abab* pattern, we might generate the *b* motivic idea by transforming *a* in some way, minor or dramatic. The *abab* pattern can be intensified through higher contrast between *a* and *b*, and greater similarity between respective repetitions of *a* and *b*. The same pattern can be made more subtle by reducing the contrast between *a* and *b* motives (moving toward *aaaa*), or by loosening the match between *a* and/or *b* repetitions (moving toward *abcb*, *abac*, or *abcd*). I like to compare such variations to color patterns in textiles: e.g., setting blue against red, vs. pastel blue against sky blue.

There's an almost limitless variety of these motivic relations and operations. As with learning a library of larger song forms, it will greatly enliven your songwriting to learn and practice a repertoire of these structuring and transformation moves. Many have been examined extensively in literature on classical composition or jazz improvisation. Jack Perricone's *Melody in Songwriting* (Berklee Press, 2000) discussed some of these devices in a songwriting context, primarily in melody; while their aesthetic effects in rhyme schemes, sectional line-length patterns, and other lyric aspects have been explored by authors such as Pat Pattison (*Songwriting: Essential Guide to Rhyming* 2nd edition, Berklee Press, 2014) and Andrea Stolpe (*Popular Lyric Writing*, Berklee Press, 2007). The 360° framework allows us to work more independently with motivic patterns, and to better understand their common and varying effects in each facet, and at different levels of structure.

Question/Answer Phrases

The smallest scale at which you can see unfolding take place is at the level of a *couplet* (extending this notion beyond lyric only): a matched set of lines, or phrases, that sound connected as question and answer, call and response. In theory, you could build a section entirely from phrases with little or no motivic connection, or *through-composed*. But humans are pattern makers; this applies to listener's ear and composer's voice alike. In practice, it's almost impossible to generate an answering phrase without applying some structural or motivic transformation to the question. Even a short melodic or rhythmic seed of a few bars' length may form around a motivic device that gives it integrity and interest.

EXERCISE 8.3. ANSWER THE QUESTION, QUESTION THE ANSWER!

Start with a beginning phrase in any facet—your motivic statement. First treat it as a question, and generate, responsively, an answer to it. Try for a response between a direct repetition with minor variation and a through-composed response (answer with an idea of the same length!). Allow your answer phrase to arise by free association and improvisation. Let the original phrase resonate in your mind; wait till you "hear" an answer in mind's ear, then quickly record or transcribe it, without thinking much about it. Try several of these, then reflect on them. You'll likely find you've applied some motivic development techniques, even without realizing it. Motivic operations name and formalize patterns we use and hear intuitively—the natural ways we think musically.

Now for the most important part of the exercise! Go back to your starting motive, but this time treat it as the *answer phrase*—that is, generate a "question" phrase to precede it, and that makes it sound like an "answer" heard in that new context. To do this, you must be able to hear the motive in a fresh way.

Unfolding in All Directions

Through exercise 8.3, you experience an important aspect of working with motivic structure. Most motivic operations are reversible, and so the same musical material can feel like a question or answer depending on context. When we unfold structure in a bottom-up way, we need to keep this principle in mind. Often, our seed ideas will be the answers to which we must find the questions, rather than the other way round! That is, in composing, we must often work in the *opposite* direction from how time will flow experientially for the listener in the final song.

This principle holds true whether working bottom up or top down, and at every hierarchical level of structure in the song. A structure can be fulfilled in *any sequence* during composition. For example, to properly set up a lyric title, hook, or refrain line, we often think *backward* in the flow of the song, working like detectives from the last line to earlier lines, or from the chorus to the first verse. And often, the first verse we actually *write* winds up *not* the first verse of the finished song.

Fulfilling: Structure into Motives

Unfolding is a bottom-up, exploratory, incremental style of structuring activity. We can also work in a top-down, structure-first way. Like an architect planning a building, you conceive a song or section's overall form or *architecture,* then fill in the pieces. Once you've architected your song plan or structural map, you *fulfill* that structure—either by generating new material, or by selecting from existing seeds and motives. (The latter process may feel more like stitching a quilt together than architecture.)

You may believe working from a structural plan in this top-down way will confine your creative work. But we always write to a structure of some sort; the choice is whether we *choose* our structures with informed artistic intent. If we don't, we fall back on a small repertoire of comfortable forms that tend to make our songs sound similar, and may or may not suit the song's content. This way of working also limits our ability to experiment and innovate with new forms.

Example: Fulfilling a Structure in All Facets

In the following extended example, we'll fulfill a structural pattern with *independent* attempts in all facets, using the simple pattern *aaba* involving just two contrasting motives.

Here's an *aaba* structure in melodic phrases:

FIG. 8.2. An *aaba* Structure Expressed in a Melodic Phrase

Note that the *a* pattern is repeated most directly in the melodic *rhythm*. Pitches are subjected to various melodic transformations: sequence, intervallic augmentation, etc. The *b* motive contrasts with, yet is audibly similar to, the *a* motive in both contour and melodic rhythm.

Here's the *aaba* pattern expressed in, or *fulfilled* by, a chord progression. Note that this is an *independent* attempt, not a harmonization of the first example:

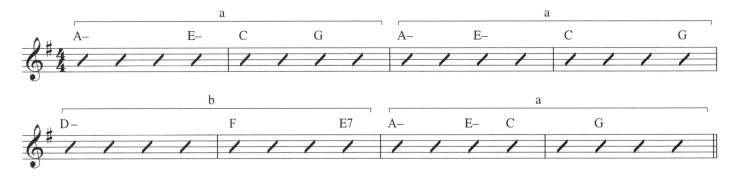

FIG. 8.3. Fulfilling an *aaba* Motivic Structure in a Chord Progression

In figure 8.3, the chordal motives are short *sequences of chords*: *a* = A– E– C G, *b* = D– F E7. As with the melody example in figure 8.2, the repetitions of *a* are not exact. Here, the variations are created by *rhythmic* placement of the chords, with a kind of retrograde or mirroring of harmonic rhythm in the first four bars, and an even more dramatic displacement in the final *a*. The *a* and *b* "chord motives" contrast strongly, both in terms of the chords used and in harmonic rhythm. Thus, the *aaba* phrase pattern is still clearly audible.

In these first two examples we see the notion of a *motive* extended to apply to a melodic phrase or a chord sequence. Rhythmic aspects are interwoven into each. We can also fulfill the *aaba* pattern directly with a rhythmic phrase, possibly to be set later to material in other facets:

FIG. 8.4. Rhythmic Phrase Fulfilling an *aaba* Pattern

In figure 8.4, both repetition and contrast seem exacting, yet with a few quirks that make a less straightforward mapping of motivic units in rhythm to metric structure. Is the trailing eighth note at the end of bar 2 part of the second *a*, hence a variation? Or is it the start of the *b* motive? Similarly, the tied note at the end of bar 3 sounds like part of the *b* motive—until it's revealed as an anticipated first note of the final *a* repetition. These ambiguities suggest a key aspect of structure: motivic units can be ambiguous, emergent, elided, or overlapping, and in the "ear of the be-hearer."

We'll now fulfill the *aaba* pattern in lyric. Structural patterns are familiar to songwriters and listeners in the context of lyrics, especially rhyme schemes:

I'm talkin' to my friendly *neighbors*	*a*
I'm restin' from my weary *labors*	*a*
Lazy summer *day*	*b*
Grillin' dogs down at the *river*	*a*

This shows another potent aspect of structure. Familiar, expected structures play a shaping role in making other connections audible. *Neighbors* and *labors* is perfect rhyme, easy to hear. *Neighbors/labors* and *river* is a looser rhyme connection, involving subtractive (losing the "s"), assonance, and consonance rhyme ("ay" vs. "ih") effects. But the expected fulfillment of an *aaba* pattern invites the ear to catch the looser rhyme, even when distanced by the intervening unrhymed line.

Besides (or independent from) its rhyme scheme, the verse also expresses (or fulfills) the *aaba* pattern in line length. Heard in terms of the *number of stressed syllables in the line*, the section has the pattern 4434— also an *aaba* pattern, now expressed in lyric *rhythm*. In this case, rhyme scheme and line-length scheme coincide and reinforce the same *aaba* pattern. That need not be the case:

Talkin' to my friendly neighbors	4
Restin' from my weary labors	4
Love these lazy days of summer	4
Grillin' dogs down at the river	4

Here, the third line is now set to the same line length (four stresses) as the others, and the *aaba* effect expressed only by rhyme scheme, not line length. Here, the choice of "summer" works against us; we no longer have *enough* sonic contrast between the *a* and *b* line-end sounds. "Summer" is an even looser rhyme to "labors" than "river," but the regular line-length rhythm lulls the ear into hearing it as a semi-rhyme, creating an undulating *aaa"a'* rhyme scheme effect rather than the desired *aaba*. This illustrates a central principle in all work with structure: *Make similar elements sufficiently similar, and contrasting elements sufficiently contrastive, to fulfill the pattern at the desired degree of intensity vs. subtlety.*

Putting It All Together

That *aaba* pattern, though clearly audible in each case, isn't fulfilled strictly in any facet. There are minor variations in *a* repetitions and connections between *a* and *b* motives. In each facet, subsidiary patterns can be expressed or suggested. When you put all the elements together, other connections and resonances emerge.

Here, to finish, is one possible way of putting together some of our separate *aaba* explorations. Since these were generated *independently*, rather than in response to each other, combining them is a bit of a "crapshoot." There's no particular reason they *should* fit together thematically. Still, sometimes chance collisions create interesting effects.

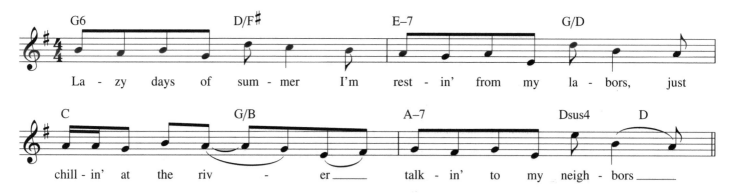

FIG. 8.5. Structure Expressed in Multiple Facets

In figure 8.5, we see material from the melody and lyric experiments, rearranged and integrated into a single-section passage. The chords, instead of mirroring the *aaba* structure, create a single narrative arc with a descending bass-line/chord cliché. Though not intended to be striking or original, it does create interest with non-chord tone relations against the melody in a few spots. Note that lyric lines were rearranged in this version. You can revise and rework any structure consisting of a sequence of units by changing the sequence—a process skill we can compare to a kind of juggling.

EXERCISE 8.4. JUGGLE PHRASES IN A SECTION

Start with a short section in a given structure: e.g., *aaba*. We'll demonstrate with a lyric section; you can try it with material in any facet. Work through different *orderings* or sequences (formally, permutations) of the lines, placing them into different structural configurations. (This works best if each line is a separate "thought phrase.") Reflect on the effects of each structure; pick the best and know why. Generating such alternatives is particularly useful when matching to material in other facets. Your best choice may depend on these interactions. Here are just a few of the 24 (that is, 4 factorial or 4!: 4 x 3 x 2 x 1) ways we can arrange the four lines of our earlier example lyric.

A	Talkin' to my friendly neighbors	*a*	
B	Restin' from my weary labors	*a*	
C	Love these lazy days of summer	*x*	or loose *b*
D	Grillin' dogs down at the river	*x*	*b'''*!

D	Grillin' dogs down at the river	*x*
A	Talkin' to my friendly neighbors	*a*
B	Restin' from my weary labors	*a*
C	Love these lazy days of summer	*x*

A	Talkin' to my friendly neighbors	*a*
D	Grillin' dogs down at the river	*b*
B	Restin' from my weary labors	*a*
C	Love these lazy days of summer	*b'*

Each sequence reveals connections and parallels, both sonic and semantic, between lines we might not have seen before. The first version feels grounded, ending with a line of sense description, and conversational, with a tight rhyme couplet followed by a very loose one. The second puts the most reflective "thought and feeling" line at the end, and shifts the rhyme scheme to stagger the close rhyme in the middle couplet. The last version transforms the second by simply swapping the lines of the first couplet. This creates a satisfying *abab* rhyme scheme, reinforcing the loose rhyme. The surprise here? These rewrites and revisions create rich resonance in imagery, narrative, theme, and emotion. Yet, they are arrived at primarily through simply messing about with the structure.

COUNTERPOINT IN MOTIVIC STRUCTURE

In the "Melody/Harmony Connections" chapter, we examined relationships between vocal melody and various "melodic" aspects of the chord progression in the song, in terms of the four canonical voice-leading relationships of traditional counterpoint: parallel and similar motion, oblique motion, and contrary motion. Here, we extend this analogy to counterpoint one step further—as a way to characterize effects of various interactions of *different* motivic structures, expressed in elements both within and across facets.

Counterpoint within Facets

Each facet has multiple internal elements. Lyrics, for example, involve rhyme scheme, line-length scheme, and phrasing, among other elements. In a given lyric section, each such element can express distinct patterns that carry their own effects. These patterns can be worked with independently, and taken together, can create either aligned or contrasting patterns.

We can recognize different kinds of "contrapuntal" effects between these patterns, treating each element as a "voice." Each voice's "melody" is its respective pattern of motivic repetition and contrast. The listener's ear can discern when these *patterns* or "motivic melodies" move in similar or independent ways, even though the patterns are expressed with different elements. We discuss these in order of increasing skill level required, using rhyme scheme and line length in lyric as our working example of the elements "in counterpoint" within a facet.

Parallel and Similar Motivic Motion

Working independently and simultaneously with differing patterns requires a high degree of skill. Thus, by far, the most natural tendency in writing is to move patterns together. The more improvisationally based and "composite" your writing process, the more likely you'll use structures in this parallel way.

Admittedly, there's no exact correlation between melodic pitch and the varying qualitative ways different motivic elements can repeat or contrast. Since elements such as rhyme and metric length are qualitatively quite different, the distinction between "parallel" and "similar" motion may appear less salient here. (Or perhaps this extended analogy with traditional counterpoint is only a similarity—not a parallel.)

We can, however, distinguish degrees of closeness in a match. An *abab* rhyme scheme moves "in parallel" with a 4343 pattern in line length; an *xaxa* rhyme scheme can be heard as a looser match, not parallel but still similar. Relative degrees of contrast in elements of each pattern, and closeness of the match across the patterns, offer a range of subtly differing effects.

Parallel or similar effects support unity and integrity in the section, but also risk making the structure too heavy-handed and obvious when not employed with care. The general principle is: *Stating a given structure in multiple song elements intensifies that structural effect—for good or ill.*

Oblique Motivic Motion

Oblique motion is activity in one voice, quiescence in the other. What does this mean in motivic terms? What's the motivic analogue of a melodic voice "staying still"? Patterns do not always draw the listener's attention. Here, two contrasting structural options have the effect of moving a given element to the relative background of attention. The first is simple repetition: when every line ends with the same sound or is of the same length, we stop listening for changes, and accept the texture as backdrop. With *no* repetition at all, our ears stop listening for repetition or pattern to emerge, and eventually "zone out" or accept the "through-composed" texture.

Oblique motion, in motivic terms, can be an effective texture for spotlighting the "moving" pattern against the backdrop of the element carrying less structure. However, both repetition and through-composed or "chaotic" structure carry their own meaning and emotion. Thus they can distract rather than spotlight, if used as "filler" rather than with intent.

Contrary Motivic Motion

It's also possible to superimpose or layer *different patterns* at the same time—a kind of independent or "contrary" motivic motion with the potential to create intriguing and subtle effects. Working with these fully "contrapuntal" motivic effects can require considerable skill, given the relative complexity of each individual pattern and their interactions. Where parallel/similar or oblique textures tend to spotlight an entire pattern to varying degrees, contrapuntal (contrary motion) patterns create spotlighting effects on specific points in the structure. These spotlight points come at points of "deceptive resolution"— where *expectation of parallel motion is created, then not fulfilled.* (Fulfilling such a "non-fulfilling" structure is tricky work indeed—but quite fulfilling if you can pull it off!)

For example, if we set an *abab* rhyme scheme against a 4344 (thus, in effect, *abaa*) line-length scheme, the surprise or "shearing point" comes on the *last stress* of the last line, where a three-stress line was expected but an extra stress provided. Here, occurring at the last line of the section, the shearing point reinforces sectional form and closure as well. In working with contrary-motion or "counterpointing" motivic structure, care must be exercised that the resulting texture isn't too muddy and confusing to the ear.

The following exercise is an aid to creating *contrapuntal* relationships in structure, first within, then across facets:

EXERCISE 8.5. CONTRAPUNTAL STRATEGIES IN A LYRIC SECTION

Take a short lyric section (say, four lines). Working with the two structural elements of rhyme scheme and line length, create *three* versions of the section: with similar, oblique, and contrasting/contrary relationships respectively between the elements. In the example versions below, the line length indicated reflects the number of stressed syllables in the line. The + symbols indicate unstressed syllables at the start or end of the line.

	Stressed Syllables
I'm talkin' to my friendly neighbors	+4+
I'm restin' from my weary labors	+4+
Lazy summer evening	3+
Grillin' dogs down at the river	4+
Talkin' to my friendly neighbors	4+
Restin' from my weary labors	4+
Love these lazy summer evenings	4+
Grillin' dogs down at the river	4+
I'm talkin' to my neighbors	+3+
I'm restin' from my weary labors	+4+
Lazy summer evenings	3+
Grillin' dogs down at the river	4+

In the example, each variant retains the *aaba* (or *aaxa*) rhyme scheme. In the first variant, the line-length scheme, basically 4434, is also an *aaba* structure, thus creating a similar or parallel effect with the rhyme scheme. That makes the third line contrast strongly with the other lines, by both rhyme sound and line length. In the second variant, line length is uniform, creating constant motion and moving line length as an element of attention to the background: oblique motion that spotlights the rhyme scheme. Finally, the third variant creates true "counterpoint" or contrary movement between the *aaba* rhyme scheme and the 3434 or *abab* line-length scheme. This contrapuntal relation creates spotlights where the two patterns diverge. For example, at the end of the second line, "labors" surprises by rhyming but arriving later than expected. In these examples, the presence or absence of upbeat syllables in each line is yet another subsidiary element that carries structure. In the last version, this element creates a third contrasting pattern, *aabb*.

You can do this exercise the other way round: holding the line-length pattern constant while changing rhyme scheme. You can also extend the exercise to other facets.

Counterpoint Across Facets

Let's extend our exploration of contrapuntal relations to structural relationships *across facets*, with an example between the facets of melody and chords. To be clear, we're still focusing on counterpoint of *motivic structure*. This is tricky when melody and harmony are our example facets, since traditional counterpoint deals with melody and also takes harmonic relations into account. In the chapter on melody/harmony connections, we applied this view of counterpoint in a songwriting context, treating vocal melody as one melodic line, the chord progression as a whole as another "line." Now, we look at *motivic structure* reflected in vocal melody and chords. In figure 8.6, an *abab* melodic phrase structure is combined with an *aaab* pattern in the chord progression.

FIG. 8.6. Contrasting Motivic Structure in Melody and Chord Progression

The chords resolve into repeating two-chord motives: C A– and D B7, suggesting an *aaab* pattern. This is set against melodic motives (of the same length, one measure) forming an *abab* pattern. The first "pull" or "tug" between patterns comes in measure 2, while a "convergence" of the patterns occurs in measure 4. (Note that rhythmic aspects of both melody and harmony are uniform, hence parallel here.) What happens if we "thin" the chord progression a bit?

FIG. 8.7. Thinning Chord Progression Changes Motivic Structure

Now, in figure 8.7, motivic structure in the chords is less obvious. Has *aaab* shifted to *aa'ab* (hearing the C chord in measure 2 as the repetition, the following A– as the variation) or *abac* (hearing C A– as a unit, and a new idea, contrasting with D B7)? Here, a *simplifying* move has increased asymmetry and rhythmic interest in the chord progression, and overall contrapuntal interest in its relation to the melody. Harmonic rhythm now plays a role in how we hear the structure, though it's obscured a bit by the notation: the C chord restated on beat 1 of measure 2 is a *continuation* chord (/); the D chord on beat 1 of measure 4 is a *change* (X). The apparent *motivic* match hides a *rhythmic* asymmetry between measures 2 and 4. A *third* structural pattern, *abac*, is thus created by the harmonic rhythm. This is shown in figure 8.8, mapped at a half-measure pace (X: chord change, \: continuation):

Changes	X	\	\	X	X	\	X	X
Motives	*a*		*b*		*a*		*c*	

FIG. 8.8. Motivic Aspects in Harmonic Rhythm

Motivic structure is not deterministic; it can be emergent and ambiguous in the ear of both composer and listener. And the counterpoint of structural patterns can move at different paces in different elements and facets. Of course, in writing a song, you don't think about all this consciously, at every moment. Since we can delve endlessly into the interactions of these patterns, there's no way to figure them out completely anyway! The point is that by working independently with material in different facets, and following different pathways, you can build up sectional structures with rich, interlocking patterns to delight and intrigue the listener's ear, mind, and heart—even when the elements appear simple on the surface.

CHAPTER 9

Using the Compass: Further Steps

We've now toured through the four songwriting facets and the central aspect of structure that unifies them. With the songwriter's compass as a lever, and a place to stand on, you can now move the world—with your songs. (Sorry, Archimedes.) In this final chapter, we'll revisit the compass model and discuss some implications for further steps you can take to advance your songwriting using 360° strategies.

REVISITING THE COMPASS

A model need not be true in all respects, but it should be useful. Having worked through the material in this book, my pictorial model of the songwriter's compass may or may not resonate for you. You may believe I've left out some essential facet, or that structure, or content and the World should be facets in their own right. You might need to shift the model if your concerns are broader than songwriting in the strict sense I've taken as my scope for this book—such as songwriting in connection with production and sound design, or in the dramatic context of opera or musical theater.

Nevertheless, the model as presented here offers a rich set of strategies to help you write better songs, and to advance the productiveness, innovation, and versatility of your writing. Here are some ways to go deeper with the facets and pathways of the compass.

The Compass as a Unity

The circular arrangement of the compass is intended to illustrate that facets are not in a hierarchy of importance, but are peers or comrades: knights of the Songwriter's Round Table. (My last mixed metaphor, I promise.)

The circle's unbroken circumference further suggests that the divisions or boundaries between facets are inherently fuzzy. In fact, facets undeniably do form a continuum or seamless creative space. This matches the intuition of songwriters who experience verbal and musical materials as a seamless whole. Words dissolve into rhythms; melodies move toward chords or towards words. A given musical expression can flow from pitchless rhythm to rhythmic melody, to harmonically driven melody. Songwriters employ intermediate forms between verbal and nonverbal material, as I've approximated with tools and techniques such as "word buds" and "syllable buds," dummy lyrics and melodies, etc.

The 360º songwriting approach and the structure of this book reflect a general learning principle in artistic work: sometimes, we break up a unity into isolated aspects in order to gain better control over the elements. As you master these elements and their relations, you can gradually move back toward a more seamless and integrated way of working. At the end, the isolated elements might appear as inseparable as you experienced them at first—yet, you have become a different writer.

From Compass to Tetrahedron

Since every facet is creatively equidistant from each of the others, any flat rendering of their relationships, as in the compass picture, must fib a little. Geometrically astute readers may have gleaned that a more precise and accurate spatial arrangement of the songwriting facets requires three-dimensional space, with the circle as a sphere. In this space, the facets are inscribed, not in a flat plane as with the compass, but as a *tetrahedron*—a pyramid with a triangular (rather than a square) base, and four points (or vertices). The points correspond respectively to rhythm, lyrics, melody, and harmony.

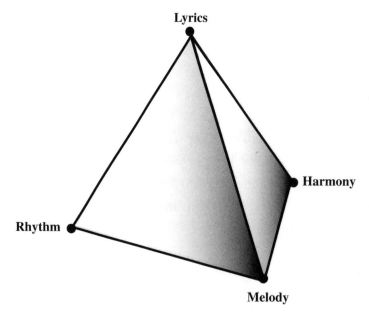

FIG. 9.1. The Songwriter's Tetrahedron

You can flip this tetrahedron around, putting any point on top, with the others providing the base. Each facet is a viable jumping-in point from the world; each facet touches that world of content *directly*; and there is a pathway from each facet directly to each of the others. And, if you'll bear with me, we'll see that each aspect of this more well-rounded spatial metaphor illustrates more advanced songwriting strategies that you can cultivate. This is 360° songwriting in a nutshell (or a tetrahedron).

Facets: From Vertices to Edges

Continuing our geometrical analogy: a tetrahedron has four vertices, but *six* edges (lines between vertices). These correspond, in terms of songwriting, to six distinct connections between facets: for example, the pairings of melody/lyric, or harmony/rhythm.

In this book, we've explored some of these "edges" in a directional sense. We've seen, for example, that the creative *process* of setting from a lyric to a melody is dramatically different from moving the other way, from a melody to a lyric. The term "setting" has been an intentional oversimplification of (or placeholder for) a repertoire of different techniques for combining material along the various facet "edges." These include the following:

- *Generate.* Starting with a seed in one facet, create brand-new material in the related facet in response to that seed material. This involves a kind of free association, an intuitive leap to generate responsive material.

  We can always take this intuitive strategy one step farther and generate material in a blended form at the start. For example, when jamming over chords, it's natural and comfortable to blend melody and lyrics. As we've seen, it's also a good skill to be able to isolate these, for example, to refine lyric or melodic ideas. That skill should increase your ability to generate in a more organic way as well.

- *Match.* With a disciplined approach to seed catching, we have another option any time we need to set to a new facet. We start with our source seed in one facet, and turn to our "catalogue" of seeds in the target facet. For example, given a melodic line we might glance down a list of titles, hooks, or individual lyric lines, looking for a hit or a match. We can "scan and match" many combinations of seeds in this way until we get something we like. This can also lead to surprising but effective juxtapositions that we'd not get to by generating material responsively.

  By extension, if we're ever stuck with writer's block, or simply want to write and have no particular project or task to write to, we can always practice matching seeds in different facets via chance collisions. This can also be a great skill-building exercise, or an ice-breaker or warm-up for a co-writing session or team writing "camp."

- *Transform.* We can also move along a facet-to-facet edge by *transforming* material in an incremental way, by degrees. Rather than taking a generative "flying leap," with this strategy we traverse the edge as a continuum, along which we can create hybrid or composite material, including "composite seeds" that blend the facets involved. This was the approach explored in the chapter on "Melody/Harmony Connections." This was not really "setting" in the sense of putting chords to a given melody or melodies to a given progression, but *transforming* a given melody to be progressively more or less "chord-driven," or revising a chord progression to be less dependent on an implied linear melody. This skill is essential in later stages of writing, when we want to polish, revise, or respond to critique.

Facets as Faces: Facet Triads

We're not quite done with our tetrahedron analogy. You'll be happy to know the tetrahedron is the simplest Platonic[19] solid, with one unique feature: it's the only regular solid with an equal number—four—of corners (vertices) and sides (faces). Thus, we can visualize our Fab Four friends as not vertices but faces (hey—facets!) of the tetrahedron.

This flipped view asks us to pay attention, not to the vertices, but the faces. Each face is, in effect, a triad: a triangular area bounded by three distinct vertices, the elemental facets we've been working with up until now. Just as the six edges represent intuitive combinations of songwriting elements, the four faces of the tetrahedron correspond to four distinctive, higher-level songwriting strategies. Some of these "triad" strategies match familiar, intuitive ways that songwriters work, and well-known and very practical writing practices. Others suggest more innovative possibilities and techniques.

Another way of viewing each triad is in terms of the individual facet that it *excludes* or withholds from foreground attention. This is fairly intuitive: in many ways it's easier to work on isolation skills by thinking about what you're *not* working with. When you try to write "melody only," it's always an abstraction and a fiction to some degree. There will inevitably be a harmonic and rhythmic aspect to your melody. But you *can* at least hold back the lyrics. In effect, you're now working with the "triad" of melody/harmony/rhythm, sans lyric.

This grouping actually corresponds pretty closely to our conventional associations of "the music" of the song, with lyric being the facet held back. This strategy reflects the traditional composer/lyricist division, used from librettist and composer in opera through musical theater, Tin Pan Alley, and the Great American Songbook era. Of course, in much contemporary songwriting, the writer is both composer and lyricist. And much co-writing, whether of band members in the Lennon/McCartney model or the Nashville "two writers in a room with guitars" model, involves collaboration on both lyrics and music by

---

19. *Platonic* here meaning: talk about this at a party, and that's the kind of friend you'll make that night....

all partners. Much of my task in this approach has been to give writers a more integrated way to work on these elements of songwriting. The foundation 360° songwriting skills and strategies should make you a stronger and more versatile composer and lyricist, solo songwriter, and co-writer.

Two other triad groupings correspond to strategies that reflect real songwriter practices for which there are no familiar names. Consider melody/chords/lyric sans rhythm. This is how you work when you have the "bones" of a song but are keeping strict temporal decisions fluid—time signature, phrase lengths, harmonic rhythm, etc. It's working your song in a rhythmically malleable, mercurial state. Recognizing this as a distinct strategy helps you apply it more effectively: to shift rhythmic settings of melody or lyric in flexible yet prosodically sound ways. A good example of how critical such rhythmic reshaping can be to great songwriting is "I Can't Make You Love Me" by Mike Reid and Allen Shamblin—a breakthrough hit song for Bonnie Raitt as a slow ballad, but first written as a fast bluegrass-tempo song.

Similarly, you can work with rhythmically spoken lyrics over a chord progression, while holding back melody. This helps you steer clear of a throw-away "filler" melody that tracks too closely to the chords, especially when your attention is focused on the lyrics. If you temporarily hold melody in abeyance, then later explore alternative melodic settings, you have a better chance of finding that compelling, unexpected melody—perfectly complementing the lyric's emotion and meaning, while moving independently with and against the chord progression.

Lastly, let's consider melody/rhythm/lyric, sans chords. Surprisingly, this is a good description of the practice of contemporary top-line writing. The topline writer creates lyrics and melody set to a distinct vocal rhythm; the chords (along with many timbral, orchestration, and form decisions) are generally the province of the "production track." Topline writers typically develop their melody, lyrics, and vocal rhythm simultaneously and improvisationally. However, the more fine-grained 360° songwriting skills and strategies can be helpful here, e.g., to refine a lyric beyond easy "filler" cliché lines, or experiment with subtle rhythmic shifts in the hook. Your effectiveness with any of the composite-facet strategies discussed here will be greatly augmented by the work with the individual facets we've done in the main chapters of this book.

Curiously, this same functional grouping—melody/rhythm/lyric sans chords—also takes us into a very different genre and cultural context: folk music. As discussed in the chapter on melody/harmony connections, the a cappella songs and ballads and archaic dance tunes in many world music traditions were, by and large, composed without dependence on harmonic accompaniment. The melodies are often modal or pentatonic in quality; because they're composed and learned only by ear, they also rely strongly on motivic rather than harmonic structure for their interest and integrity.

Unlike the contemporary topline writing/production split, this is not just division of labor leaving chords to a different collaborator, or a process strategy of holding back harmonization until later stages of composition. Here the final song or tune can stand alone, performed without chordal accompaniment. Yet these songs and tunes require close integrity with lyric and/or rhythm. Thus, despite their independence from harmonic underpinnings they represent, not melody in an isolated and abstract sense, but melody, lyric, and rhythm as a unity.

Even more curiously, these two worlds of production-driven, topline writing and traditional modal folk may have more common ground than either camp suspects! From a musical perspective, I think it's more revealing to consider much contemporary popular music in modal terms, rather than from the standpoint of functional harmony. (And don't be surprised if some fiddle tune toplines hit the charts soon!) But there's also an intriguing link in process terms.

In mainstream pop writing, the current convention is for track writers to develop tracks first and for topline writers to compose melodies and lyrics in response to those tracks. In theory, you could flip this process, writing toplines first and then creating the track. Some production companies specifically request "a cappella toplines" with the intent of adding the final track later in the pipeline. In practice, this works more via a kind of pivoting: a topline is written to a track, then the track gets swapped out (perhaps by prior arrangement, perhaps through the vicissitudes of production and pitching), and another track matched or written to the topline.

When I first heard about this emerging creative/production model, I was mystified by the question: what about the chord progression? If a topline is written to a track that embeds a progression, wouldn't any swapped-in replacement track need to copy that progression? What I learned—from practitioners I consider highly informed—was that "a good topline hook melody shouldn't be dependent on the chords." That response gives me the hope that foundation questions we've wrestled with in this book—such as how to write a great melody that isn't driven completely by preconceived chords— are absolutely relevant to issues in contemporary songwriting.

FROM COUNTERPOINT TO IRONY: BACK TO THE WORLD

We've applied and stretched the concept of counterpoint to various aspects and levels of songwriting: first, to interactions of vocal melody with the chord progression of the song; then, to motivic patterns within and across facets. At higher levels of phrasing and form, the same principles are at work when counterposing *cyclical* with *narrative* structure. After all, no motivic patterns contrast more strongly than *aaaaaaa* and *abcdefg*!

Through all these explorations, I've avoided speculating about what given structures "mean" or assigning them direct emotional connotations. In my own writing and in teaching, I encourage an experiential approach: play with structures, create interesting effects, then *attend to your emotional and associative reactions as a listener* to effects created, to determine how and where to use them.

Nevertheless, all these forms and interactions do create emotional responses and thematic associations. The very presence of audible structure itself, and the degree of intricacy of that structure, is a "telling detail" with prosodic import. However we arrive at the final song, we certainly seek integrity in those responses. A tacit implication might be that all elements should *tell the same story* in the song—providing an unambiguous, compelling emotional experience for the listener.

But it's not quite that simple! Interactions of a song's elements are not always direct. They can be complex and subtle, ambiguous, shifting through repetition, even apparently contradictory. I reserve the term *irony*, as distinct from *counterpoint*, to refer to tension or mismatch between emotional connotations of varied musical or lyrical aspects of the song and theme or content. Irony need not involve detailed motivic counterpoint as discussed in the "Structure" chapter. It can be expressed in overall relationships between melody and lyric, for example, or between lyric tone and subject matter. The key is that tension kicks in through contrasting and conflicting content or emotional associations.

Sometimes, we'll intentionally mismatch elements for purposes of humor, disorientation, surprise, or shock value. Extreme ironic effects invite little "explosions," often humorous in effect. When you write a happy, jaunty song about a tragic murder, you're probably trying to be funny (or perhaps you're just a bluegrass musician). If you write a lyrical, sexy torch ballad from a potato to a potato, you're likely going for a laugh ("I Only Have Eyes for You"? "I've Got You Under My Skin"?). But ironic juxtaposition need not be humorous or obvious in effect. Consider how the soothing lullaby-esque music of John Lennon's "Imagine" sets off the lyrics—which ask us some of the hardest and most thought-provoking (in the best sense) questions a songwriter has ever asked.

Acknowledging counterpoint and irony as an integral aspect of songwriting broadens our vision of integrity in the song. This world is a complicated and bewildering place. If our task as songwriters is to be "on call" to write in a songwriterly way about any aspect of the world, we need to be able to convey confusion and contradiction as well. In that noble work, it's fine for us to be just as confused and conflicted as our fellow humans—about life. But it won't hurt to be a little *less* confused about songwriting.

SOUND AND SENSE: FACETS, WORLD, AND STRUCTURE

There are infinite aspects to explore in connections between the "real" sensory and referential world and creative work we do with the facets. I've bounded discussion of these connections with the simplifying process notions of *casting* and *framing*. When you work from story, theme, project, or narrative to musical or lyrical material for the song, you're casting. When you look for real-world or narrative associations for musical material, or for the sonic or just ambiguous aspects of lyric material, you're framing. A 360° approach challenges you to work across *all* facets in making these connections. Now, we see that in casting and framing, we can work in not only direct ways but also more surprising ways, through *ironic reversals:* "half-twists" between theme and emotion and material in one, or all, facets.

As a songwriter, I'm intrigued with deeper, even philosophical questions raised by these connections. I've claimed everything in the song *means*. Yet clearly, lyrics, melody, harmony, and rhythm each carry meaning in distinctive ways. What kind of thematic material lends itself most readily to melodic vs. harmonic, modal, or rhythmic associations? Here's a speculative account of how this might work, grounded in recognizing a deep asymmetry in ways we work with language (via the lyrics facet) vs. music (via other facets).

Imagine a "criss-cross" between sense and sound aspects of lyric vs. musical facets, and a polarity in how these facets connect, respectively, to the World (content) and to structure:

- *Lyrics connect to the world through sense: to structure through sound.*
- *Musical facets connect to the world through sound: to structure through sense.*

To elaborate: referential aspects of lyrics draw us toward the sensory world, while sound aspects of lyrics take on their strongest role for songwriting in connection to *structural effects*, both within the lyric itself and in relation to other facets.

This insight runs counter to a naïve notion: that great lyrics come from "word painting" or direct imitation of real-world effects with lyric sounds. Such onomatopoetic relationships certainly occur in lyrics, but are tangential rather than essential. Your primary concern with lyric sounds should be patterning them to resonate against accompanying structures in melody, chords, and rhythm. This both links lyric writing to some aspects of poetry and highlights ways in which the arts differ.

Conversely, for a songwriter's purposes, musical materials take on meaning, and perhaps even emotion, primarily via *self*-referential associations and resonances created by structural effects. These "sense" aspects of a chord progression, for example—whether lying in a functional harmonic vocabulary or more impressionistic modal palette—give it meaning in the musical world and its reflection in structure. This insight runs counter to another tendency—to correlate musical aspects too literally to narrative or emotional associations. To the extent that music does relate directly to the sensory world, it may be primarily—and somewhat paradoxically—through *sound* aspects. As with lyric word painting, these are special effects, best used sparingly: an occasional melodic line that soars like a bird in the sky; a rhythmic riff evoking a heartbeat.

Consider this tidy scheme of symmetries an area of ongoing research, a jumping-off point for inquiry through your own experience and creative investigations. I include it here mainly as a cautionary note against too enthusiastic an embrace of only surface elements of a 360° songwriting approach.

I've placed strong emphasis on the sound aspects of lyrics, the nonharmonic possibilities of chords, the potential to work on songs in an "impressionistic" way, prior to a thematic focus. While this emphasis is perhaps a corrective to overly "rationalized" explanations and prescriptions for songwriting, we can take it too far. Simmering every note and chord into a direct sensory study could lead us to an artificial, overly illustrative kind of "tone poem" songwriting.

We can avoid such pitfalls by cultivating respect for the power of structural patterns themselves to carry a kind of meaning. Trust that writing to a rhyme scheme or a melodic phrase structure is more than a display of craft and technique; it contributes actively to the emotion and meaning of the song. I'm hesitant, though, to explain this by searching for too direct a link between the meanings carried by structures and referential meanings in the world. Let the structures do their own work.

From a Song to the World

One big lesson of 360° songwriting is that you don't always know what the song is "about" when you start. Strategies of song seed catching and starting songs from any direction mean the material itself can lead us to themes and content to write and sing about—or (and you're doing well if it feels like this) *what the song itself asks us to write it into being about.*

In the songwriting strategies presented in this book, you can apply this not only to initial song seed catching, but potentially to *any* compass move, such as setting *from* one facet *to* another. You can treat such moves as assignments to *generate* material afresh, such as writing a new melody to a lyric line, or finding new words to a melody, aligning the material emotionally as best you can. Alternatively, you can treat this work as a kind of *bricolage*, collage, or quilt-making: searching your (oh so efficiently compiled!) lists of song seeds for the facet of interest, and letting these collide serendipitously with the material you're matching to—in surprising, maybe even ironic ways. Working with counterpoint and irony further extends this discovery-based approach to songwriting. Compositional techniques that rely on "chance operations" (to borrow a phrase from John Cage, a most "un-caged" composer) allow and invite mismatches and ironic juxtapositions—and through these happy accidents, perhaps unexpected new truths.

I believe certain human truths, vital to our future, can *only* be conveyed through song—and that the songs can tell us what to sing. It's this songwriter's crazy faith that these connections are there to be experienced, in different ways, with every facet—and that every pathway expands our scope and voice as writers. Doing this work, we'll be trying to answer the big questions: *Why* write songs? Why write a song about *this*? Why a *song* about this? Wrestling with these questions expands us outward—from the only songs we can write, to songs only we can write. Why? Write songs! Welcome to our proud tribe of *songwriters*: comrades to creative writers and composers, but with our own work to do.

ABOUT THE AUTHOR

Photo by Phil Farnsworth

Mark Simos, associate professor in songwriting at Berklee College of Music, is a renowned songwriter, composer and tunesmith, teacher, and writer. Over four-plus decades, Mark's songs and "tunes from imaginary countries" have stretched musical boundaries with innovative melodies and harmonies and intricately crafted lyrics, bringing a contemporary sensibility to "neo-traditionalist" forms. Over one hundred of Mark's compositions have been recorded by artists, including Americana supergroup Alison Krauss and Union Station, Ricky Skaggs, Del McCoury, and Laurie Lewis. He's co-written with artists/writers such as Australian rock icon Jimmy Barnes, Catie Curtis, and the Infamous Stringdusters' Andy Hall. He's featured on many recordings as fiddler and guitar accompanist, and has recorded an acclaimed song-cycle album, *Crazy Faith*, and four albums of original and traditional fiddle music.

At Berklee, Mark creates innovative curriculum in 360° songwriting, collaboration, guitar techniques for songwriters, and tunewriting, and leads Berklee's American Old-Time Ensemble. He also continues to perform and teach at workshops, camps, festivals, and retreats worldwide.

INDEX

360° songwriting approach, ix, xx
  concept seeds in, 5–8
  discovering the song, 201–203
  facet triad strategy, 196–98
  harmonic aspect, 123–54
  ironic reversals, 200
  irony and, 198–99
  lyric aspect, 65–93
  lyric seeds in, 8–12
  melodic aspect, 95–121
  melody/harmony connections, 155–74
  melody/lyric connections, 108–10
  melody/rhythm connections, 105–8
  musical seeds in, 12–15
  rap and hip-hop and, 48
  rhythmic aspect, 41–63
  song seed catching in, 1–20, 32
  songwriter's compass and, 21–40, 193–201

A

accompaniment rhythm, 43, 53–54, 147
Agans, Jen, 179
aleatoric discoveries, 124, 128–30, 202
alternate harmonizations, 73–74, 168, 172, 174
anchor tones, 162
Arlen, Harold, 108–9
arpeggios in melodic shape, 99–102
"As Tears Go By," 127
assonance
  effects, 185
  lyric rhythm and, 76
  in lyric seeds, 11

B

bagpipe notation style, 46–47
Beatles, the, 2, 10, 24, 120, 130–31, 142
Beethoven, Ludwig van, 132
bend melodic shape, 99–102
Bergson, Henri, 83
breaths and rhythm, 57
bricolage, 202
Buckland, Ellie, 130

C

caesura, 66, 67
Cage, John, 128, 202
call and response songs, 48
cantus firmus, 157
Carmichael, Hoagy, 27
Cash, Johnny, 140
casting technique, 27–28, 32, 200–201
  from concept seed, 39–40
  from groove, 54
  to chords, 125
"Catch the Wind," 160
challenge writing, 177
chanting tones, 112–13, 117–21
chord progressions, 136–46
  analyzing, 144–45
  chord roots as scale degrees, 137–38
  with diatonic intervallic moves, 146
  directional effects of root movement, 139–40
  falling motion, 142
  functional considerations, 144
  intervallic motion in, 138–39
  rising motion, 141–42
  root tone contours, 145–46
  simple chords, 136–37
  transitions in, 144
chord seeds, 13
chordal seeds, 126, 127–36
  aleatoric discoveries, 128–30
  away from instrument, 132–36
  finding from instrument, 128–31
  as sound, shape, and feel, 127
  using, 131
  using notation, 133–35
  using recording technology, 132
chord-driven melodies, 165–67
circle of fifths pattern, 142
circle of fourths progression, 142
clichés, avoiding, 10, 28
"Come Together," 2, 41, 131
concept seeds, 5–8
  casting from, 39–40
  mistaking for title or hook, 6–7

consonance
  effects, 185
  lyric rhythm and, 76
  in lyric seeds, 11
consonant buds, 90, 91
consonant contours, 89–90
consonants
  clusters of, 77
  rhythmic aspects of, 77–78
  sound colors of, 76
constraints, creativity and, 31
content's place in songwriter's compass, 23–24
context, song seeds and, 8
contrary motivic motion, 189–90
counterpoint, 157–59
  across facets, 191–92
  contrary motivic motion, 189–90
  within facets, 189–90
  irony and, 198–99
  lazy melodic lines against chords, 163–65
  in modal melody/harmony, 170–72
  motion between voices, 159
  in motivic structure, 188–92
  oblique motivic motion, 189
  ostinato melodies, 160–61
  parallel and similar motivic motion, 188–89
  parallel textures, 161–63
  pedal-point melodies, 159–60
  species, 158–59
  textures, 159–69
co-writing sessions
  capturing context in, 8
  collaboration models, 196–97
  paraphrasing strategies, 79–80
cyclic progressions, 149–50, 152–53, 198

D

Davis, Sheila, 65
disorientation strategies, 124
Donovan, 160
dry lyric, 74, 96
dummy lines and gibberish as lyric writing strategies, 80–84, 194
duple pulse, 50
Dylan, Bob, 177

E

"Eight Days a Week," 10
energy contour of a rhythmic phrase, 88–89
enjambment, 66–67
environmental sounds, song seeds from, 44
essential melody, 96–97

F

figures in melodic shape, 99–102
filler
  chords for musical seeds, 16
  distinguishing from seed, 3–5, 12, 107
  dummy lines vs., 80
  lyric, 17, 80
folk music
  independence from harmonic structure, 169–74, 196
  originality and, 14
"For the Benefit of Mr. Kite," 2
framing technique, 28–29, 32, 33–34, 37, 200–201
  alternate settings, 73–74
  from chord progression to narrative, 144
  from harmony, 125
  in setting from rhythm to lyric, 87
  triangulating/converging strategy and, 31
fricatives, 77
fulfilling structural strategy, 32, 175, 176, 183–186

G

Gaffney, Henry, 61
gamelan music, irama concept in, 52–53
Gaye, Marvin, 130–31
"Girl," 120
Grandmaster Flash and the Furious Five, 41
Great American Songbook repertoire, 142, 169, 170, 174
groove, 51
Guthrie, Woody, 65

H

Harburg, Yip, 108–9
"Hard Day's Night, A," 2, 11
harmonic facet of songwriting, 21–23, 123–54
  aleatoric and disorientation strategies, 124, 128–30
  chord progressions, 136–46
  chord seeds, 13
  chordal song seeds, 127–36
  cyclic vs. narrative progressions, 149–51, 198
  harmonic rhythm, 147–49
  independence from melody, 156–57, 167–69
  jamming, 126
  melody/harmony connections, 155–74
  melody/harmony counterpoint, 157–59
  "mind's ear" skills, 135–36
  motivic progressions, 151–54
  process considerations, 125
  rhythm and, 44
  sound and sense in chords, 123–26
  structure and, 185
harmonic rhythm, 44, 147–49
Hendrix, Jimi, 142, 150

"Hey Joe," 142
hip-hop, 48, 60
hocketing technique, 47–48
hook melodic shape, 99–102
hooks, mistaking song seeds for, 6–7

I

"I Can't Make You Love Me," 197
"I Heard It Through the Grapevine," 2, 130–31
"I Walk the Line," 140
"Imagine," 199
Indonesian gamelan music, 52–53
instrumental articulation, 114
instrumental rhythms, 58
intervallic movement in melodies, 99–100
irama concept in Indonesian gamelan music, 52–53
Irish *séan-nos* ballads, 169
ironic reversals, 200
irony in songwriting, 198–99
iterating strategy, 28, 30, 32, 33, 39, 80–81

J

Jagger, Mick, 127
jamming, 126
Jobim, Antonio Carlos, 160
juggling, 179
    as process technique, 186, 187
junctures, 67, 78

K

Knack, the, 41

L

Laughter (Bergson), 83
Lennon, John, 41, 131, 199
Lil' Wayne, 65
line endings and rhythm, 57
linear melodic shape, 99–102
"Little Wing," 150
"Lucy in the Sky with Diamonds," 2, 142
lyric facet of songwriting, 21–23, 35–40, 65–93
    dummy lines and gibberish, 80–84
    harmonic rhythm and, 147
    harmonic setting, 38–39
    lyric sounds and melody, 108–9
    lyrics as sound, 65–69
    making adjustments, 92–93
    mapping lyrics to syllabic rhythm, 69–75
    melodic setting, 36–37
    paraphrasing, 79–80
    rhythmic implications of sounds, 77–78
    rhythmic setting, 35–36, 39, 41–63

setting from rhythm to lyric, 86–93, 105
    sonic contours, 84–86
    sound and sense strategies, 78–86
    sound aspects of, 65–69, 76–78
    sound elements vs. meaning, 21–22
    structure and, 185–86
    syllabic anatomy, 76–78
    thought phrase, 66–67
    word painting, 37
lyric pace, 55
    comfort zones in, 120
    melodic pace and, 113–14, 119–20
lyric rhythm, 69
    attributes of, 55–58
    developing from syllabic rhythm, 74–75, 111–12
    independent movement from melodic contour, 116, 119–20
    melodic contour and, 111–16
    pace and, 61
    regular to irregular, 58
lyric seeds, 8–12
    attributes of good, 9–12
    collisions of sound and sense, 10–11
    compactness, 10
    emotional resonance, 9, 39
    filler and, 17, 80
    individuality/voice, 9
    novelty/surprise/unexpectedness, 9–10
    recontextability, 10
    rhyme connections, 11–12
lyrical patterns, 56

M

McCartney, Paul, 14
melismas, 112–13, 118–21
melodic contour, 99–102
    avoiding monotony, 121
    independent movement from lyric rhythm, 116, 119–20
    lyric rhythm and, 111–16
    modal interchange and, 104
    sequences and, 103
melodic design, 98–104
    contour, 99
melodic facet of songwriting, 21–23, 95–121
    challenges, 96–98
    chord-driven melodies, 165–67
    essential melody, 96–97
    harmonic rhythm and, 147
    independence from other aspects, 95, 119–20, 156–57, 167–69
    lyric rhythm and melodic contour, 111–16
    melismas and chanting tones, 112–13, 117–19

melodic contour, 99–102
melodic design, 98–104
melodic memory, 97–98
melodic range, 104
melodic texture effects and uses, 117–21
melodic transformations, 102–3
melody/harmony connections, 155–74
melody/harmony counterpoint, 157–59
melody/lyric connections, 108–9
melody/rhythm connections, 105–8
natural intonation and speech melody, 109–10
ostinato melodies, 160–61
pedal-point melodies, 159–60
pentatonic modes and, 102
rhythm in vocal writing, 58–59
rhythmic setting, 43–44
setting from melody to rhythm, 106–8
setting from rhythm to melody, 106–8
shifting figure and field, 103–4
structure and, 185
melodic memory, 97–98
melodic pace
comfort zones in, 120
lyric pace and, 113–14, 119–20
melodic range, 104
melodic rhythm, 114–16
melodic sequence, 103
melodic shape
bend, 99–102
hook, 99–102
linear, 99–102
sawtooth, 99–102
slope, 99–102
melodic textures
effects and uses of, 117–21
process considerations, 117
melodic transformations, 102–3
Melody in Songwriting (Perricone), 167, 182
melody/chords/lyric triad, 197
melody/harmony connections, 155–74
alternate harmonizations, 73–74, 168
chord-driven melodies, 165–67
contrapuntal textures, 159–69
counterpoint, 157–59
independence of, 156–57
independent tonal melody, 167–69
modal melody/harmony, 169–74
melody/harmony/rhythm triad, 196–97
melody/lyric connections, 108–10
melody/rhythm connections, 105–8
melody/rhythm/lyric triad, 197
Mercer, Johnny, 27

"Message, The," 41
Messiaen, Olivier, 132
modal and pentatonic modes, 169–70
modal interchange, 104
modal melody/harmony, 110, 169–74
counterpoint in, 170–72
expanding songwriting possibilities through, 170
palettes and mosaics, 172–74
model songs, song seeds from, 2, 14
harmonic seeds, 130–31
rhythmic seeds, 45
monorhythm, 121
motivic motion
contrary, 159, 189–90
oblique, 159, 189
parallel or similar, 159, 188–89
motivic progressions, 151–54
motivic structure, 176, 181–87
counterpoint in, 188–92
fulfilling structure, 183–87
motives vs. song seeds, 181
question/answer phrases, 182–83
unfolding directional strategies, 183
unfolding motives into structure, 181–83
musical seeds, 12–15, 96
filler chords for, 16
guidelines for catching, 13–15, 97
instrument dependence and, 12
instrumental phrases with, 17–18
isolating from filler, 12
notating, 12
originality of, 14
overworking dangers for, 14
quality of, 13–14
sense and sound in, 13
simplifying rhythm in, 16
"My Sharona," 41

N

narrative progressions, 144, 150–51, 152–53, 198
nasals, 77
Nashville-style notation system, 134, 148
natural intonation, speech melody and, 109–10
"Nice Day till the Hurricane" (example), 9–11
framing, 33–34
setting, 35–40
notation
for chordal seeds, 15, 133
as first strategy, 135
harmonic rhythm, 148
Nashville-style, 134, 148
of rhythm, 46–48

O

oblique motivic motion, 159, 189
"One Note Samba," 160, 167
ornamental tones, 162
ostinato melodies, 160–61
ostinatos, 100
"Over the Rainbow," 108–9, 167

P

parallel or similar motivic motion, 189–90
parallel textures, 161–63
  effects and uses of, 162
  risks with, 162–63
paraphrasing in lyric writing, 79–80
Pattison, Pat, 65, 182
pedal-point melodies, 159–60
pentatonic modes, 15, 102, 110, 170
  sequences and, 103
Perricone, Jack, 167, 182
phrasal rhythm, 59
phrase structure, 59, 175, 177–80
  independence in, 178–80
phrasing templates, 120–21
pitch space, 99
pivoting strategy, 31, 32, 93
plagal cadence, 142
plosives, 77, 90
polarity, 22
Popular Lyric Writing (Stolpe), 182
Prince, 41
process language, x
pulse
  continuum, 50–51
  importance of, 50

R

radiating strategy, 31, 32
rap, 48
recitative, 110
Reid, Mike, 197
rhyming dictionary, 12
rhyming in lyric seeds, 11–12
rhythm/chords/lyric triad, 197
rhythmic duration, 59
rhythmic events, 58–60
rhythmic facet of songwriting, 21–23, 41–63
  accompaniment rhythm, 53–54
  challenge of rhythm, 41–44
  dimensions in song, 43–44
  interlocking accompaniment and vocal rhythms, 47–48
  notating rhythms, 46–48

  rhythmic events, 58–60
  rhythmic pace, 60–61
  rhythmic patterns, 62
  setting from melody to rhythm, 106–8
  setting from rhythm to lyric, 86–93, 105
  setting from rhythm to melody, 105–6
  as shadow facet, 41–42
  song seeds, 44–48
  structure and, 185
  temporal framework, 49–53
  working with rhythm, 42
rhythmic melody, 100
rhythmic pace, 60–61
  norm vs. mean, 60
  relation to metrical framework, 61
rhythmic patterns, 62
rhythmic phrase, 43–44, 55–63
  attributes of lyric rhythm, 55–58, 111–12
  casting to, 54
  concept of, 59
  energy contour of, 88–89
  framing, 87
  vowel and consonant contours, 89–90
  working with, 63
rhythmic placement, 59
rhythmic seeds, 42, 44–48
  catalogues of, 45
  composing, 45–46
  sources of, 44–45
rhythmic template, 63
Richards, Keith, 127
Robinson, Smokey, 2
rubato, 59
Rubber Soul, 120

S

sawtooth melodic shape, 99–102
scale degrees, chord roots as, 137–38
scales in melodic shape, 99–102
scansion marks, 67
sequencing strategy, 30, 32
setting technique, 26–27, 32, 40
  between harmony and other facets, 125
  between lyrics and other facets, 26–27
Shamblin, Allen, 197
signature style, 97
Simon, Paul, 1
simple chords, 136–37
"Sir Duke," 102n10
"Skylark," 27
slope melodic shape, 99–102
song form, 176

song seeds, 1–20
  catching, 2–5, 15–20, 32, 97–98, 124, 126, 202
  catching regime for, 18–20
  chordal, 126, 127–36
  concept, 5–8
  context and, 8
  different starting points for, 1
  from environmental sounds, 44
  filler vs., 3–5, 107
  inspiration points, 2
  irreducibility of, 15
  lyric, 8–12
  from model songs, 2
  motives vs., 181
  musical, 12–15
  for "Over the Rainbow," 108–9
  personal voice and, 3
  remembering, 3
  rhythmic, 44–48
  simplifying rhythm in, 16
  as term, 2
  varieties of, 5–15
song titles
  lyric seeds and, 8
  mistaking song seeds for, 6–7
songwriter's compass, 21–40, 193–201
  content as world, 23–24, 40
  edge approach, 195–96
  facet triads, 196–98
  four facets, 21–23, 40
  general creative strategies, 30–31
  independence and flexibility in, 40, 95, 119–20
  revisiting, 193–98
  shadow facet, 41
  signature style, 97
  songwriting strategies, 26–31
  sound and sense, 22–23, 78–86, 200–201
  sound and timbre, 24
  structure, 25–26, 40
  summary of elements and moves, 32
  as tetrahedron, 194–95
  as a unity, 193–94
  words and music, 21–22
Songwriting: Essential Guide to Rhyming (Pattison), 182
songwriting strategies. *See also specific facets*
  casting and framing techniques, 27–29, 32, 33–34, 39–40
  irony in, 198–200
  setting techniques, 26–27, 32, 40, 86–93
  structuring strategies, 29–30, 32
sonic aspects in lyric seeds, 11
sonic contours, 84–86

speech duration variations, 56
speech melody, natural intonation and, 109–10
speech rhythm proportions, 56
speech-tone melody, 48
Stolpe, Andrea, 182
Strong, Barrett, 130–31
structuring strategies, 29–30, 32, 175–92
  challenges, 177
  into chord progression, 184
  irony and, 198–99
  juggling phrases, 187
  into lyric, 185–86
  into melodic phrase, 184
  into motives, 183–87
  motivic structure, 176, 181–87
  phrase structure, 175, 177–80
  place in songwriter's compass, 25–26
  rhythm and, 59
  into rhythmic phrase, 185
  song form, 176
  starting from structure, 176–77
swing, 50
syllabic pace, 60
syllabic rhythm
  developing alternative, 73–74
  example, 70–74
  lyrical rhythm contrasted with, 69, 74–75, 111–12
  mapping lyrics to, 69–75
syllabic stress patterns, 67–69
  primary stress, 68
  secondary stresses, 71–72
syllable buds, 83, 91–92, 194
syllables, anatomy of, 76–78
  sound color aspects, 76

T

"Tangled Up in Blue," 177
tempo of song, 51
temporal framework
  phrase structure and, 177
  rhythm in, 43
temporal framework of song, 49–53
  flow of musical time, 49
  pulse in, 50–51
  strict vs. loose time, 49
  time signature and tempo, 51
  working with, 51–53
tetrahedron, 194–95
thought phrase, 66–67
through-composed music, 151, 182
time signature, 51
tonic drone, 166–67

triangulating/converging strategy, 31, 32, 80–81
    syllable buds to words to lyrics, 91–92
triple pulse, 50
"Tunesmith Telephone" game, 98
twelve-bar blues progression, 142–43

U

unfolding structural strategy, 32, 175, 176, 181–83
unvoiced consonants, 77–78

V

verse/chorus form, 25
vocal interpretation and rhythm, 57
voiced consonants, 77–78
vowel buds, 90, 91
vowel contours, 89–90
vowels
    rhythmic aspects of, 77–78
    sound colors of, 76

W

Warren, Diane, 1
"When Doves Cry," 41
Whitfield, Norman, 130–31
Wonder, Stevie, 102n10
woodblock notation style, 46–47
word boundaries, 67
word buds, 82, 194
word painting, 37
wrenched stress, 57
"Write the Letter" technique, 79
writer's block, unfreezing, ix

Y

"Yesterday," 2, 14

More Fine Publications
from BERKLEE PRESS

GUITAR

BEBOP GUITAR SOLOS
by Michael Kaplan
00121703 Book.....................................$14.99

BERKLEE BLUES GUITAR SONGBOOK
by Mike Williams
50449593 Book/CD.........................$24.99

BLUES GUITAR TECHNIQUE
by Mike Williams
50449623 Book/CD.........................$24.99

BERKLEE GUITAR CHORD DICTIONARY
by Rick Peckham
50449546 Jazz................................$10.99
50449596 Rock...............................$12.99

BERKLEE JAZZ STANDARDS FOR SOLO GUITAR
by John Stein
50449653 Book/CD.........................$19.99

THE CHORD FACTORY
by Jon Damian
50449541 ....$24.95

CREATIVE CHORDAL HARMONY FOR GUITAR
by Mick Goodrick and Tim Miller
50449613 Book/CD.........................$19.99

FUNK/R&B GUITAR
by Thaddeus Hogarth
50449569 Book/CD $19.95

GUITAR CHOP SHOP – BUILDING ROCK/METAL TECHNIQUE
by Joe Stump
50449601 Book/CD $19.99

JAZZ IMPROVISATION FOR GUITAR
by Garrison Fewell
A Harmonic Approach
50449594 Book/CD $24.99
A Melodic Approach
50449503 Book/CD Pack $24.99

A MODERN METHOD FOR GUITAR
by William Leavitt
Volume 1: Beginner
50449400 Book...............................$14.95
50449404 Book/CD $22.95
50448065 Book/DVD-ROM $34.99
Volume 2: Intermediate
50449410 Book...............................$14.95
Volume 3: Advanced
50449420 Book...............................$16.95
1, 2, 3 Complete
50449468 Book...............................$34.95
Jazz Songbook, Vol. 1
50449539 Book/CD $14.99
Rock Songbook
50449624 Book/CD $17.99

PLAYING THE CHANGES: GUITAR
by Mitch Seidman and Paul Del Nero
50449509 Book/CD $19.95

THE PRACTICAL JAZZ GUITARIST
by Mark White
50449618 Book/CD...............................$19.99

THE PRIVATE GUITAR STUDIO HANDBOOK
by Michael McAdam
00121641 Book....................................$14.99

BASS

BASS LINES
by Joe Santerre
50449542 Fingerstyle Funk:
 Book/CD $19.95
50449478 Rock: Book/CD $19.95

FUNK BASS FILLS
by Anthony Vitti
50449608 Book/CD.............................$19.99

INSTANT BASS
by Danny Morris
50449502 Book/CD $14.95

READING CONTEMPORARY ELECTRIC BASS
by Rich Appleman
50449770 Book....................................$19.95

DRUMS

BEGINNING DJEMBE
by Michael Markus & Joe Galeota
50449639 DVD....................................$14.99

DOUBLE BASS DRUM INTEGRATION
by Henrique De Almeida
00120208 Book....................................$19.99

DRUM SET WARM-UPS
by Rod Morgenstein
50449465 Book....................................$12.99

DRUM STUDIES
by Dave Vose
50449617 Book....................................$12.99

EIGHT ESSENTIALS OF DRUMMING
by Ron Savage
50448048 Book/CD..............................$19.99

PHRASING: ADVANCED RUDIMENTS FOR CREATIVE DRUMMING
by Russ Gold
00120209 Book....................................$19.99

WORLD JAZZ DRUMMING
by Mark Walker
50449568 Book/CD $22.99

KEYBOARD

BERKLEE JAZZ KEYBOARD HARMONY
by Suzanna Sifter
50449606 Book/CD $24.99

BERKLEE JAZZ PIANO
by Ray Santisi
50448047 Book/CD $19.99

CHORD-SCALE IMPROVISATION FOR KEYBOARD
by Ross Ramsay
50449597 Book/CD Pack....................$19.99

CONTEMPORARY PIANO TECHNIQUE
by Stephany Tiernan
50449545 Book/DVD $29.99

HAMMOND ORGAN COMPLETE
by Dave Limina
50449479 Book/CD $24.95

JAZZ PIANO COMPING
by Suzanne Davis
50449614 Book/CD $19.99

LATIN JAZZ PIANO IMPROVISATION
by Rebecca Cline
50449649 Book/CD $24.99

SOLO JAZZ PIANO – 2ND ED.
by Neil Olmstead
50449641 Book/CD..........................$39.99

VOICE

THE CONTEMPORARY SINGER – 2ND ED.
by Anne Peckham
50449595 Book/CD $24.99

VOCAL TECHNIQUE
featuring Anne Peckham
50448038 DVD................................$19.95

VOCAL WORKOUTS FOR THE CONTEMPORARY SINGER
by Anne Peckham
50448044 Book/CD..........................$24.95

TIPS FOR SINGERS
by Carolyn Wilkins
50449557 Book/CD..........................$19.95

YOUR SINGING VOICE
by Jeannie Gagné
50449619 Book/CD $29.99

WOODWINDS

FAMOUS SAXOPHONE SOLOS
arr. Jeff Harrington
50449605 Book................................$14.99

IMPROVISATION
by Andy McGhee
50449810 Flute...............................$14.99
50449860 Saxophone $14.99

THE SAXOPHONE HANDBOOK
by Douglas D. Skinner
50449658 Book................................$14.99

SAXOPHONE SOUND EFFECTS
by Ueli Dörig
50449628 Book/CD $14.99

Berklee Press Publications feature material
developed at the Berklee College of Music.
To browse the complete Berklee Press Catalog, go to
www.berkleepress.com

ROOTS MUSIC

BEYOND BLUEGRASS
Beyond Bluegrass Banjo
by Dave Hollander and Matt Glaser
50449610 Book/CD $19.99

Beyond Bluegrass Mandolin
by John McGann and Matt Glaser
50449609 Book/CD $19.99

Bluegrass Fiddle and Beyond
by Matt Glaser
50449602 Book/CD $19.99

THE IRISH CELLO BOOK
by Liz Davis Maxfield
50449652 Book/CD $24.99

BERKLEE PRACTICE METHOD

GET YOUR BAND TOGETHER
With additional volumes for other instruments, plus a teacher's guide.
Bass
by Rich Appleman, John Repucci and the Berklee Faculty
50449427 Book/CD $14.95
Cello
by Matt Glaser and Mimi Rabson
00101384 Book/CD $14.99
Drum Set
by Ron Savage, Casey Scheuerell and the Berklee Faculty
50449429 Book/CD $14.95
Guitar
by Larry Baione and the Berklee Faculty
50449426 Book/CD $16.99
Keyboard
by Russell Hoffmann, Paul Schmeling and the Berklee Faculty
50449428 Book/CD $14.95
Viola
by Matt Glaser, Mimi Rabson and the Berklee Faculty
00101393 Book/CD $16.99

WELLNESS

MANAGE YOUR STRESS AND PAIN THROUGH MUSIC
by Dr. Suzanne B. Hanser and Dr. Susan E. Mandel
50449592 Book/CD $29.99

MUSICIAN'S YOGA
by Mia Olson
50449587 Book $14.99

THE NEW MUSIC THERAPIST'S HANDBOOK – SECOND ED.
by Dr. Suzanne B. Hanser
50449424 Book $29.95

EAR TRAINING, IMPROVISATION, MUSIC THEORY

BEGINNING EAR TRAINING
by Gilson Schachnik
50449548 Book/CD $14.99

THE BERKLEE BOOK OF JAZZ HARMONY
by Joe Mulholland & Tom Hojnacki
00113755 Book/CD $24.99

BERKLEE MUSIC THEORY – 2ND ED.
by Paul Schmeling
50449615 Rhythm, Scales Intervals: Book/CD $24.99
50449616 Harmony: Book/CD $22.99

BLUES IMPROVISATION COMPLETE
by Jeff Harrington
Book/CD Packs
50449486 B♭ Instruments $19.95
50449488 C Bass Instruments $19.95
50449425 C Treble Instruments $22.99
50449487 E♭ Instruments $19.95

A GUIDE TO JAZZ IMPROVISATION
by John LaPorta
Book/CD Packs
50449439 C Instruments $19.95
50449441 B♭ Instruments $19.99
50449442 E♭ Instruments $19.99
50449443 ℣ Instruments $19.99

IMPROVISATION FOR CLASSICAL MUSICIANS
by Eugene Friesen with Wendy M. Friesen
50449637 Book/CD $24.99

REHARMONIZATION TECHNIQUES
by Randy Felts
50449496 Book $29.95

MUSIC BUSINESS

THE FUTURE OF MUSIC
by Dave Kusek and Gerd Leonhard
50448055 Book $16.95

MAKING MUSIC MAKE MONEY
by Eric Beall
50448009 Book $26.95

MUSIC INDUSTRY FORMS
by Jonathan Feist
00121814 Book $14.99

MUSIC MARKETING
by Mike King
50449588 Book $24.99

PROJECT MANAGEMENT FOR MUSICIANS
by Jonathan Feist
50449659 Book $27.99

THE SELF-PROMOTING MUSICIAN – 3RD EDITION
by Peter Spellman
00119607 Book $24.99

MUSIC PRODUCTION & ENGINEERING

AUDIO MASTERING
by Jonathan Wyner
50449581 Book/CD $29.99

AUDIO POST PRODUCTION
by Mark Cross
50449627 Book $19.99

MIX MASTERS
by Maureen Droney
50448023 Book $24.95

PRODUCING AND MIXING HIP-HOP/R&B
by Mike Hamilton
50449555 Book/DVD-ROM $19.99

PRODUCING DRUM BEATS
by Eric Hawkins
50449598 Book/CD-ROM Pack $22.99

RECORDING AND PRODUCING IN THE HOME STUDIO
by David Franz
50448045 Book $24.95

UNDERSTANDING AUDIO
by Daniel M. Thompson
50449456 Book $24.99

SONGWRITING, COMPOSING, ARRANGING

ARRANGING FOR LARGE JAZZ ENSEMBLE
by Dick Lowell and Ken Pullig
50449528 Book/CD $39.95

COMPLETE GUIDE TO FILM SCORING – 2ND ED.
by Richard Davis
50449607 .... $27.99

JAZZ COMPOSITION
by Ted Pease
50448000 Book/CD $39.99

MELODY IN SONGWRITING
by Jack Perricone
50449419 Book/CD $24.95

MODERN JAZZ VOICINGS
by Ted Pease and Ken Pullig
50449485 Book/CD $24.95

MUSIC COMPOSITION FOR FILM AND TELEVISION
by Lalo Schifrin
50449604 Book $34.99

MUSIC NOTATION
PREPARING SCORES AND PARTS
by Matthew Nicholl and Richard Grudzinski
50449540 Book $16.99

MUSIC NOTATION
THEORY AND TECHNIQUE FOR MUSIC NOTATION
by Mark McGrain
50449399 Book $24.95

POPULAR LYRIC WRITING
by Andrea Stolpe
50449553 Book $14.95

SONGWRITING: ESSENTIAL GUIDE
by Pat Pattison
50481582 Lyric and Form Structure: Book $16.99
00124366 Rhyming: Book – 2nd Ed. . $16.99

SONGWRITING STRATEGIES
by Mark Simos
50449621 Book/CD $22.99

THE SONGWRITER'S WORKSHOP
by Jimmy Kachulis
50449519 Harmony: Book/CD $29.95
50449518 Melody: Book/CD $24.95

AUTOBIOGRAPHY

LEARNING TO LISTEN: THE JAZZ JOURNEY OF GARY BURTON
by Gary Burton
00117798 Book $27.99

HAL•LEONARD® CORPORATION
7777 W. BLUEMOUND RD. P.O. BOX 13819 MILWAUKEE, WI 53213

Prices subject to change without notice. Visit your local music dealer or bookstore, or go to **www.berkleepress.com**

0214